LEO XIV.

-Tasks, goals and expectations.

LEO XIV.

- Tasks, goals and expectations.

This volume is also published in German Language (ISBN 978-3-8192-4845-0).

In the theological book series DEUS EX MACHINA have been published:
- DEUS EX MACHINA - Or: On questioning life (Part I). ISBN 978-3-7583-4022-2.
- Homecoming from the Pope - A Quintessence of Charity (Part II). ISBN 978-3-7693-5795-0
- Faith is like dancing – (Glauben ist wie Tanzen) - Moved by faith to grow as a Christian. Training book for building religious skills (Part III). ISBN 978-3-8192-9630-7.
- I will be a female bishop! – The Basics of Sermons on Happiness and other religious policy field analyses (Part IV). ISBN 978-3-8192-2914-5.

<u>Imprint</u>

Circe, Eureka: **LEO XIV - Tasks, goals and expectations.**
Hamburg, 2025.
ISBN 978-3-8192-4848-1

Publisher: BoD · Books on Demand GmbH, Überseering 33, 22297 Hamburg, bod@bod.de
Print: Libri Plureos GmbH, Friedensallee 273, 22763 Hamburg
© 2025 Eureka Circe in documentation and translation with AI.
Bibliographical references at the German National Library at: https://portal.dnb.de

Eureka Circe is the editor and curator of the book series "DEUS EX MACHINA.

The series includes: "DEUS EX MACHINA - Or: On questioning life" (Part I), "Homecoming from the Pope - A quintessence of charity" (Part II), "Glauben ist wie Tanzen - Vom Glauben bewegt als Christ:in wachsen. Training book for building religious skills" (Part III), and "I will be a female bishop! - The Basics of Sermons on Happiness and other religious policy field analyses (Part IV)".

With the work "DEUS EX MACHINA", the curator is committed to documenting and, if necessary, discussing the texts of artificial intelligence in a religious and theological context. Her thesis: "Artificial intelligence (AI) represents a profound turning point because it fundamentally changes the relationship between humans, knowledge and access to the world - not only technically, but also culturally, epistemologically and socially. It opens up new access to knowledge and leads to its multiplication and democratization: AI systems make information available at a low threshold - often without traditional reading or in-depth prior knowledge. This fundamentally changes how we think, learn and understand, and at the same time promotes a new form of individualization of thought - which can also be exemplified by spiritual belief. What's more, machines are now generating meaning - texts, images, arguments - where previously only human expertise was required. This has long-term consequences for education, science, politics and religion."

Right at the beginning, LEO XIV greeted the world with "Peace be with you all" and emphasized that this greeting of peace should reach "all nations and all people". Echoing Pope Francis, Leo XIV emphasized that God's love is *"unconditionally for all people"*. He literally assured: *"God loves you all. Evil will not win"*. These words implicitly *include all* people - including *queer* people - as no exception is made before God and now also before the Vatican. The universal formulation makes it clear that no one is excluded from receiving divine love.

"To be called 'woke' in a world that sleeps through suffering is no insult - it is Gospel. ... Be awake. Be loving. Be woke."

Finally, in the early days of LEO XIV's pontificate, a quote widely circulated on social media attributed to Pope Leo XIV also emerged. In it, he first thanks everyone for prayers and love at the beginning of his ministry and then formulates a passionate appeal that reinterprets the term *"woke"* positively in a Christian sense. An excerpt from this circulating quote reads: *"To be called 'woke' in a world that sleeps through suffering is no insult - it is Gospel. ... Be awake. Be loving. Be woke."*. These drastic words, including *"Woke means to be awakened by compassion... We will not build the kingdom [of God] with walls, but with love... Be awake. Be loving. Be woke."*, were shared thousands of times on Facebook, Instagram & Co. Although the alleged "woke" quote - "woke" comes from "awake", meaning "to be awake", "to be alert" to social injustice and discrimination - reflects the social and compassionate tone that many believe Leo XIV to have, it is not one of the Pope's confirmed statements. The Vatican has therefore not yet published any official communication for this quote, and others have also made it clear that there is no evidence for this statement, but that it could only be an expectation of the new pontificate.

Contents

Introduction: Quod formandum esset
"What needs to be shaped...:
Tasks, goals and expectations
- The new Pope LEO XIV.

In turbulent times, orientation, clarity and courageous visions are needed. With the election of Robert Francis Prevost as Pope Leo XIV in May 2025, the Catholic Church is once again at a significant turning point in its history. Pope Leo XIV is taking on a difficult yet inspiring legacy: After the era of Francis, which was characterized by strong pastoral impulses, a clear option for the poor and the attempt to build bridges between tradition and modernity, the new pope is faced with the task of safeguarding these achievements and at the same time paving new paths that will enable the Church to have a sustainable future.

This book aims to be more than just a first portrayal of Leo XIV. Rather, it sees itself as a companion that guides readers through the challenges, potentials and expectations of the new pontificate. The focus is on the tasks, goals and expectations that Leo XIV himself formulated and already made visible in his first official acts - as well as the hopes, expectations and demands that society, the public, journalists, theologians and, last but not least, the faithful placed on him as tasks and needs. A comprehensive picture emerges of a Pope who is not afraid to tackle burning issues and always seeks dialog - both within the Church and with society as a whole.

Leo XIV brings a wide range of personal qualities to his office: The missionary dedication from his long years in Peru, the diplomatic skills from his time as head of a global religious order, the academic depth of a canon lawyer and a deep spiritual rootedness in the Augustinian tradition. All these aspects come together to make him a leader who is both visionary and pragmatic. The present chapters span an arc from his biography to his theological and spiritual accents to concrete, necessary, urgent and unavoidable reform issues, where clear expectations of the faithful and pressing social realities demand convincing answers.

None of the big questions are to be shied away from: How will Leo XIV deal with the central reform issues, such as the ordination of women, the role of the laity, the inclusion of LGBTQIA+ people, for example in the sacramental celebration of their marriages, or compulsory celibacy? What measures does he take to prevent sexual abuse and abuse of power? How does it manage the balancing act between tradition and necessary modernization - in a church that is increasingly diverse, digital and globalized?

The questions of ecological responsibility, inclusive sexual ethics, financial transparency and synodal decision-making structures are also dealt with in depth and transparently. In the final section of the book, we also venture an outlook on possible scenarios for the long-term development of the Church under Leo XIV, with concepts such as network church, participatory leadership, digital transformation, the recognition of same-sex partnerships and protection against abuse of power at the top of the agenda.

This volume aims to offer all interested parties - Catholics as well as socially engaged readers - a well-founded and exciting insight into the world of Catholic thought, the experiences and goals as well as the personality of Leo XIV. It aims to inform, inspire and encourage readers to play an active and critical role in shaping the future of the Church.

May reading this book give you many ideas and insights and at the same time strengthen your own commitment to a lively, (gender) just, inclusive and authentic church.

We hope you enjoy reading the individual chapters and wish you much reflection and insight.

Eureka Circe, at the beginning of May 2025.

15

16

🕊 *Chapter 1:*
Introduction and biographical basics - LEO XIV.

Robert Francis Prevost, the current Pope Leo XIV, can look back on an unusually varied life. Born in Chicago in 1955 to a deeply Catholic family, he developed a close bond with his faith at an early age. He attended a Catholic seminary as a teenager and felt his calling to religious life. At the age of 22, Prevost joined the Augustinian order (Order of St. Augustine). There he not only found a spiritual home, but also the basis for his missionary vocation. The Augustinians, influenced by the spirit of their religious father Augustine, place great value on community and service to others - values that Prevost also internalized from the very beginning. After completing his novitiate and studying theology, he took his solemn vows in 1981 and was ordained a priest in Rome a year later. His interest in a sound education became apparent early on: At the Pontifical University of *St. Thomas Aquinas* in Rome (the Angelicum), Prevost received his doctorate in canon law in 1987. His dissertation *was entitled "The Role of the Local Prior in the Order of St. Augustine"* - a topic that indicates how much he was interested in questions of community leadership and the organization of religious life. This academic examination of the everyday life of the order was later to be of great benefit in his leadership roles.

Missionary work in Peru and social commitment

After his studies, Robert Prevost was drawn to the wider world church: he followed his call as a missionary and went to Peru in the mid-1980s. In the territorial prelature of Chulucanas, a poor rural region in northern Peru, he worked actively in pastoral care as a young religious priest from 1985 to 1987. This time made a deep impression on him. Prevost lived in simple circumstances with the local people and shared their worries and hopes. He was particularly committed to disadvantaged communities: He campaigned for social justice and stood by people in emergency situations. Companions from Peru describe the current Pope as *"hands-on and energetic"*, a man who did not hesitate to lend a hand when help was needed. During the severe flooding in 2017, for example, he organized relief efforts and personally helped to ensure that the victims were provided for. When many people lacked oxygen during the COVID-19 pandemic, Bishop Prevost initiated solidarity campaigns and financed the construction of an oxygen plant to save lives. Migrants and other marginalized groups also found a committed advocate in him. These practical deeds show Prevost's heartfelt concern: a church that **is there for the poor** and responds to people's concrete needs.

His years in Peru - first as a simple missionary, later in a leading position - also shaped Robert Prevost culturally and spiritually. He never saw himself there as a foreign American, but as a *"brother in faith"* who adopted the language and culture of the people. This humble closeness to the Latin American population created a mutual trust. Prevost learned to speak Spanish fluently and felt so connected to Peru that he even took on Peruvian citizenship in 2015. His time in Peru shaped him spiritually, theologically and culturally, emphasizes a Peruvian priest who experienced him there. This background explains why Pope Leo XIV is regarded today as a bridge builder between different cultures and mentalities.

Academic career and advancement in the Order

Parallel to his practical pastoral work, Prevost always pursued an academic and organizational career within the church. After completing his doctoral thesis on the role of the local religious superior, he put what he had learned directly into practice: In the late 1980s and 1990s, he took on tasks in the training of future priests and religious in Peru. He ran a training center for young Augustinian priests from various parts of the country and taught subjects such as canon law, patristics and moral theology at the seminary in Trujillo. **The good education of the clergy** was a particular concern of his - in his own words, *"the training of clergy [...] and the commitment to social justice were close to his heart"*. Prevost showed leadership qualities early on: As early as 1988, he became Prior (Superior Superior) of his order in Peru and later Provincial Superior, i.e. head of the Augustinians throughout Peru. In these roles, he promoted a *synodal*, inclusive church leadership in which priests, religious and lay people deliberate and make decisions together. This cooperative leadership model was to become a hallmark of his leadership style.

His successful work in Peru did not go unnoticed in the Order. In 1998, Robert Prevost returned to his home province of Chicago and took over the office of Provincial Prior there. But just a few years later, the Augustinians called him to lead them worldwide: from 2001 to 2013, Prevost served as **Prior General of the Augustinian Order**. In Rome, he led one of the most traditional Catholic orders with members on all continents. During this time, he traveled to many countries, visited Augustinian monasteries in Europe, Africa, Asia and America and got to know the global diversity of the church. Fluent in several languages (including English, Spanish, Italian and Portuguese), Prevost used his language skills and cultural openness to build bridges between different communities. His leadership style as Prior General was described as balanced and dialog-oriented - qualities that were as much in demand in the multicultural order as they are today in the universal church.

Career milestones (selection):

He has the following key milestones on his CV:

- 1977: Joins the Augustinian order - the beginning of his lifelong missionary commitment.

- 1985-1998: Missionary work in Peru - pastor, trainer and professor in disadvantaged regions.

- 1987: Doctorate with the dissertation "The role of the local prior in the Augustinian Order" - a sign of his interest in church structure and leadership issues.

- 2001-2013: Prior General of the Augustinian Order - worldwide leadership, reforms and renewal of the Order.

- 2014-2023: Bishop of Chiclayo (Peru) - Commitment to social programs and the expansion of the local church.

- 2023: Prefect of the Dicastery for Bishops - was responsible for the appointment of bishops and promoted the synodal orientation of the Church.

- September 2023: Cardinal - Appreciation of his key role in church leadership.

- May 2025: Election as Pope Leo XIV - continuation of his focus on mission, justice and renewal.

These life stages alone show that Leo XIV understood his entire work under the guiding principles **of mission, justice and renewal**. His decades of activity in Latin America made him a staunch advocate of social causes. At the same time, he was shaped by the Augustinian tradition with its focus on community, education and spiritual life.

From bishop to pope: serving the universal church

After more than a decade at the head of his order, a new call followed: in 2014, Pope Francis appointed Robert Prevost Apostolic Administrator - and shortly afterwards Bishop - of the diocese of **Chiclayo** in northern Peru. Prevost thus returned to the country that had become his second home, but now as the head pastor of a diocese with around three million Catholics. In Chiclayo, he took over a diocese that had previously been dominated by very conservative forces and led it with a gentle hand in a more open, dialog-oriented direction. What was particularly remarkable was how he brought together the various church groups - from grassroots communities to conservative movements. *"He built bridges between the different church movements,"* reports one observer about Prevost's work as bishop. The faithful experienced him as a pastor close to the people, who often went into the barrios (city districts) personally to talk to the people and get to know the reality of their lives. **Social justice** remained a core concern of his episcopal ministry: Prevost stood up for the poor, indigenous people and migrants and strengthened Caritas work in his diocese. He also took on responsibility within the Peruvian Conference of Bishops - at times as its deputy chairman - where he raised his voice in particular for the needs of the most vulnerable.

His integrative nature and experience led to Prevost attracting increasing attention in the Vatican. In January 2023, Pope Francis finally brought him to Rome and entrusted him with the leadership of one of the most important Curia authorities: Prevost became Prefect of the **Dicastery for Bishops**, responsible for appointing bishops worldwide. In this office, he once again demonstrated his diplomatic skills. For example, he mediated between Vatican authorities and the German bishops in the conflict over the "synodal path" in Germany and tried to defuse tensions through dialog. The international press praised him as a pragmatic diplomat who had clear principles but was also able to listen. In September 2023, Robert Prevost was elevated to cardinal by Francis. This officially made him one of the Pope's closest advisors - and one of the papal electors in the next conclave.

This next conclave was not long in coming: Following the death of Pope Francis in early 2025, the cardinals gathered in the Sistine Chapel to elect a new head of the church. Robert Prevost was considered by many to be a *middle-of-the-road candidate*. Thanks to his international experience, his religious spirituality and his ability to appeal to different camps within the church, he was seen as a bridge builder between conservative and progressive forces. In fact, the cardinals agreed on him surprisingly quickly: on May 8, 2025, they elected Robert Francis Prevost **pope** in the fourth ballot. He took the name **Leo XIV** - a deliberate choice reminiscent of Pope Leo XIII and his commitment to the Church's social doctrine. Leo XIV was the first US-American to ascend the Chair of Peter, who had also become a *"South American at heart"* through decades in Latin America. Hundreds of thousands cheered in St. Peter's Square when he appeared on the loggia of St. Peter's Basilica that evening and gave the *Urbi et Orbi* blessing. In his first address as Pope, Leo XIV called for **bridges to be built and peace to be established** - a motto that ran like a thread through his entire life.

In this first address as pope, Leo XIV also emphasized unity, peace and inclusion: "All belong to the Church," he called out to the crowd - and thus could not have excluded queer people and other clientele and target groups of the Catholic Church, for example - and called for global mercy overall. This attitude - openness to all people while at the same time maintaining a clear ecclesial identity of charity - reflects the defining values that characterize Prevost's career and his future pontificate.

Overall, Pope Leo XIV can bring all his diverse experience as Robert Prevost to his new office: His **biographical roots** - from church rector in Chicago to Augustinian missionary in Peru, from religious general in Rome to bishop on the Peruvian north coast - give him a broad understanding of the needs and hopes of people around the globe. Leo XIV embodies a church that is *"close to the people"* and knows the concerns of the poor. He is a man of tradition and at the same time an advocate of renewal in the spirit of the Second Vatican Council. His missionary passion, his commitment to social justice and his dialog-oriented leadership style give an idea of the emphasis he would like to set as Pope. In the following chapters of this book, we will go into more detail about **his tasks, goals and expectations** - but LEO XIV's life is already a living testimony to the values he stands for: faith, justice, inclusion and community, as well as the tireless will to build bridges between people.

 Chapter 2:
Theological and spiritual orientation

Following his swift election as the new head of the Roman Catholic Church in 2025, Pope Leo XIV has already made it clear what theological and spiritual accents he would like to set. As the first American to sit on the Chair of Peter and also the first pope from the Order of the Augustinians (OSA), Leo XIV brings a unique character to his pontificate. From his religious charism and his many years of missionary work in Latin America to his spiritual closeness to the course of his predecessor Francis, Leo XIV's basic principles are clear. Observers unanimously describe him as a **"man of the center"** - a balanced, spiritually inspired pope who avoids ideological extremes and instead builds bridges between the camps. His first appearances and speeches as Pope underline this profile: the **greeting of peace** and **the inclusion of all** came first, followed by appeals for justice and unity. Overall, the image that emerges is of a humble shepherd with great intellectual depth and warm-hearted charisma, who is firmly rooted in prayer. In the following, the spiritual influences and prayer life of Leo XIV, his commitment to social justice, his basic theological stance between tradition and reform and the guiding principles of his pontificate will be examined in more detail.

Spiritual imprints and prayer life

Leo XIV's spiritual roots lie deep in the tradition of his order. **As an Augustinian**, he followed the Rule of St. Augustine of Hippo, which is one of the oldest in the Western Church. After studying mathematics, philosophy and theology, he joined the Augustinian order at an early age and spent decades in the community of the friars. This influence can still be seen today in his coat of arms and motto: the papal **coat of arms of Leo XIV** contains symbols from the Augustinian emblem, which are reminiscent of the dramatic conversion of the church father Augustine. Below the coat of arms is the Latin motto *"In Illo uno unum"* - **"In him who is one, we are one"**, an inclusive quotation from St. Augustine.

This motto, which Leo XIV has kept unchanged for years, expresses his vision of an inclusive church as unity in Christ. It reflects a profoundly **community-oriented and diverse, pluralistic understanding of the Church**: the faithful should be one in the One - a reference to the togetherness of all in God.

The Marian spirituality of the new pope also stands out. His coat of arms features Marian symbols, which suggests a special devotion to the Mother of God. As a religious, Leo XIV knew the fixed rhythms of prayer life: from the Liturgy of the Hours to the community rosary and the celebration of the Eucharist, his day had always been structured by prayer. Close companions emphasize his deep piety and inner concentration. The Filipino Cardinal Luis Tagle, who has known the Pope for many years, describes Leo XIV **as a man of prayer and prudence**: he listened patiently, reflected and prayed carefully before making decisions. In encounters, he radiated a calm, cordial warmth, "**characterized by prayer and missionary experience**". This mixture of contemplation and active service characterized Prevost's decades of work as a pastor and trainer in Peru. According to Tagle, he gained a *"missionary experience"* there that taught him to combine closeness to people with a deep trust in God's guidance.

As a **religious,** Leo XIV also brought the spiritual experience of communal life to the office of pope. The President of the Central Committee of German Catholics, Irme Stetter-Karp, sees this as a great treasure: "No pope can rule alone today - the experience of Christian community life and shared spiritual responsibility helps to lead collegially. Leo XIV, who led the Augustinians worldwide for many years, embodied this *"vita communis"* at the highest level. His **humility** and **attitude to service** are characteristic of this. Even as a bishop, he warned that bishops should not be "little princesses" on their own thrones, but should above all humbly serve the people and be close to them . This attitude of simple service is rooted in his spiritual life: Like his role model Augustine, Leo XIV recognizes that true greatness for a church leader consists in serving God and his neighbour, not in external splendour.

Even though Leo XIV wore traditional regalia such as the red shoulder cape (**mozetta**) and a gold-embroidered stole on his first appearance as pope, this is less indicative of ostentation than of a **rootedness in tradition**. At the same time, he personally lived a modest lifestyle. From his religious spirituality, he brings with him the principle of *"living simply in order to serve others"*. It is therefore not surprising that Pope Leo XIV - as observers point out - combined intellectual education with spiritual profundity without boasting about it. He combined intellectual curiosity and a spirit of prayer, which gave his pontificate a solid spiritual foundation.

Last but not least, Leo XIV followed in the spiritual footsteps of his predecessor, but in his own way. After a Jesuit (Francis), there is now an Augustinian at the head of the Church - **no coincidence** for Cardinal Tagle. *"Augustine and Ignatius were both seekers [...] until they found in Jesus what their hearts longed for. Their schools are rooted in the grace of God. Leo XIV will carry on the Ignatian spirit of his predecessor in his own Augustinian way,"* said Tagle. This beautiful comparison shows: Leo XIV understands his ministry in deep continuity with the previous spiritual course, but shaped by the spirituality of St. Augustine - with a focus on the inner relationship with God, the community of believers and the humble pilgrimage of the people of God. In his first address, Leo XIV himself quoted St. Augustine: *"We are pilgrims on the way to a true home."* These words suggest that the new Pope has in mind a **pilgrim Church that is coming together** - a community that is humbly on its way, guided by prayer, always seeking its final home with God.

Commitment to social justice and charity

Shortly after his election, Leo XIV made it clear that he wanted to continue on the path set by Pope Francis in matters of **social justice and charity**. In his very first address from the balcony of St. Peter's Basilica, he expressly emphasized his commitment to **peace and justice** in the world. In fact, he already had a reputation as a committed bridge-builder between rich and poor. His religious general Alejandro Moral Anton praised him as someone who *"loves everyone, both the poor and the rich"* and immediately focused on issues such as justice and peace. This universal love can be seen in Leo XIV's biography: Born in the USA, he spent many years as a missionary and later bishop in **Peru**, where he was mainly active in poorer regions. There he experienced the social hardships of the people at first hand and was committed to helping the most vulnerable. For example, he helped refugees from crisis-ridden Venezuela and stood up for them. This heart for migrants and those in need also characterizes his view as Pope: observers even interpret his election as Pope as a signal in times of global migration movements - Prevost's commitment to refugees could be understood as a quiet criticism of a hard-hearted policy of isolation.

Another focus is the **advocacy of social justice in the sense of Catholic social teaching**. Many see the fact that the new pope has given himself the name *Leo XIV* as a deliberate program. Irme Stetter-Karp, for example, points out that **Leo XIII** is regarded **as the father of Catholic social ethics**. Leo XIII, who wrote the first social encyclical *Rerum Novarum* in 1891, was the first pope ever to stand up for the rights of workers and demand fair wages. By choosing this name, the new pope is clearly following in this tradition: Leo XIV wants a church that is clearly on the side of the disadvantaged, that stands up for **workers' rights, social balance and the dignity of every human being**. His work to date confirms this - he is considered down-to-earth and attentive to social grievances. His international experience (not only in the USA and Europe, but also in the global South of Latin America) has sensitized him to the concerns of both the North and the South. In his actions, Leo XIV tried to **connect North and South**: as the first pope from North America with a Latin American influence, he built a bridge between the continents, which also benefited global social issues.

In addition to the classic social issue, Leo XIV was strongly committed to the **protection of creation** and ecological justice. Pope Francis set standards on the climate issue with his encyclical *Laudato Si'* - Leo XIV made it clear that he wanted to continue along this path. As a cardinal in 2024, he warned that it was time *to "move from words to deeds"* in the fight against climate change. He emphasized that the God-given **authority "over nature" should not** be exercised **in a tyrannical manner** - rather, a *"relationship of reciprocity"* with the environment is needed. Such clear words show that Leo XIV took a **holistic approach**: for him, social justice and environmental responsibility belong together, as the poor in particular suffer from environmental degradation and climate change. Accordingly, he called on the Church to take decisive action against the destruction of the environment and to promote a simpler, more sustainable way of life. He shares this concern for an ecological rethink with his predecessor and - church observers agree on this - is likely to make it a hallmark of his pontificate.

Leo XIV also made his mark in the area of concrete **charity** - in other words, organized charity. He is held in high esteem by church aid organizations, particularly in Latin America. The Catholic aid organization *Adveniat* expressly welcomed his election and described him as an *"open, popular shepherd"* who understands the concerns of the poor. Indeed, during his time in Peru, the new Pope worked closely with grassroots communities and social projects, be it in educational initiatives, health programs or pastoral care among ordinary people. His ability to reach out to people on the margins sets him apart. **"He is a balanced, spiritual person who is close to everyone,"** his Augustinian confrere Alejandro Moral Anton emphasized approvingly. This closeness is expressed, for example, in the fact that Leo XIV always remained approachable even as a high-ranking churchman and took time to listen to people's concerns. It is to be expected that as Pope he will increasingly put issues such as **combating poverty, helping refugees and promoting peace on** the agenda. Cardinal Reinhard Marx expressed the hope that Leo XIV would provide strong social and peace-ethical impulses that would have an impact beyond the Church. He is already signaling that the Church under his leadership will be a **Church of bridge builders** that is there for people and works for justice and peace worldwide.

Basic theological attitude: between tradition and reform

Theologically, Pope Leo XIV is regarded as a moderate and balancing spirit. He embodied a basic attitude that did not see **tradition and reform** as contradictory, but as a field of action in which it was important to navigate wisely. On some issues, he is progressive and open, while on others he emphasizes continuity with the teachings of the church - an approach entirely in line with that of *"moderate reformers"*. Observers in the USA have already characterized him in this way: *Prevost is seen as diplomatic and pragmatic. Like Francis, he holds more progressive views on some issues and more conservative views* *on others.* This **mixture of open-mindedness and adherence to principles** characterizes his theological profile.

On the one hand, Leo XIV stood firmly on the ground of Church tradition and dogmatics. He made it clear that certain **doctrinal lines** were **hardly negotiable** for him. For example, **he still rejected the ordination of women to the priesthood a dozen years ago**, as he was of the opinion that women already had central ministries in the Church even without ordination. On this point, he is following the course of his predecessors John Paul II and Benedict XVI. He is also signaling restraint when it comes to far-reaching changes such as compulsory celibacy or questions of church sexual morality. His election initially dampened the expectations of progressive reform groups: Theologian Jacqueline Straub, for example, expressed disappointment and believed that Leo XIV would *"unfortunately not change much within the church"* in terms of, for example, the treatment of remarried divorcees or LGBTQIA+ people. Such assessments indicate that Leo XIV acted **steadily and cautiously** on controversial doctrinal issues rather than daring to do anything revolutionary or perhaps necessary and equal. His background as a doctor of canon law suggests that he would only tackle reforms within the framework of solid theological and legal foundations - but would also want to **anchor them permanently**. For example, experts expect him to transform the synodal process initiated by Francis into concrete, legally secure structures. This shows his appreciation for orderly reforms that build on the magisterium instead of undermining it.

On the other hand, Leo XIV was by no means a mere preservationist. He is regarded as a **"bridge builder" between conservative and progressive forces**, who wants to be measured by his results and who, as a cardinal, has already succeeded in keeping different currents together. As a cardinal in Rome, he was appreciated by church representatives from all camps for his diplomatic, pragmatic and at the same time modest style. His personal career reflects this middle-of-the-road attitude: many years of close collaboration with Pope Francis have shaped him in many ways, for example in terms of pastoral openness. At the same time, he remains clearly theologically rooted in the teachings of the Church. This balancing act - openness in pastoral care, presence in doctrine - could become characteristic of his pontificate. Leo XIV was thus in line with the so-called "pastoral course": the Church's message was to be translated into the present day and applied *mercifully* without abandoning the substance of the faith.

A central keyword of his theology is **synodality**. Leo XIV emphasized right at the beginning: *"We want to be a synodal church on the way"*. In doing so, he was building on his predecessor's vision of the church, which was based on more participation, dialog and listening to the Holy Spirit together. In his first message, he clearly acknowledged this openness and sent the signal that the Catholic Church should be *a people of God on pilgrimage together*. This fundamental theological conviction - that the Church finds its way by **listening and discerning** together - combines tradition (the spirit of the Council of the Apostles and the Second Vatican Council) with progress (new forms of participation by the faithful). Leo XIV seems determined not only to politely continue the synodal process that had begun, but also to fill it with life and emphasis and to implement the results. At the same time, he signaled to the more conservative forces that synodality did not mean arbitrariness: he made it clear that unity in essential matters of faith could be maintained - true to his motto *"In him who is one, we are one"*. This motto can be read as a theological program: Diversity and unity come together in Christ. In this way, the Pope wants to play an **integrating role**, both within the Church and externally, in order to bring together different, diverse cultures, mentalities and styles of piety. His international biography and multilingualism stand him in good stead; he is credited with intercultural sensitivity and a global, but pluralistic, vision of the Church.

Leo XIV's theological approach is also characterized by his **willingness to listen**. His ability to listen to other opinions and voices was already emphasized in the first reactions. Paul Zulehner, a renowned theologian, praised the new pope as a theologically profound and *"spiritually inspired man"* who was not ideologically stubborn. This praise shows that Leo XIV based his decisions less on church politics or personal preferences, but rather sought to feel out the will of God through prayer and conversation. His approach in his important role as prefect for the appointment of bishops already demonstrated this: he was considered to be someone who **carefully weighed up** and took various voices into account before submitting personnel proposals to the Pope. He even implemented a small revolution in this office by appointing women to the advisory committee for the appointment of bishops for the first time - a step that broke with traditional procedures but was in line with Pope Francis' mandate without any loud break. This example is emblematic of Leo's approach: cautious reform steps in line with doctrine to make the church more contemporary and participatory.

Overall, Leo XIV can be seen as **a "pope of the center and of inclusive cooperation".** He sought neither a sharp break with tradition nor a simple *'business as usual'*, but rather a path of **continuous renewal.** Changes should grow organically and be theologically well-founded. At the same time, he is not afraid to **set bold accents** where he considers them necessary - for example in the reform of the curia or the strengthening of the laity. His basic theological stance could therefore be described as *conservative in principle, reform-oriented in application.* The aim seems to be to keep the church authentic and yet enable **"aggiornamento"** - i.e. renewal in the present.

Spiritual and ethical guiding principles of his pontificate

Clear guiding principles emerge from all these aspects, which Pope Leo XIV based his pontificate on. A first guiding principle is the aforementioned **unity in Christ.** His motto *"In Illo uno unum"* puts it in a nutshell: In Christ, who is one, all should be one. This principle of unity permeates his vision on both a spiritual and ethical level. Spiritually, it means that the Church must always find its way back to the center, to Christ - in prayer, in teaching, in the sacraments. Ethically, it means that divisions and injustices should be overcome so that the **community of the human family** is strengthened. Leo XIV saw the Church as an instrument of unity in a divided world: it should bring people together, build bridges and act as a *"sacrament of unity".*

Closely linked to this is the principle of **bridge builders.** Even at his inauguration, Leo XIV promised a church *"that builds bridges"* - between nations, cultures, social classes and also within its own ranks. This model of building bridges is reflected both in his diplomatic skills and in his personal approach. He is committed to **promoting dialog and**

reconciliation wherever there is conflict. In a world marked by wars, polarization, separation and inequality, the Pope wants to strengthen the reconciling role of the Church. His first message to the city and the world was significant: *"Peace be with you all!"* - an appeal that was understood as a programmatic signal in the face of ongoing wars and crises. For Leo XIV, peace work was therefore not a political sideshow, but a core spiritual and ethical concern. In doing so, he built on the legacy of his namesake Leo XIII, who was already regarded as the **"Pope of Peace"** and helped to settle international conflicts.

Another guiding principle is the **option for the poor** and disadvantaged. Leo XIV repeatedly made it clear that the **church of the poor** should remain a central focus - in continuity with John XXIII, Francis and many others. His own career - from a simple missionary in poor communities to the papacy - suggests that he saw the papacy as a service to the least of these. His brother John Prevost put it in a nutshell: Leo XIV would continue Pope Francis' course *"and stand up for the disadvantaged and the poor"*. This ethos of charity is reflected in many of his statements and gestures to date: the new Pope actively seeks closeness to the marginalized, be it through encounters, through intercession in speeches or through structural decisions (such as the aforementioned involvement of lay people and women in responsible processes). For him, **charity** - understood as active love - is not merely a field of action of the Church, but an expression of its essence. He therefore also emphasizes the sacredness of every human life and the Church's duty to be an advocate for the weak, from unborn children to the elderly, sick or refugees.

One of Leo XIV's guiding principles that should not be underestimated is **humility and a willingness to serve in leadership**. After his election, he himself humbly described himself as a *"pilgrim"* on the way with the faithful. This image shows that he did not see the office of pope as an earthly position of power, but as a spiritual ministry. His understanding of authority is essentially defined by the example of Christ, who washed the feet of his disciples. This is why Leo XIV is often quoted with the admonition that bishops - and even more so popes - should **approach** people **authentically and humbly** and *"suffer with them"* instead of acting as rulers. This attitude should characterize his leadership style: collegial, listening, serving. It creates trust - both among the bishops worldwide (many of whom already know him because of his work in the Congregation of Bishops) and among the people of God, who can sense whether a shepherd truly shares in their joys and hopes, grief and fear.

Leo XIV also shows that he attaches great importance to **credibility** and **transparency**. He belongs to a generation of church leaders who are very aware of the church's credibility crisis - for example due to abuse scandals involving sexual violence or abuse of power. In Peru, he did not shy away from taking action against influential conservative networks such as the scandalous *Sodalicio* order, which signals courage and loyalty to principle. Such experiences could underpin his maxim that spiritual authority only endures through moral integrity and dealing honestly with failure. It is therefore to be expected that **reappraisal and prevention** will remain important in his pontificate agenda, coupled with a simple, credible lifestyle in the spirit of *"poverty of spirit"*, as exemplified by Francis.

After all, one of Leo XIV's guiding principles was the **openness of his faith to the world**. As Regina Polak described him, he saw himself as *a "man of the world"*: less charismatic and extraverted than his predecessor, but universally approachable and sustainable in his mission. His international profile (multilingual, interculturally adept) comes to the fore here. Leo XIV clearly wanted to find a **universal approach** that would reach people from different backgrounds. This was already evident in the fact that his first blessing *Urbi et Orbi* ("to the city and the world") was introduced by a simple, general wish for peace - not an extravagant theological manifesto, but an understandable message for all people of good will. It resonates with the desire to present the Church as the *mother and teacher of all peoples*, who speaks to hearts in simple language and stands credibly on the side of humanity.

In summary, **Leo XIV** thus presents a holistic image of a pope who is spiritually rooted in the Augustinian tradition, theologically seeks the center and pastorally focuses on the margins. His **spiritual orientation** - characterized by prayer, a sense of community and trust in God's grace - lends depth and direction to his work. His **theological orientation** - characterized by loyalty to doctrine and a simultaneous will to reform - shows him to be a guardian of tradition who wants to creatively carry it forward into the future. And his **ethical orientation** - visible in his advocacy of justice, inclusion, peace and the integrity of creation - indicates the direction his pontificate was likely to take: towards a church that is an advocate for the weak, that **builds bridges** and sets *signs of hope* in the world. Leo XIV unites many threads of recent church history in his person and program: the social teachings of Leo XIII, the pastoral spirit of the Second Vatican Council, the spiritual legacy of great religious and the new beginnings of the present. With his **balanced, spiritual and people-oriented manner**, there is justified hope that he can - and must - lead the Catholic Church credibly into the future and set new impulses for faith and society. The universal church can look forward to seeing how Leo XIV will bring these guidelines to life in the coming years and achieve documented results, such as the necessary changes to canon law - signs of a promising new beginning are already clearly visible.

 *Chapter 3:*

Continuity and differences on Pope Francis

Pope Leo XIV is taking on a difficult legacy: His predecessor Pope Francis shaped the Catholic Church for over a decade with a new style and a focus on mercy, closeness and a spirit of reform. Francis - the first pope from Latin America and a Jesuit - pursued **a theology of mercy** that often set aside dogmatic strictness in favor of pastoral compassion. He emphasized a *"church as a field hospital"*, which should primarily serve the wounded and marginalized.

Theological and pastoral line in comparison

His pastoral approach was strongly characterized by personal **closeness to the faithful**: Francis sought direct contact, used simple language and broke with many a traditional protocol in order to be close to the people. This human and humble manner was reflected, for example, in the fact that he often gave impromptu speeches and sent inviting signals to groups of Catholics (e.. in formulations such as *"Who am I to judge?"* with regard to queer LGBTQIA+ people). Francis also emphasized openness in his theology: he stressed the **importance of discernment of conscience and spiritual discernment** - an approach that stems from his Jesuit heritage - and placed topics such as social justice, environmental protection and the poor at the center of his teaching (for example in the encyclicals *Laudato Si'* on responsibility for creation and *Fratelli Tutti* on fraternity). Overall, Francis was seen as a pontiff who broke new ground in order to perceive the *"smell of the sheep"* - i.e. the concerns of the simple faithful - even if he had to accept conservative criticism.

How does Pope Leo XIV fit in here? Initial indications suggest that he will continue Francis' course in many respects, but with his own accent. Leo XIV is not only the **first US-American on the papal throne** and a religious (Augustinian) who worked in **Latin America** for a long time. His international biography (USA, Peru, Vatican) clearly shaped his understanding of the universal church. Theologically and pastorally, he is said to be very close to Francis - he is regarded as a *"moderate reformer"* who shares many of the late pontiff's concerns. Leo XIV thus appeared emphatically humble and made gestures close to the people. In his very first address as Pope, for , he greeted the faithful of his former Peruvian diocese in **Spanish**, which made the audience sit up and take notice: for the first time, Italian (and Latin) was not heard at this traditional blessing ceremony on the loggia of St. Peter's Basilica. This detail signals that Leo XIV takes into account the **multilingualism and global diversity** of the Church and - like Francis - consciously breaks with conventions in favor of closeness to the people. Georg Bätzing, the chairman of the German Conference of Bishops, describes Leo XIV **as "reserved and friendly"**, but at the same time ready to speak plainly when it matters. Here, a pope is emerging who shares Francis' warm cordiality, but who may be more conflict-averse and diplomatic. Indeed, Prevost is described as a **pragmatist and diplomat**: He mediated behind the scenes between the reform-minded German bishops and the Vatican in 2023, for example, when Germany's *Synodal Way* met with resistance in Rome. This mediating role fits in with his image as a *man of the middle ground* who wants to keep different church camps together. Francis, on the other hand, did not shy away from polarizing decisions - such as his harsh criticism of curial abuses or his initiative to restrict the traditional liturgy - which earned him much support as well as significant opposition. Leo XIV was likely to proceed more cautiously here: His election itself was seen as a **compromise and a signal of unity** in the divided College of Cardinals. Overall, it can be said that **theologically**, both popes remain in line with Catholic doctrine, but there are small differences in their **pastoral style** - Francis as a charismatic "outsider" and apostle of mercy, Leo XIV as a consensus-oriented bridge-builder and citizen of the world. However, the real continuities and differences are particularly evident in their approach to specific reform issues.

Differences in dealing with key reform issues

Both Francis and Leo XIV are/were faced with similarly pressing reform issues that have been the subject of controversial debate within the

Church for years - and have not progressed. These include, above all, the **strengthening of synodal structures**, the **role of women in church ministries such as the office of popes**, the treatment of **LGBTQIA+ people** (i.e. the question of ecclesial, sacramental recognition and inclusion of homosexual, bisexual, trans* and queer believers) and compulsory celibacy for priests. Francis has initiated debates in all of these areas - albeit to varying degrees - and Leo XIV must now decide how to take up these impulses for renewal or, if necessary, adjust them in a new and better way. A closer look at the positions of the two shows both **continuity** and **differences** in nuances.

Synodality: participation of the faithful

Synodality - i.e. a more synodal, consultative and faithful-inclusive decision-making structure of the Church - was a hallmark of Francis' pontificate. The predecessor of Leo XIV repeatedly emphasized that the church must become "a **church of participation**", in which clergy and laity listen together to the Holy Spirit. Specifically, Francis convened numerous synods and expanded their influence: Most recently, for example, women and non-clergy were allowed to vote for the first time at the 2023 World Synod in Rome. Francis even initiated a worldwide **synodal process** lasting several years, which involved the entire Church in a dialog on pressing issues and was to culminate in two assemblies in 2023 and 2024. Shortly before his death, he laid the foundations for another major ecclesial assembly in 2028 to continue this path of participation. Leo XIV clearly signaled that he wanted to continue this synodal course. He is considered a staunch advocate of a more transparent, listening church: even as a cardinal, he emphasized the need **to include** the **voices of the faithful more and to change the hierarchical style of leadership** in favour of more listening. Immediately after his election, Leo XIV made it clear that he would continue on the path of synodality set out by Francis. Observers such as Father Mauritius Wilde even expect Leo to conduct the synodal consultations in the Franciscan spirit of listening, but to **act more decisively** in the end: As an American, he attaches importance to concrete results and outcomes. This pragmatic approach - *listen, include, then decide* - could mark a slight difference in style. In principle, however, Leo XIV stands for **continuity**: the opening towards regular consultations with the universal church and more co-determination of the laity is likely to progress further under him. The challenge will be to implement synodality in such a way that it unites the Church worldwide instead of creating new divisions. This is where Leo's diplomatic skills come into play, which he has already demonstrated. He will have to master the balancing act **between** the call for genuine participation - for example from the church base and progressive circles - **and** the concern of some traditionalists that synodal processes could jeopardize the hierarchical order and unity of faith.

Women in church offices: between equality and dogma

Hardly any other topic symbolizes the reform backlog as much as the question of **equal rights for women** in the church and in the office of popes. Under Francis, there have been cautious changes in this regard: It is true that Francis also upheld the **non-admission of women to ordained** ministries (priesthood and episcopate), as his predecessors had defined it magisterially. He did, however, promote the **advancement of women in church leadership positions** - he appointed women to leadership positions in the Roman Curia and to advisory bodies and opened up official (albeit non-ordained) ministries such as lector *and acolyte* to women for the first time. Francis also set up commissions to research, for example, the historical question of the diaconate of women (deacons in the early church). These cautious steps showed his willingness to **involve** women **more**, but without yet touching the ban on ordaining women . Leo XIV followed this line of cautious reform - perhaps with a little more restraint. **Until now, Robert Prevost, now Leo XIV, has rejected the ordination of women** and has even hinted at this: at the World Synod of 2023, he warned against the *"clericalization of women"*, i.e. against wanting to give women more influence simply by giving them the priesthood. This is not a solution and would rather create new problems, he emphasized - women already have a variety of central roles in the church. However, he left open which solutions could be considered in the event of a shortage of clerical staff and which paths could be taken to implement equal rights - for example in accordance with the German Basic Law. This statement suggests that Leo XIV **was not** seeking **any short-term changes** to the admission of women to the diaconate or priesthood. Rather, as predicted by experts, he was likely to continue **pragmatic upgrades**: For example, it could appoint more women to positions of responsibility and consolidate the openings that have already begun (women's right to vote in synods, leadership of authorities by laywomen, etc.). This would be a change to the **Definiendum** without at the same time adapting the **Definiens** accordingly: Introduction in practice, without adapting the written defining doctrine - it would thus correspond to the possibility of simultaneously being believers (**credens**) without actively participating in the church's Sunday life (**practicans**) - a separation that is increasingly the reality of many people's lives, like the default of supposedly heterosexual clergy who, however, know to have same-sex feelings. Georg Essen, professor of theology at the HU Berlin, for example, expects Leo to "pragmatically enhance" the role of women without changing the fundamental ban on ordination. A balancing act in which content does not follow form. There will therefore - in all likelihood - be no great leaps such as the ordination of women to the priesthood from this pope if he remains in the mindset status of his cardinal position and does not live up to his own vision of the Father for all with restrictions.

On the other hand, pressure from grassroots movements is growing, especially in Europe: Groups such as the Katholische Frauengemeinschaft Deutschlands (kfd) and initiatives such as *Maria 2.0* have long been calling for **women** to be **admitted to all ordained ministries**. They hope that Leo XIV will "open the doors of the church wide - for all people. For example, the *Maria 1.0* initiative - which expects the new Pope to put his foot down **against the false hopes of the unrealistic conservatives**. Leo XIV must therefore find a middle way between reformists and traditionalists. There is **continuity** insofar as Francis also had to perform this balancing act and ultimately stuck to the no to the ordination of women - but the emphasis may be **different**: Francis at least left the theological debate (e.g. on deacons) open, while Leo XIV was already more skeptical in this regard. In the end, the decisive factor will be whether Leo XIV can credibly convey to the many committed women in the Church that their contribution is dispensable if the **sacraments** and the office of popes are reserved for men only.

LGBTQ inclusion: welcoming without changing teaching?

Nowadays, much attention is focused on how open the church is towards **queer people** - that is, people with different sexual orientations and gender identities. Pope Francis was characterized by a much **more dialogical and compassionate tone** in this area, but without fundamentally revising traditional doctrine (which classifies homosexual acts as "disordered", for example). His statement *"Who am I to judge?"* with regard to a believer with same-sex feelings became famous. Under Francis, there were isolated tendencies towards openness: he encouraged pastors not to turn the door on same-sex loving people and spoke out in favor of legal protection for same-sex partnerships. In 2023, Francis hinted that **blessings for same-sex couples** could be possible under certain circumstances - even if others put the **sacramental marriage of queer couples** on the agenda for full equality and inclusion. This at least pastoral flexibility was seen by many as a step towards more inclusion, although Catholic moral teaching remained formally unchanged.

Robert Prevost's previous statements indicate that Leo XIV **needs to be more involved in the topic** than Francis. LGBTQIA+ Catholics expressed concern after his election and referred to previous statements by the new pope. In fact, Prevost had polemicized against the introduction of gender issues in school lessons during his time as Bishop of Chiclayo (Peru) many years ago: *"The promotion of gender ideology is confusing because it tries to create genders that do not exist,"* he said at the time. Prevost became even clearer in 2012 at a synod of bishops in Rome: the Western media, he said, were *"arousing enormous sympathy for beliefs and practices that contradict the Gospel - for example abortion, homosexual lifestyles, euthanasia"*.

The earlier equation of same-sex love with euthanasia appears today to be a misguided path that is difficult to comprehend and a mistake made by a young man at the time. It may be credited to him that he was socialized at that time in the context of a province in Peru and lacked the corresponding perspectives and experiences. Today, however, as **Pope,** he is **faced with the task of going beyond personal attitudes to**

have an institutional and integrative impact, negotiating positions in dialog with affected interest groups, church-related associations and the faithful and facing up to their critical questions. In retrospect, such early formulations, which brand certain lifestyles as immoral across the board, appear much less experienced than the conciliatory tone of an experienced official such as Pope Francis. It is clear that these quotes were made several years ago.

Whether Leo XIV can and will nuance his stance as Pope remains to be seen - his first speeches indicated that he wanted to begin his pontificate under the banner of reconciliation, inclusion and peace, which gives us hope that these groups of the faithful will also be included. Whoever begins his pontificate in this way must follow up with results, or as we say in the vernacular: whoever says A must also act with and according to B. The sacramental marriage ceremony is the symbol of **full equality for queer people in the Catholic Church**.

For the time being, however, **continuity** is recognizable above all in that Leo XIV - like Francis before him - does not seek to change the Church's teaching on sexual morality - including for heterosexuals, contraceptives or divorcees: after all, he still has a few days for an initial assessment of 100 or more days. It will probably remain the case that marriage is defined by the Church as a union between a man and a woman and that a sacramental marriage ceremony for same-sex couples remains excluded: therefore, one must ask why love should be different or discriminate against sexual orientation. However, Leo XIV, like Francis, is faced with the task of **pastoral ways for LGBTQIA+ believers and queer marriage partners** to be welcomed into the church on an equal footing. He does not fundamentally reject the tension between an appreciative welcome and the preservation of traditional morals - but it does require sensitivity. Leo XIV could continue the dialog with LGBTQIA+ groups begun by Francis and make it clear that every person - regardless of their sexual orientation - is loved and respected in the Church, i.e. is not excluded sacramentally. It therefore remains an open question as to how Leo XIV will clearly answer the pressing question of church recognition of homosexual couples in some countries, or whether he will leave a certain pastoral **gray area** like his predecessor.

Compulsory celibacy: celibacy put to the test

Priestly celibacy - the mandatory celibacy of Catholic priests in the Latin Church - has been the subject of reform debates for decades. Francis has maintained the existing regulation and has not generally abolished compulsory celibacy. However, he was open to discussion: At the 2019 Amazon Synod, for example, he had the ordination of proven married men (so-called *viri probati*) discussed in order to counter the extreme shortage of priests in remote areas. This concept has recently been expanded to include *"homines probati"* and *"laici probati"* by recruiting previously marginalized members of the Catholic Church, such as lay women.

In the end, Francis decided against allowing such an exception in his post-synodal letter *Querida Amazonia* - much to the disappointment of those who had hoped for movement on this issue. Nevertheless, Francis repeatedly emphasized that celibacy is **"not a dogma"**, but an ecclesiastical discipline. He thus made it clear that the rule of celibacy could be changed in principle - albeit not lightly. Under Pope Leo XIV, the question now arises anew: will he maintain the status quo on celibacy like his predecessors, or are there signs of change?

As a religious, Leo XIV was personally committed to the ideal of celibacy, but from his practical pastoral work he was aware of the need for a shortage of priests, especially from Latin America. Some churchmen **consider it conceivable** that cautious openings were considered under Leo XIV. Theologian Thomas Söding, himself a member of the Central Committee of German Catholics, said it was *"not impossible"* that Leo XIV would bring movement to the question of celibacy - precisely because he knew the pastoral reality and, as a canon lawyer, knew that celibacy was not an irrevocable dogma. Of course, such an intention has not been confirmed. Rather, it should be noted that Leo XIV came from a rather conservative US church spectrum, where celibacy is less questioned than in Europe, for example. However, the Western and American idea of equality between women and men hits a pope all the harder today.

Like Francis, Leo XIV will probably **have to weigh things up carefully**: On the one hand, there are loud calls - even from prominent church representatives such as Cardinal Reinhard Marx - for celibacy to be abolished in order to allow priests to lead a more "normal" life and perhaps also attract more vocations. On the other hand, celibacy stands for a centuries-old spiritual tradition that is closely linked to the identity of the Catholic priesthood. Francis ultimately decided not to loosen this tradition yet, and Leo XIV could act similarly out of a sense of unity and due to his formative socialization. Church historian Hubert Wolf, for example, **does not** expect Leo XIV **to make any radical reforms** with regard to married priests. Continuity would therefore mean that compulsory celibacy would remain for the time being. However, Leo XIV had to take reality seriously: There is a lack of priests in many parishes, and not least the sexual abuse scandal of male priests against children and adolescents has brought the celibate lifestyle back into the discussion (without a causal connection being conclusively proven, but a proximity to sexual violence under further conditions must and can be established). A possible **compromise solution** would be to give more room to the already existing exceptions - for example, to use married permanent deacons more in pastoral care, or in special cases to ordain experienced married people as priests, as is customary in the Eastern churches united with Rome. It remains to be seen whether Leo XIV will dare to take such a step, but it is certain that the issue will remain on the agenda and must at least be **given further consideration** by the new pope - something that every woman has long since thought through.

Francis' reform impulses and their further development under Leo XIV.

If you look at Pope Francis' entire agenda, it becomes clear that he has embarked on a comprehensive reform course - from reforming the Curia to setting new priorities in doctrine and changing the image of the Church. Pope Leo XIV largely **inherited** a **legacy of renewal** and has signaled his intention to continue much of it, but also to set his own accents in the reform agenda. Some central *Franciscan* reform impulses and how Leo XIV dealt with them:

- **Curia reform and decentralization of power:** Francis fundamentally restructured the Roman Curia with the

Apostolic Constitution *Praedicate Evangelium* (2022) - authorities were merged, lay people (women as well as men) can now take on top positions, and the mission of the Curia should be more focused on serving the universal church. Leo XIV adopted this reformed administrative structure and now had to **fill** it **with life**. As the former head of the Congregation of Bishops, he knows the work of the Curia inside out and is considered a capable organizer. He is expected to continue Francis' course, for by continuing to appoint **competent lay people to leadership roles** and strengthening cooperation between the Vatican and the local conferences of bishops. His diplomatic nature could help to continue the **decentralization** begun by Francis in a balanced way - that is, to give the local churches more autonomy without jeopardizing unity.

- **Social and environmental commitment:** One of the hallmarks of Francis' pontificate was his focus on the pressing **social and environmental issues** of our time. He published the first papal encyclical devoted entirely to climate change and environmental protection (*Laudato Si'*) and took sides with the poor, migrants and other groups. Leo XIV explicitly showed **continuity** here. Even as a cardinal, he, like Francis, repeatedly expressed the need for decisive action against climate change. The choice of his name is also noteworthy: **Leo XIV** deliberately refers to Pope **Leo XIII** (pontificate 1878-1903), who published the Church's first social encyclical, *Rerum Novarum*, in 1891. This letter laid the foundation for Catholic social teaching and was dedicated to the situation of the impoverished working class. By naming himself after this Leo XIII, Robert Prevost at least signals a **program continuity in social doctrine** - namely the commitment to social justice, the rights of workers and the option for the poor. If there is no other new Novarum - nomen est omen: and if he chooses the name Leo in this tradition and with the knowledge and the urgent reform issues, it should not remain an empty shell like an unattended service in the local parish church. In fact, Leo

XIV is already being described as **the "most international pope"**, who knows the concerns of ordinary people ("the heart of the little people") as well as the world of diplomacy. We can therefore expect him to continue and renew Francis' commitment to peace, justice and the preservation of creation - more than the minimum. Even in his very first words as Pope, Leo XIV placed the **peace of all** at the center. In view of wars and conflicts worldwide, many believers see him as a possible *"Pope of Inclusion"* and *"Pope of Peace"*, who carries on the appeals for peace and attempts at integration of his predecessor. There is no difference here, but rather a closing of ranks: Both popes recognize that credibility today is also measured by how the Church stands on global humanitarian challenges - be it the climate crisis, social inequality, equal rights, women and men or war and peace.

- **Dealing with sexual abuse and transparency:** The worldwide **church scandal of sexual abuse** is a sad, ongoing topic that has already preoccupied Francis intensively. Francis took a number of important steps to improve the investigation - for example, he lifted papal secrecy in abuse proceedings so that internal church files could be passed on to the state judiciary and obliged clergy worldwide to report suspected cases. Nevertheless, much remained to be done under Francis: victims' associations criticized his hesitant approach, and in many countries an independent investigation into clerical offences is still pending. Leo XIV will have to **act urgently** to restore lost trust. He has a certain amount of experience - during his time in Peru, Prevost supported victims of abuse and was seen as someone who took their concerns seriously. However, there are also points of criticism: He is accused of not having taken consistent action in every case as bishop in Chicago and Chiclayo, which he denies. The fact is that Leo XIV can build on the structures created by Francis (such as new ecclesiastical penal norms and commissions). The new pope has the chance to tackle the **"hot potato"** of abuse even more resolutely - for example by holding male bishops who have covered it up to account and promoting transparent investigations worldwide. It remains to be seen to what extent he will carry on and perhaps strengthen the reform impulse of his predecessor: Francis has laid a foundation, but the **zero-tolerance culture** must be implemented consistently in order to be credible. Leo XIV has already signaled that the Church should follow in the footsteps of Francis; this is particularly true in this area, which determines the moral integrity of the Church.

In summary, it can be said that Leo XIV clearly stands on Francis' shoulders in many reform concerns - he **takes on** his central concerns such as synodality, social justice, climate protection and a pastoral church of closeness. At the same time, he will set his own **priorities** - and will have to do so with concrete, effective and sustainable results - in terms of implementation: possibly in a more sober, mediating manner and with the eye of an experienced administrator. Precisely because Francis outlined such great visions, it is now up to Leo XIV to translate these visions into the administrative and everyday reality of the Church. The stakes are high - as are the problems: acting may mean making fewer media gestures, but securing administrative reforms in the background and moderating dialog processes in a results-oriented manner. Just like in a state parliament: Only written amendments to laws create a new reality-

New challenges and necessary answers

Even if there is much to suggest boring **continuity**, Leo XIV faces a series of new or intensified challenges, some of which were already virulent under Francis, but now demand answers even more urgently. Groups close to the Church are asking very clearly. The following is an overview of key problem areas in which the new Pope will have to find solutions - without anticipating how he *will* decide, it is possible to outline the **options** on the table and the **challenges that** lie ahead:

- **A divided church:** The universal Catholic Church is fragmented into different camps - **progressive** forces demand reforms (women's ministries, LGBTQIA+

recognition, democracy in the church), while **conservative** circles call for a return to traditional teaching without transformative interpretation and recognition of a newer reality. Especially in Leo XIV's homeland, the USA, the Church is *"deeply divided"* as a reflection of political polarization. The new pope must counteract this division. The option is an **inclusive leadership style** that listens to both sides and tries to emphasize common concerns (e.. commitment to life, justice). The challenge remains that compromises in matters of faith are difficult to achieve - Leo XIV must therefore above all create confidence that reform and fidelity to the core of the faith are not mutually exclusive.

- **Women and equal rights:** The issue of **gender equality** continues to loom large. It is hardly understood in society that women are excluded from important offices; this contributes to the alienation of many believers in Western Europe. Leo XIV must find new answers as to how women can receive equal participation and recognition. One option (in addition to the leadership roles already mentioned) would be **the theological upgrading of their ministries**: Women could, for , officially become baptizers, preachers or church leaders, even without ordination to the priesthood. Taking the second step here requires an answer to the question of why women should not become popes but are given ministries at grassroots level. It would also be conceivable to revisit the topic of **the diaconate for women** - a decision that Francis has left open. The challenge lies in achieving changes without causing a break with the previous doctrinal tradition. Leo XIV will have to proceed cautiously but swiftly in order to both take the call for equality seriously and avoid a **break** with the Catholic Church's **understanding of the priesthood.**
- **Dealing with LGBTQIA+ people:** At a time when many states recognize marriage and rights for same-sex couples and diversity of identities is socially accepted, the Church is under pressure to communicate its stance convincingly.

Leo XIV must decide whether and how he will shape **pastoral openings** for LGBTQIA+ people. Options would be, for , an official handout that allows pastoral **sacramental celebrations** for loving, committed same-sex partnerships (as individual bishops would like to practice), - Can it be a commandment of charity not to define this as a church wedding ceremony when even God loves everyone as he created them? Another addition is the drafting of a pastoral letter on the appreciation of people with a homosexual orientation in order to reduce discrimination within the church. The challenge is to keep **the universal Church, social reality and the Magisterium in harmony:** In some cultures (especially in the global North) the pressure for recognition is growing, while in others (Africa, Asia) even a slight opening could incorporate reflections. Leo XIV must find a course that takes the universal Church with him - possibly by resolving this issue more strongly at the level of the respective regions (keyword: **differentiation according to cultural groups**). Irrespective of structural solutions, it is expected that he - like Francis - will at least make it clear in his tone that **every person, every married couple is loved by God** and that the Church excludes no one. This is his vision of the inclusive church.

- **Lack of priests and celibacy:** The worldwide **decline in priestly vocations** - particularly in Europe and America, but also in parts of Latin America - is coming to a head. Parishes are being merged, and Eucharistic celebrations can only take place rarely in some places. This raises the question of whether compulsory celibacy is still in keeping with the times or whether the Church must take alternative paths and abolish it. Leo XIV will have to find solutions to the shortage of priests, according to many calls. In addition to a stronger pastoral care of vocations, there is the option of **extending the conditions for admission** to the priesthood: for example, ordaining selected married deacons or proven parents as priests in exceptional cases. This option was openly advocated on the German Synodal Path and elsewhere. The challenge is that a softening of the celibacy requirement would be seen in conservative circles as a transformation of a sacred tradition, which they would have to go along with in terms of their world view. It is also unclear whether allowing married priests would actually significantly increase the number of vocations. Leo XIV had to weigh up between **preserving a spiritual, imposed way of life** and the pragmatic need for pastoral care. Alternative approaches - e.. greater involvement of lay pastors or new models of parish leadership in which priests are relieved - could also be part of the answer. However, going down this path shows that people are sewing on the edge and are not prepared to change in the hope of the older or more conservative that it can meet the expectations of the younger or more progressive - although this does not have to coincide.

- **Crisis of confidence due to abuse scandal**: One of the main reasons for the church's massive loss of credibility is the sexual abuse scandals and its inadequate handling of the past. Society expects the Pope to act with **zero tolerance** and maximum transparency. Leo XIV is faced with the task of establishing globally binding standards for dealing with the past. Necessary steps could include: the establishment of independent investigation commissions in every conference of bishops, more decisive action against cover-up bishops (up to and including dismissal from office) and closer cooperation with state authorities. Francis has opened important doors (abolition of papal secrecy, new canonical norms), but the implementation is now in the hands of Leo XIV. The challenge will be to bring the **global church** - with very different legal systems and mentalities - onto a consistent course and to show the victims that the church has learned from its mistakes. There is zero room for whitewashing here; Leo XIV's pontificate will have to be measured by whether it succeeds in regaining the lost trust bit by bit through measures.

- **Social and global political expectations:** In addition to the issues of reform within the Church, Leo XIV was confronted with great **global political and social expectations.** Many people - including those outside the Church - hoped for a strong moral compass in a crisis-ridden world. Peace, as mentioned, is a central theme: Leo XIV is expected to make a name for himself as a **peacemaker** and to continue his mediation efforts, for example in the Ukraine conflict or other wars. His voice could also carry weight in the **global economy and social policy** when it comes to combating poverty, migration or global justice. The challenge for the new Pope is to bring **faith and ethics into the public discourse** without allowing himself to be taken over by political actors. As the first pope from the USA, Leo XIV has a special role to play here: He knows the Western world power from his own experience and could - it is speculated - represent a counterpoint to tendencies towards isolation and division. At the same time, he had to be careful to maintain a global perspective and not be seen merely as the "American pope". Leo XIV has the chance to continue the **Franciscan openness to the world** (Francis reached out to both the powerful and the marginalized) and to build new bridges with his cosmopolitan biography.

In summary, Pope Leo XIV faces a balancing act of embodying **continuity and renewal** in equal measure. In many respects, he is following in the footsteps of Francis: both are united by a heart for people on the margins, a sense of justice and the will to bring the Church closer to the faithful. Differences are more apparent in style and emphasis: Leo XIV acts more diplomatically and moderately - a *"moderate reformer"* who wants reforms, but without media publicity and a break with tradition. The coming years will show whether he succeeds in resolutely tackling the church's unresolved issues - from the question of women to abuse. What is certain is that **social realities** demand answers - because everyone has questions. Leo XIV will not be able to use personal preferences as a yardstick, but rather the good of the whole Church and its faithful. History teaches us that every pope is different. But the tension between continuity and change will determine whether Leo XIV can lead the Church credibly into the future. The world looks to this new pontiff with high expectations - as a *reformer, cosmopolitan and pragmatist* - and in his work, the **lines of Francis** will have to be continued and developed in new ways.

🕊 *Chapter 4:*
Personal qualities and leadership style

When Leo XIV gave the blessing "Urbi et Orbi" on the loggia of St. Peter's Basilica on the evening of his election and even addressed a few words in Spanish to his former diocese, a few nuns thousands of kilometers away burst into tears. These sisters from Chiclayo in Peru had recognized their former bishop - **a pastor "who was close to the people"**, as Sister Karina Gonzales Risco reported. In fact, the new pope was already considered to be **close to the shepherds and humble** in Peru: He rode for hours on the back of a mule along dirt roads to reach remote villages, **"used the people's means of transportation"**, as the nun recounted - this is how he wanted to *"be one of us"*. His close connection with the simple people and the poor even earned him the nickname **"Saint of the North"**, as he was known in Peru. *"He had time for everyone"*, recalls an Augustinian priest from Peru, *"he was someone who would pick you up on the way"*. This spirit of **closeness and humanity** still characterizes Leo XIV today.

Character and personal values

Robert Francis Prevost comes from Chicago, but Peru became his second home. The young Augustinian priest came to Latin America as a missionary in 1985 and fell in love with the country and its people. **With his open nature and charisma**, he quickly gained access: *"He had this aura that spoke to people. People flocked to him,"* recalls a former altar boy of the young Padre Prevost. Despite initial language barriers, Prevost made an effort to live, learn and even play with the locals - he organized sports and excursions for young people to keep them away from crime. He showed **courage and loyalty** in dangerous times: When the terror of the *Sendero Luminoso* (Shining Path) shook Peru in the 1980s and missionaries were threatened with death, **Prevost steadfastly stayed with the people** instead of fleeing to safety . *"What made them stay were the people,"* says a priest about Prevost and his fellow brothers and sisters. This **deeply felt solidarity** with the local faithful runs through Prevost's life.

Modesty, dedication and a sense of justice were among the defining values of Leo XIV. During his time as Bishop of Chiclayo, he lived the *option for the poor* in the spirit of Pope Francis: *"Many people are poor. Bishop Prevost lived the option for the poor in the spirit of Pope Francis and was always there for everyone, even the poorest people,"* reports Jürgen Huber, a German expert on the Peruvian church. Prevost did not hesitate to raise his voice against social grievances - *"time and again, the bishop addressed politicians with admonishing words,"* says Huber. **Environmental and climate protection** were also close to his heart: his diocese suffered from extreme weather and flooding caused by *El Niño*, and Prevost organized aid for the victims and denounced the neglect of public infrastructure. This hands-on approach earned him great esteem - *"everyone liked him"*, recalls Sister Gonzales Risco. Even when he had already been appointed as a senior curia official in Rome in 2023**, Prevost stayed with his people in Peru until the very end** to deal with the consequences of heavy rainfall. *"He wanted to help until the end, even when he had already been appointed to Rome,"* says the nun about that time. This sense of duty and **empathy for the suffering** are qualities that now also characterize Leo XIV in the office of Pope.

Management style and leadership competence

Leo XIV brought with him an impressive wealth of experience in leading positions - from the leadership of the order to the administration of the Curia. Prevost was twice elected **Prior General of the Augustinian Order** and thus stood at the head of a worldwide order with a centuries-old tradition. In this role, he learned to **lead internationally and collegially**, in constant exchange with brothers and sisters from different cultures. Augustinians - just like the Jesuits, from whose ranks his predecessor Francis came - cultivate a community spirit: faith is shared and decided together. You can see this imprint on Leo XIV. He is regarded as a **team player** who can listen to and focuses on balance rather than authoritarian intervention. **His winning manner** creates trust - qualities that were also evident in the conclave: Observers see the fact that the cardinals agreed on Prevost as the new pope unusually quickly as a sign of the great support and trust he enjoys among church leaders.

Prevost has proven himself not only in the spiritual community, but also as an **administrator and manager**. *"He is a religious man ... and ultimately he is a manager,"* commented Vatican expert Tilmann Kleinjung after the election, as Pope Francis had brought Prevost to Rome in 2023 and *entrusted* him *with one of the most important offices in the Vatican: the Department for Bishops - the personnel department* of the universal church. As Prefect of the Dicastery for Bishops, Cardinal Prevost was responsible for the selection of new bishops worldwide - a task of enormous responsibility that requires diplomatic skills, knowledge of human nature and decisiveness. Colleagues attest to his great sensitivity in this area: *"As head of the bishops' authority in the Vatican, Cardinal Prevost enjoys great trust within the Catholic Church,"* said one Austrian bishop approvingly. Prevost is regarded as someone who can **reform structures in a well thought-out manner** and at the same time seeks personal encounters. As prefect, for example, he oversaw a small revolution when women were given the right to vote in the selection of bishops for the first time - an initiative by Pope Francis that Prevost put into practice.

Prevost's **dynamic leadership style** was also evident at diocesan level. In Chiclayo, where he became bishop in 2015, **he brought a breath of fresh air to a rigid local church**. *"Chiclayo used to be an Opus Dei diocese, very conservative and clerical,"* explains Jürgen Huber. But under Prevost's leadership, **the local church opened up**: *"Today there are many active and committed lay people there..."* These are all things *that Bishop Prevost has sown there.* In particular, he set new accents in the training of priests. Many of the young priests who were trained during his time were **open and synodal** - which Huber explicitly attributes to Prevost's influence: *"This is due to the way Bishop Prevost set up his seminary and organized ".* Instead of promoting clerical elitism, the Augustinians under Prevost emphasized **education and humility**, Huber continues. Prevost successfully practiced this cooperative understanding of leadership based on the Gospel and today's world in Peru - and it seems to have carried over seamlessly into his pontificate. Many observers see his election itself as a **signal for balance and unity** in the Church: *"His election is seen as a compromise*

- *and at the same time as a signal of unity"*, wrote one magazine about Leo XIV, *"Prevost combines American origins, Latin American influence and Roman experience"*. He does not fit into any simple pigeonhole and can build bridges. Or as *Stern* put it pointedly: *"He is not a liberal. But neither is he a concrete head... Pope Leo XIV does not fit into any pigeonhole"*. It is precisely this **ability to strike a balance** - to act neither rigorously tough nor ultra-liberal - that defines his leadership style and gives many hope that he will be able to navigate the Church through turbulent times.

Communication skills and external impact

Already in the first days of his pontificate, Leo XIV showed that he was **a master of communication** - not of pompous words, but of simple gestures and dialogues. The new pope **spoke several languages** fluently: In addition to English and Spanish - his two "home languages" - he also speaks Italian and probably some French. His manner is both urbane and close to the people. During the first blessing at St. Peter's Basilica, he greeted the crowd in several languages and focused on a simple but central core of the message: *"God loves us, God loves everyone,"* he called out to the people in the square. This unmistakably echoed the legacy of his predecessor Francis, who always placed **God's mercy** at the center. Leo XIV also paid homage to Francis in terms of content, but he did so in **his own, heartfelt way**.

Shortly after his election, he demonstrated a sense of **humor and humanity in his dealings with the media**. In his very first audience for the 3,000 or so journalists present at the Vatican, he drew laughter and applause when he jokingly remarked in English: *"They say it doesn't matter if people clap at the beginning. If you are still awake at the end of my speech and would like to applaud - thank you very much"*. With such spontaneous words, he won the hearts of the media representatives. But Leo XIV didn't just have a joke in his luggage, he also had a **weighty message about the responsibility of the media**. *"We must say no to the war of words and images. We must reject the paradigm of war,"* he warned and called for communication to always be geared **towards the search for truth, dialog and peace**. The media and the public should not allow themselves to be driven by aggressive language and pure sensationalism, the Pope said. *"Peace begins with each and every one* *of us, in the way we look at, listen to and speak about our fellow human beings,"* Leo XIV declared emphatically. These words were echoed enormously - they underline his reputation as a **bridge builder and peacemaker** who wanted to set a conciliatory tone in polarized times.

The public image of the new pope has so far been characterized by great open-mindedness. Even secular media are amazed at how balanced and unbiased Leo XIV appears. *"Born in the USA - at home in Latin America. He doesn't fit into any pigeonhole,"* is how *Stern* characterized him, emphasizing that Prevost was not a dogmatic hardliner, but also not an outspoken progressive. This middle ground, which is difficult to categorize, seems to be his strength: he sends signals to **all parts of the church**. For example, it was emphasized that, as a North American, he is also *"part of a worldwide religious community"* - his roots and experiences reach far beyond the USA. Many Catholics in Latin America feel truly represented by him in the papal office for the first time; after all, Leo XIV even has Peruvian citizenship. **The joy in Peru** at his election was enormous: in Chiclayo, his former diocese, thousands celebrated their "adopted son" on the streets and praised his *"big heart"* for the people. The election was also greeted with interest in the United States, where many hope that a pope from Chicago will be able to build bridges between the conflicting wings of the American church.

Within the Vatican Curia and among bishops worldwide, Leo XIV is already regarded as a **strong communicator and approachable**. Numerous church people report that Prevost is *"very competent, listens well and understands situations quickly"*. This praise comes from someone who should know: Jürgen Huber got to know Prevost as a papal representative in a complicated church situation and was impressed by how calmly and understandingly the current Pope tackles even complex problems. Leo XIV's **ability to listen** - an often invoked virtue of Pope Francis - continues. In Rome, as in Peru, he has gained a reputation for being approachable: not an aloof hierarch, but an **advocate of human dignity** who prefers to engage in conversation, even with questions. This openness is felt by ordinary believers as well as journalists and dignitaries. One Austrian bishop praised Leo XIV as a *bridge builder, peacemaker and advocate of human dignity and justice,* convinced that he would continue the course of dialogue and reconciliation set by Francis. Such voices show that the new Pope has already won the **trust and sympathy** of many different camps in the first few days.

Dealing with challenges and crises

Despite all his popularity, enormous tasks await Leo XIV - *"almost superhuman tasks"*, according to commentators. The Catholic Church is facing challenges that require the new pope's full **will to lead and his ability to withstand crises. Within the Church, tensions threaten** to tear unity apart: *between the South and the North, reformers and preservationists, diverse women and diverse men.* Bridging these rifts was perhaps the greatest test for Leo XIV, who now *had to be "a pope for all".* However, his previous stations have virtually prepared him for this. In Peru, he experienced what it means to **overcome cultural differences** - as a North American, he won the trust of the people there without denying his identity. He knows the concerns of the young churches in Latin America and Africa as well as the issues of the old churches in Europe and North America. This global perspective could help him to moderate conflicts. His election itself is seen by many as a compromise between different directions, which raises the expectation that Leo XIV will have a **reconciling and conciliatory effect, but not a consoling one.** A first indication of this: following the conclave, the new pope expressly prayed for his predecessor Francis and his missionary legacy, **but also struck a new note**, for example by choosing his papal name Leo in deliberate reference to Leo XIII. Leo XIII is the pope who wrote the first social encyclical in 1891 and sensitized the church to the rights of workers. Leo XIV's choice of name can therefore be understood as **a program:** Like his predecessors, this pope wants to stand up for **social justice** - a clear message in a world full of inequality - and not just in financial terms.

One pressing challenge is to consistently **deal with the abuse scandal** in the Church - a *"darkest chapter"* that has only been partially overcome under Francis. Francis has issued stricter rules and laws against sexualized violence; now it is up to Leo XIV to ensure that they are **applied across the board and without compromise.** How does the new Pope himself deal with this sensitive issue? His record is not free of criticism: specifically, three women religious complained that he had not sufficiently followed up a report of abuse against a priest in Chiclayo in 2022. However, well-known voices on the ground are supporting the new pope: Edinson Farfán, Prevost's successor as Bishop of Chiclayo, firmly rejected the accusations. *"That is a lie. He listened, he respected the procedures,"* Farfán clarified. On the contrary, Prevost had *"reacted **the fastest of all in** the Peruvian church to these cases"* and made justice possible. One snail doesn't peck at another? - This view is also supported by an independent source: Father Hans Zollner, one of the best-known church abuse experts, considers the accusations made against Prevost to be *"slanderous"* and emphasizes that Prevost acted correctly in both cases in question. The background to the accusations is apparently a conflict with the scandal-ridden Sodalitium Christi cult, a group in Peru that Pope Francis has dissolved. Prevost had played a key role in cleaning up this powerful network, which had been tainted by serious cases of abuse. The fact that he is now being accused of a cover-up is seen by experts such as Huber as a **tit-for-tat response from disempowered circles**. Leo XIV is therefore unlikely to be a naive figure in this area in particular, but someone who knows the **power struggles for transparency and responsibility** from his own experience. Expectations are high that he will emphatically continue the course set by Francis - *"tightening the rules is not enough, they must finally be applied consistently"*. Victims' associations and reformers hope that Leo XIV **will not** allow **any leniency towards perpetrators or cover-ups**, but will consistently pursue the *zero-tolerance line*.

Another major construction site is the **reform of the curia and financial restructuring** of the Vatican. This is where Prevost's *managerial talent* comes into play. The Vatican is struggling with considerable financial deficits - the most recent annual deficit amounted to around 80 million euros. Leo XIV is expected to continue the administrative reforms that have been initiated, ensure **transparency and professionalism** and stabilize the finances. As a former general of a religious order, he has experience in budgeting, and as the bishop of a missionary diocese, he knows how to achieve a lot with scarce resources. He also has a good overview of the **global human resources** of the Church thanks to his time in the Dicastery of Bishops - he knows many dioceses and their challenges from a personnel perspective. This knowledge could be helpful in putting the right people in the right places, be it in the Curia or in important dioceses.

Finally, Leo XIV also faced **pastoral tensions** that required sensitivity. One example is the equality - and not the role - of women in the Church. Francis has appointed some women to leadership positions in the Vatican, but they are still denied ordained ministries - *"For how much longer?"* asked commentator Kleinjung. **Expectations of change** - for example in the diaconate of women or the inclusion of laywomen in leadership roles - are high, especially in Europe and North America. At the same time, there was fierce resistance to any expansion of lay rights or liturgical reforms, especially from traditionalist circles. Leo XIV will have to proceed with caution: **Pursue reforms without jeopardizing church unity**. His CV suggests that he is **ready for a synodal style** - in other words, he wants to work together with bishops and the faithful to find solutions . In Peru, he has focused on the participation of lay people and young people. And the ongoing worldwide synodal process of the Church (the "World Synod") is now in his hands. Many hope that Leo XIV will promote the cause of a *"synodal church"* with conviction. *"I hope that he will advance the synodal church throughout the world,"* says Father Szeles hopefully. It is fitting that Prevost has always sought exchange even as a bishop - with Protestants, for example: When the anniversary of the Reformation and Martin Luther, the Augustinian monk, were discussed at retreats in 2017, Prevost *"smiled broadly, with that welcoming smile that we now also know from the media"*. This smile perhaps symbolizes his **willingness to engage in dialogue**: he does not shy away from difficult topics, but is increasingly approaching them openly - without prejudice.

Leo XIV also observed the world outside the Church with great expectations. He had already made his mark, particularly on issues of **peace and social justice**. The fact that he began his pontificate with an extended greeting of peace - *"May the Lord give you peace"* were his first words to the city and the world - is seen by many as a powerful sign. *"How desperately this world needs a strong advocate for peace,"* commented one television station, and Leo XIV seems determined to be that advocate. At a time when war is raging in Europe and conflicts are smouldering in many places, the **Pope's voice for reconciliation** is urgently needed. Leo XIV has also signaled that he wants to speak (and write) plainly on the international stage. Even as a cardinal, he was not afraid to take a clear stance on the issue of migration, for example. *"Trump will be surprised what the Pope has to say to him,"* predicted Jürgen Huber with a wink, referring to Prevost's commitment to migrants in Peru. In fact, Leo XIV uniquely combines the background of an American with the heart of a Latin American. He knows **both worlds**: the affluent society and the reality of the poor. This gives him credibility when he wants to build bridges between North and South.

In summary, Pope Leo XIV is characterized as a **man of balance and committed action**. His personal path - from a youth missionary in the Peruvian Andes to a doer of bishops in Rome - gave him skills that are now in demand: Empathy and determination, humility and leadership, the ability to engage in dialog and adherence to principles with a successful capacity for reform. Companions praise his humanity and closeness, the media praise his open-mindedness and willingness to compromise. One thing is certain: the coming years will show how Leo XIV uses these qualities to master the various crises and tasks. The advance praise is considerable - now **Catholics all over the world are praying and looking hopefully to Leo XIV**, who is preparing to lead the Church into the present as a *bridge-builder* and *benevolent shepherd*.

🕊 *Chapter 5:*
Pastoral goals and priorities

When Pope **Leo XIV** appeared on the loggia of St. Peter's Basilica on the evening of his election, he greeted the world with a simple, profound word: *"Peace be with you all."* He thus outlined a pastoral vision of *reconciliation, inclusion, justice and openness*. His missionary self-image, his option for the poor and inclusive pastoral care, i.e. also queer pastoral care, his dialog with society and cultures as well as his commitment to education and social justice intertwine and shape the mission of this pope.

Missionary self-image and vision

Leo XIV is a pope with **a missionary heart** - shaped by decades as a pastor and missionary in Peru, where he *"hoped, cried and learned with the people"*. These experiences have matured in him the vision of a *"church that goes forward"* and is with the people. It was no coincidence that he chose the motto *In illo Uno unum - "In the One we are one"*, a quote from St. Augustine. Unity in Christ and a common journey characterize his self-image as a shepherd. In his first address to the cardinals, Leo XIV reaffirmed his *"total dedication"* to the path laid out by **the Vatican II Council** and praised Francis' vision of a renewed Church in accordance with the program of the joy of the Gospel (*Evangelii Gaudium*, 2013).

The ideal of a **synodal, missionary church** was central to Leo XIV. *"We want to be a synodal church for all you brothers and sisters (...), a church that is on the move,"* he proclaimed. He thus emphasized that the Church should set out together with the faithful and listen to them. Leo XIV stood in the line of the *"Church on the move"*, as described by Pope Francis: boldly proclaiming the Good News, opening the doors, going out. In his first message, he also listed the leitmotifs that he had in mind: Christ as the *"light that the world needs"*, a church that is **open and willing to engage in dialog with** people, **faithfulness to the Gospel**, a common *"advance in synodality"*, a united church that works for **peace and justice**, closeness to those who suffer - and, time and again, the admonition *not to be afraid*. This *"do not be afraid"* echoes John Paul II, but Leo XIV fills it with the spirit of Francis: trust in God's help in *building bridges* so that *"we* may *all be one people, always at peace"*. Leo XIV's **pastoral vision** is thus clearly outlined: a missionary church that reaches out to the world in unity and mercy, rooted in the Gospel and open to the signs of the times.

His name signals his agenda: like Leo XIII, he wants to promote the Church's dialog with the modern world and translate faith into concrete acts of justice. Artificial intelligence, **globalization**, new social disruptions - he sees all of these as challenges that the Church must meet with its teaching and its commitment to human dignity. *"The Church offers everyone the treasure of its social doctrine in response to a new industrial revolution and developments in the field of AI, because these pose new challenges for the defense of human dignity, justice and work,"* Leo XIV declared programmatically. This already resonates with his option to continue the course *"that Pope Francis began with his option for the poor"*. His missionary self-image is therefore inextricably linked to his commitment to social justice - a point that will be examined in more detail in the following section.

Option for the poor and inclusive pastoral care

The **"option for the poor"** - giving priority to the oppressed, marginalized and weakest - is a hallmark of Leo XIV's pastoral work. Even as a bishop in Peru, he exemplified a church *"for the poor"*. Observers note that Leo XIV thus continued *the church* propagated by Francis *as a "field hospital"* - a healing church at the side of the wounded. His name Leo ties in with Leo XIII and thus with a long tradition of social justice; Andreas Frick of Misereor called Leo XIV a *"pope of peace"* who, with his program *"Peace in justice and freedom, for all, especially the poor"*, ties in with Francis and Leo XIII. In fact, Leo XIV had *"all men of all nations, who are one people"* in mind - no one should be overlooked.

This inclusive attitude is evident in word and deed. Leo XIV paid special attention to the **poor, the marginalized and other groups of believers**, whether homeless people, individual groups or **people with disabilities**. At the same time, he emphasized that *all* members of society are children of God who are close to the heart of the Church. In an early address, the Pope made it clear: *"No one is exempt from working for respect for the dignity of every human being, especially the most fragile"*. He listed the many often overlooked groups that need to be protected and accompanied: *from the unborn to the elderly, from the sick to the unemployed, both citizens and migrants*. The **comprehensive protection of life** and the social ethics of the church clearly resonate here - from advocating for the dignity of the unborn child to caring for the unemployed or refugees who have been left alone.

Leo XIV's pastoral style is characterized by his **openness towards the marginalized**. This also included groups that had long been on the margins of the church, such as **LGBTQIA+** people. Pope Francis had always emphasized that homosexual people were welcome in the church. Leo XIV took the same line: he **combined a welcoming pastoral approach with previous teaching**. Right at the beginning of his pontificate, he reaffirmed the Church's traditional view that the family is based on the *"stable union of man and woman"*. At the same time, however, he also emphasized that *no one* should be excluded from the Church solely because of their lifestyle. This statement is remarkable in light of the fact that Robert Prevost (Leo XIV's real name) had spoken even more critically in 2012 and had probably become more accepting of same-sex partnerships in the meantime. Now, however - around a decade later, influenced by Francis' attitude - he even speaks of **a welcoming culture** and of not condemning people, but including them pastorally. This inclusion-oriented pastoral care also extends to other formerly marginalized groups: Divorced remarrieds, single mothers, people who have had premarital sex or take the pill - Leo XIV wants *everyone to* feel that the Church wants to offer them a home. In doing so, he remained on a classical course in terms of doctrine (such as rejecting abortion and euthanasia), but the **tone** was one of mercy and respect. *"God cares for you, God loves you all,"* he called out to the people, echoing Francis - a key sentence that sums up his pastoral program: God's love is for everyone, especially the vulnerable and lost, and the Church must reflect this in its actions and decrees.

Dialogue with society and intercultural dialog

Leo XIV clearly acted as a **mediator between the Church and the world**. His pontificate came at a time of global tensions - wars, polarization, cultural conflicts - and the Pope saw it as his task to build bridges and promote dialogue. Just a few days after his election, he met the diplomatic corps accredited to the Holy See and called for international cooperation to be revitalized and **dialogue between religions** to be intensified in order to seek peace together. These words underline Leo XIV's conviction: The Church must not close in on itself, but must actively reach out to **politics, civil society and other faith communities**. He has announced that his first trip abroad will take him to **Turkey** of all places - where he wants to commemorate the 1700th anniversary of the Council of Nicaea together with other Christians. This move is highly symbolic: a pope from America celebrating shared Christian history with Orthodox brothers and sisters in Asia Minor - a sign of Leo XIV's commitment to **ecumenism** and building intercultural bridges.

In general, Leo XIV is predestined for **intercultural dialog** due to his life's journey. He is the first pope from the **USA** and at the same time deeply familiar with the southern hemisphere thanks to his long career in **Latin America**. His knowledge of languages is a polyglot matter of course, which allows him to approach people of the most diverse origins directly. The *Neue Zürcher Zeitung* described him as a *"pragmatic man of the middle and mediator between the worlds of American Catholicism"*, indeed as a cosmopolitan. In fact, Leo XIV's biography combines the most diverse cultural experiences: the intellectual influence in North America, the pastoral influence in the Andean villages of Peru, the administrative experience in Rome. This mixture makes him a Pope who thinks and acts *in terms of the universal Church*. For him, **the universal Church** means valuing the diversity of cultures in the Church and at the same time preserving unity in faith. In this way, he continued what the Second Vatican Council had begun: the opening of the Church to a *culture of dialog*. Leo XIV repeatedly emphasized the importance of *encounters* - encounters with political decision-makers, with other religions, with non-governmental organizations and grassroots movements. Early on, he met with representatives of Jewish and Muslim communities for courtesy visits and reaffirmed his desire for friendly exchange (in continuation of Francis' interreligious dialog, such as the *Abu Dhabi Document* of 2019).

Leo XIV also intervened within society with a clear moral voice. **Social actors** such as politicians, associations and NGOs listened carefully when he took a stand. In the first weeks of his pontificate, for example, Leo XIV **condemned** the Russian war of aggression against Ukraine as *"imperialist"* and made an urgent appeal for peace efforts in Ukraine and the Middle East. These clear words attracted worldwide attention. At the same time, he advocated a culture of non-violence: *Not only weapons, but also words can hurt and kill*, he warned - peace means more than the absence of war, it is a task for everyone. His appeal to *"build bridges, not walls"* resonates with both political and interpersonal dimensions. Leo XIV sought to join forces with all people of good will, be they heads of state or simple believers, in order to work towards a fairer world. In doing so, he did not shy away from **denouncing grievances**: In previous years, for example, he has repeatedly criticized the policies of US President **Donald Trump** on his personal Twitter account (now **X**), instead showing **sympathy for refugees** and compassion in the George Floyd case - suggesting that he is not indifferent to global refugee issues as well as issues of racism and police violence. Such statements from a curial bishop and now pope signal: The Church under Leo XIV wants to be a **prophetic voice** in the political public sphere, intervening, but always with the aim of giving a voice to the weak, integrating and promoting peace and the common good.

The fact that **church aid organizations and social organizations** see him as an ally was evident immediately after his election. The international alliance of Catholic development organizations CIDSE welcomed Leo XIV and emphasized that his name program (in succession to Leo XIII) is both an encouragement and a mandate to continue the work for *justice, peace, inclusion and the preservation of our common home* with renewed vigour. Josianne Gauthier, Secretary General of CIDSE, praised the Pope's first words, which raised hope for *a shared and just world and for peace for all people*, and emphasized the need for a *"synodal church that welcomes all and includes the* *voices of the most distant"*. Misereor in Germany was also pleased: Leo XIV followed Francis' course, had *"the people of all nations in mind"* and his message of peace included *"all, especially the poor"*. Such voices from observers and companions make it clear that Leo XIV is perceived as an *advocate for the poor* and *an admonisher of dialog* - someone who builds bridges between the Church and the world, North and South, rich and poor, believers and those of other faiths.

Educational programs and promotion of social justice

Another focus of Leo XIV's pastoral work is **education** - understood in the broadest sense as education, training and awareness-raising - and its connection with social justice. The Pope was convinced that education was the *key* to a fairer world and that the Church had an important role to play here. Even as a young religious, Robert Prevost (Leo XIV) worked as a **seminary teacher** in Peru and later headed a seminary for the training of clergy - so he knows educational work from the ground up. He now encourages Catholic schools, universities and parishes to set up educational programs that **combine faith and society**. He speaks of *"evangelization through education and education through evangelization"* - in other words, the transfer of knowledge and values should go hand in hand. In this way, young people should be empowered to go their **own** way **independently and responsibly**, rooted in ethical principles.

In an address to the **brothers and sisters of the Christian schools** - a traditional teaching order - Leo XIV made clear the challenges facing young people today: *"Think of the isolation caused by superficial relationship models, of individualism and emotional instability; of thought patterns weakened by relativism; and of the rhythm of life that leaves little room for listening and reflection"*. However, the Pope combines this unsparing analysis of the *"culture of arbitrariness"* with confidence: it is precisely these challenges that must become *"stepping stones"* in order to break new ground in pedagogy. He called on Christian educators to be creative and to speak the language of young people in order to really touch their hearts. Leo XIV understood **education** as a *service and a mission: "Teaching must be understood* *as a service and as a mission to help young people to give their best according to God's plan*," he appealed. In concrete terms, this means emphasizing **the teaching of values and character development** alongside academic education. The Pope recalled St. John Baptist de La Salle, who founded free schools for the poor in the 18th century - a role model for today. Like La Salle, Leo XIV envisioned an *inclusive education that was open to all*, especially disadvantaged children and young people.

For Leo XIV, the **promotion of social justice** is closely linked to education. In the tradition of Catholic social teaching, educational programs should enable people to work for the common good and practice **solidarity**. The Pope encourages, for example, to make Catholic social teaching - often described as the "best kept secret of the Church" - better known. Topics such as **human dignity, labor rights, peace, diversity and inclusion, the option for the poor and the integrity of creation** should be taught in catechesis, schools and youth work so that faith does not remain abstract, but has concrete social consequences. Leo XIV sees young people as an important partner in this endeavor: *"The young people of today are a volcano of life, energy, feelings and ideas*," he said enthusiastically. This potential must be nurtured and at the same time accompanied so that it develops harmoniously and for the good. He therefore promotes **youth ministry** programs that not only provide young people with catechetical instruction, but also actively involve them in social projects - from environmental protection to feeding the poor. **Vocational training initiatives** in disadvantaged regions or scholarships for poor students are also close to his heart, as they open up ways out of poverty.

Leo XIV devoted particular attention to **environmental education and ecological awareness**. True to the guiding principle of Francis' encyclical *Laudato si'*, he regarded care for creation as an integral part of social justice. *"He repeatedly spoke out - while still a cardinal - in favor of decisive action against man-made climate change*," notes the press. Having barely become Pope, Leo XIV warned that the Church must make greater efforts against the *"destruction of the earth"*. He warned against **tyrannically dominating** the creation entrusted to us by God, as if man were above everything. Instead, he advocates a relationship of *responsibility and "reciprocity"* with nature. He wants to see this attitude anchored in education: Children and adults should learn to respect the environment as a common home. He expressly acknowledged and supported the initiatives of his predecessor - such as the **Laudato-si action plan** and ecological projects in the Vatican and the Church. Experts expect Leo XIV to follow in Francis' footsteps - which may be quite large in some respects - and act as a *"guardian of creation"*. As a cardinal, he has already shown that this is not just theory: In November 2024, for example, he called for a move from *"words to deeds"* at a climate conference in Rome and praised practical measures such as solar panels in the Vatican. Such examples should set a precedent throughout the world church.

Leo XIV thus combines education with **empowerment**: people - especially young people, the poor and marginalized groups - should be empowered with knowledge, values and concrete skills to take their destiny into their own hands and contribute to building a more just society. This approach reflects the Pope's deep conviction that true evangelization always means *liberation* - liberation from ignorance, exploitation and injustice. When the Church educates, heals and reconciles, it is faithfully fulfilling its mission. And Leo XIV himself sets the example: as a humble teacher and shepherd who listens and leads by example to make the vision of an inclusive, just and philanthropic church a reality.

In this pope's **missionary zeal**, in his **option for the poor**, in his **dialog** with the world and in his **commitment to education**, a common thread emerges: Leo XIV was always concerned with making the message of the Gospel concrete - in love and service to others. In doing so, he built on the legacy of his predecessor and continued it in his own way. The challenge of his term of office will be to implement these high ideals with concrete deeds in the structures of the Church and in the everyday lives of the faithful. But the direction has been set: a pastoral church that goes out of itself, *"welcomes all"* and credibly stands up for faith, love and hope in the world of the 21st century - now it still needs to be implemented in writing in canon law and dogma as well as in the socialization of the clergy.

 *Chapter 6:*

Dealing with key reform issues: women's ordination and gender justice

The question of **women's ordination** - i.e. the admission of women to the ordained ministries of the Catholic Church and in particular the office of Pope - is one of the most controversial reform issues of our time. Inseparably linked to this is the issue of **gender justice** in the Church, i.e. the full recognition of the dignity and equal rights of women in all areas of Church life. After the election of Pope **Leo XIV**, many people are asking themselves: How will the new pope deal with these central concerns? What attitude has he shown so far, what possibilities does he open up for legal equality and not just the participation of women - and what would have to change in terms of theology and canon law so that priests or one day a female pope are conceivable in the near future?

Leo XIV's previous stance on the ordination of women

Pope Leo XIV, whose real name is Robert Francis Prevost, is regarded in many respects as a consensus-oriented **central figure** of the Church - but not as a revolutionary radical reformer. Shortly after his election in May 2025, he made it clear that he would take a cautious approach to sensitive issues. Particularly on the issue of **ordination of women to the priesthood**, Leo XIV has so far adopted a more reserved and **reflective tone** rather than offering a clear perspective of openness. Something that may not be possible before the election - but is within the power of decision in office and may need to be assessed more comprehensively.

In his first days as Pope, there was still no official doctrinal letter or authoritative speech on the ordination of women - understandable, so soon after the conclave. However, conclusions can be drawn from earlier statements by the new pope. **As Cardinal Prevost**, for example, he commented on this topic at the World Synod in October 2023. In a press conference during the synod assembly, he was asked what his position was on women in leadership positions in the church and on ordination in particular. His answer was unequivocal: *"The clericalization of women will not solve the existing problems of the church,"* he explained at the time. This sentence - roughly translated into German: *Ordaining women as priests will not solve the church's current problems* - sums up his skeptical view. Prevost wanted to say that mere **structural changes** such as opening up the priesthood to women would not automatically eliminate all the challenges facing the church. On the contrary, he warned that such a measure could *"perhaps create a new problem"*. He thus positioned himself critically against the demand to simply make women equal in all ministries without questioning the underlying understanding of power and service in the church. He was not speaking against women, but about the continued lack of solutions. Whether women as popes could be a solution - it would not only depend on a pilot project, but would in any case address gender justice in the Catholic Church. Because there is no solution to this either, not just a new or upgraded role realized. Who would want to do without full equality today? This is the point that needs to be conveyed to male clergy.

Leo XIV justified his position **theologically**, above all with reference to the **apostolic tradition.** He emphasized that the Catholic Church had only ordained men as priests for 2,000 years because Jesus Christ himself had called twelve men as apostles - a finding that the Church has always understood as normative. Prevost said verbatim in the synod briefing on October 25, 2023: *"We are all aware of the very significant and long tradition of the Church, and the apostolic tradition is something that has been very clearly articulated, especially if you want to talk about the question of women's ordination to the priesthood."* He was implicitly referring to the official teaching of the Church, which was laid down by Pope John Paul II in the 1990s. In 1994, John Paul II declared in the letter *Ordinatio Sacerdotalis* **that the Church had no authority to** ordain women to the priesthood and that this decision should be definitively accepted by all the faithful. Shortly afterwards, the Vatican Congregation for the Doctrine of the Faith confirmed that this was a "definitive teaching" - in other words, practically irrevocable. At the time, Cardinal Prevost was clearly fully in line with this teaching. His own choice of words "apostolic tradition" indicates that he is continuing **the line of his predecessors**: According to this, women cannot be ordained as priests due to the authoritative tradition, which is traced back to Christ and the apostles. Nevertheless, there were female clergy in history and women had such a role, for example as deacons, which was suppressed from the history books by patriarchy. In order to gain time, Pope Francis also commissioned explanatory studies on the subject.

Interestingly, however, Leo XIV also hinted at a broader perspective: he suggested that perhaps the understanding of **leadership, power, authority and service** in the church as a whole needed to be rethought - including the gifts and perspectives of both women and men. In other words, instead of simply inserting women into an existing, possibly **clericalist** system, he advocated changing the church structure itself to make it less power-oriented and more open to diverse charisms. This statement shows Leo XIV as someone who, while adhering to the sacramental tradition, nevertheless saw a **need for reform** in the understanding of ecclesiastical roles. In his opinion, women should increasingly participate in positions of responsibility - not necessarily through ordination or in the office of a female pope, but through a changed interaction between clergy and laity. After all, Prevost conceded: *"Women can contribute a great deal to the life of the Church at many different levels"*. This confession "women remain laywomen" underlines that Leo XIV explicitly recognized the value of women in the church - even if he saw a limit to the **priesthood** (at least for the time being).

While still a bishop in Peru, Prevost experienced that women often effectively took over the leadership of parishes in remote communities when priests were absent. Despite this, he did not allow himself to be persuaded to call for the ordination of women to the priesthood. His statements to date on the **role and equality of women in the church** are generally rather **cautious and reserved**. However, this does not mean that he was indifferent to the concerns of women - rather, Leo XIV probably preferred a gradual, possibly synodally agreed approach. A senior Swiss church representative commented on Prevost's election with the words: *"Expectations should be high, but not naïve. Pope Leo XIV is no revolutionary. He would hardly be the first to proclaim the ordination of women. But he is a man of processes, not of quick slogans"*. This quote puts it in a nutshell: under Leo XIV, we cannot expect a bang in the short term when it comes to women's priesthood. However, the new pope could create space within the framework of a longer process to continue talking about the difficult issues - a **snail mail without prohibitions on thinking**, but also without rash actions. His ability to listen is seen as a great strength.

In summary, everything points to Leo XIV **personally adhering to the Church's Yes - No - Maybe to the ordination of women to the priesthood with an unsurprising No or sitting it out**, justifying this theologically with tradition and scripture and not wanting to break it on his own authority. At the same time, he shows respect for women in the Church and prefers **evolution rather than revolution**: changes yes, but in harmony with the unity of the Church, the patriarchy and previous teaching.

Perspectives for women in the Church under Leo XIV.

Even if Pope Leo XIV has not yet signaled a rapid opening of the ordained ministry to women, **new perspectives for the participation of women** in church life have emerged under his pontificate - even if the prospects for equality of all genders are lacking. **Pope Francis** has already set a decisive course here, which Leo XIV will continue and possibly expand. One example is the **inclusion of women in leadership positions** in the Curia and the universal church. As a curial cardinal, Robert Prevost himself was involved in one of the most "revolutionary" reforms initiated by Francis: He **had women included in the commission for the appointment of bishops**. Until recently, only male cardinals and bishops were allowed to participate in the committee that proposes new bishops for all dioceses in the world - in other words, a purely male domain. In 2022, however, Francis appointed **three women** to this influential commission for the first time, including religious sister and women's association president Maria Lia Zervino. Cardinal Prevost took over the leadership of this dicastery (the Vatican authority for bishops) at the beginning of 2023 and thus worked directly with these women. According to Zervino, Prevost treated them with great **appreciation, openness and equality**. She reported that Prevost listened to women, took their opinions seriously and allowed them to participate in decisions as a matter of course - as if it were the most normal thing in the world. This experience feeds the expectation that Pope Leo XIV will continue to promote women **in church leadership in the** future. Zervino was convinced immediately after his election: *"I'm sure he doesn't have to learn how to work with women and involve them in decisions - he already does that anyway."* Such statements from female insiders suggest that Leo XIV Francis will maintain his course of more inclusive church leadership. He will probably continue to **appoint women to positions of responsibility** wherever this is possible without an ordained ministry. Francis has already opened up a number of key positions to women - for example as undersecretaries, as advisors in important councils or as heads of departments in Vatican authorities. Leo XIV could perpetuate or even strengthen this path.

A concrete example: in 2021, Pope Francis appointed the French nun **Nathalie Becquart** as Undersecretary of the Synod of Bishops - the first woman in church history to have the right to vote at a Synod of Bishops. Sister Becquart worked closely with Cardinal Prevost at the 2023 Synod Assembly and describes him as a cooperative colleague. She and other high-ranking women in the Vatican expected Leo XIV to allow women not only *to "have their say"* but also *to "co-decide"*. **Synodal participation** is a key concept here: Leo XIV has a positive attitude towards the worldwide synodal movement (the "Synodal Process" of 2021-2024). The 2023 Synod, in which Prevost took part, was characterized by the fact that women - religious women and laywomen - also participated as full voting members for the first time. Prevost expressly welcomed this opening and described it as *"work in progress"*, i.e. a process that will continue. It can be assumed that Pope Leo XIV will continue to shape future synods **with women's voices and voting rights.** This will make the participation of women in important consultations and decision-making processes the **norm.**

In addition to the curia and synod level, the local level also comes into focus. Leo XIV came from the USA and worked as a bishop in Latin

America for a long time. In both contexts, there are already many ways in which lay people, and women in particular, bear responsibility in parish leadership. Think of **pastoral workers**, parish coordinators or catechetical leaders who work in parishes. In rural regions of Peru, for example, where Prevost was bishop, women served as so-called *"catechists"*, overseeing parishes over long distances, leading celebrations of the Word of God and acting as central contact persons for the faithful. Such **non-ordained ministries** have long since become indispensable in the Catholic Church. Pope Francis has recognized this and in 2021 created the office of **catechist** as an official appointment - open to both women and men. In addition, Francis has already opened up the formerly ordained lower ministries of **lector and acolyte** (reader or helper at the altar) to women. This means that women can now officially recite Bible texts in the liturgy, serve as communion helpers or take on the service of church care, which was previously symbolically reserved for men. Leo XIV will certainly confirm and continue these measures. It is even possible that he will strengthen other **lay ministries for women** - such as *"parish leadership in team form"* in parishes without priests, which is being tested in some countries. Such models give women de facto leadership authority without affecting the ordained priesthood. A caterpillar without a cocoon, so to speak.

The **ordination of women as deacons** is also a much-discussed topic. The permanent diaconate is the lowest ordained office, below priest, with duties such as baptizing, officiating at weddings, preaching and working in social ministry. Currently, in the Roman Catholic Church, **married men** may become deacons, but **women** may not. Interestingly, however, there were *deacons in* the early church: In the New Testament , for example, **Phoebe** is mentioned as a *"deaconess of the church of Cenchrea"* (Rom 16:1), and historical sources show that women held the office of deacon well into the early Middle Ages. This is precisely why Pope Francis set up two commissions (2016 and 2020) to research the role of women deacons in history and to examine whether this office could be reintroduced today. The results of these studies were inconclusive, and Francis himself - despite his openness - did not make a decision to admit women to the diaconate until his resignation. Cardinal Prevost was more cautious in 2023: he said that the question of deacons was "still open", but again warned that **clericalizing women**

would not automatically solve problems. However, "open" also means that the possibility has not been definitively rejected. Should the current World Synod come to the conclusion that the **ordination of women to the diaconate** would be a viable option, Leo XIV would have to deal with it. Observers expect that he will at least **listen to and examine** what the "people of God" want and expect on this point. As a "man of processes", he could also rely on a broad consensus here: for example, a worldwide consultation process or a council before a decision is reached. In the short term, however, Leo XIV was more likely to focus on **upgrading non-consecrated roles** rather than introducing sacramental ordination straight away.

Under Leo XIV, women could therefore increasingly **take on leadership roles** - in councils, in administrative positions, as advisors, theologians, church lawyers or in preaching and charity. All of this contributes to *gender equality*, insofar as women's voices become more audible and their influence grows. Nevertheless, the sore point remains: as long as the **priesthood and all higher ordinations** are **reserved for men - the patriarchy -** many committed Catholics in their own church continue to feel like *"second-class women"*. They are second-class people. And that doesn't work. It's not complicated - for example, in terms of global human rights. This sentiment has been articulated more and more loudly in recent years - by Catholic women's associations, theologians, but also by many believers at grassroots level, especially in Western Europe and North America. They are calling for genuine **equality**, which they believe remains incomplete without access to all ministries. Pope Leo XIV is therefore walking an **extremely fine line**: on the one hand, he wants to ensure equal rather than greater justice for the female half of the Church, while on the other hand he is committed to tradition and does not want to jeopardize unity with the universal Church (in which there are very different points of view). His approach so far points to **cautious changes** - no quick breakthroughs, but nevertheless signs of **opening up within the bounds of what is possible.**

Church history and canon law: what needs to change?

In view of the current doctrinal situation, the **core theological question** ultimately arises: What would have to change - in the interpretation of the biblical foundations, in canon law and in the catechism - for women's ordination to be conceivable at all? In other words: What obstacles currently stand in the way, and how could they be overcome if the church were to one day come to a different assessment?

First of all, the **current legal situation**: Catholic **Canon Law (CIC)** states unequivocally in Canon 1024: *"Only a baptized man can validly receive ordination"*. This one sentence makes all ordained ministries (deacon, priest, bishop) inaccessible to women - a woman's ordination would be legally *null and void* if someone were to perform it anyway. This norm is not a new invention, but reflects a centuries-old practice. However, it was expressly reaffirmed in 1983 with the new Code of Canon Law and incorporated into the **Catechism of the Catholic Church**. The Catechism (No. 1577) explains: *"The Lord has chosen men (viri) to form the college of the twelve apostles ... therefore the Church adheres to this decision of Christ. For this reason, it is not possible for the Church to ordain women to the priesthood"*. Here it becomes clear that **Christ himself** and his alleged intention are being invoked. The issue is thus lifted out of human control - it is considered a *matter of faith*, not merely a changeable discipline. John Paul II formulated it even more sharply, as mentioned above, by wanting to put an end to any debate: *The Church has no authority whatsoever* to change this. This statement was understood by many as quasi **infallible**, even if it was not formally proclaimed ex cathedra (directly infallible). The Congregation for the Doctrine of the Faith declared it to be definitive doctrine, which suggests that it ranks right at the top. As long as this classification applies, the **ordination of women** would be **excluded from canon law and dogmatically** - any action against it would be invalid and possibly subject to ecclesiastical penalties for those involved.

In order for women to be ordained priests or deacons, **this passage of canon law** would first have to be **changed.** Canon 1024 and the corresponding sections of the Catechism would have to be deleted or reformulated. This can only be done by the Pope himself, possibly as part of a larger decision (such as a council). But a simple change in the law alone would not be enough - because behind the law there is a **theological judgment** that has so far been regarded as binding. This judgment is: *the ordination of men is divine order.* If the Church ever wanted to see it differently, it would have to **argue theologically very thoroughly** why the previous view no longer holds. It would therefore need a **new interpretation of biblical testimonies** and tradition.

What does this mean in concrete terms? First of all, the known biblical passages and historical facts would be reassessed. Up to now, the fact that Jesus only appointed male apostles has been relied upon. Proponents of an opening counter: Jesus also had reasons for not including women in the twelve in the culture of the time - for example, to ensure their safety and credibility in a patriarchal society. Nevertheless, women played a decisive role among Jesus' followers (Mary Magdalene, for example, is revered as the "apostle to the apostles" because she was the first witness to the resurrection).

Moreover, there was an apostle whose gender is discussed in theological and historical debates as possibly female: It is **Junia**.

In Romans 16:7 Paul writes: *"Greet Andronicus and Junia(s), my kinsmen and fellow prisoners, who are respected among the apostles...".*

The original Greek text gives the name Ἰουνίαν ("Iounian"). For centuries, the feminine form "Junia" was regarded as unambiguous, until from the Middle Ages onwards the interpretation spread in theology that this must be a masculine name ("Junias"), although this name is hardly documented in antiquity.

Many theologians, historians and linguists now assume that Paul is actually referring to a woman named Junia. This interpretation would mean that Junia was a female apostle, which has major implications for the debate about the role of women in the early church.

Today, many biblical scholars, including official church authorities, hold the view that Junia was indeed a woman who was recognized among the apostles. The topic is often discussed, especially in the context of current debates about the ordination of women and equality in the church.

This key renders the entire doctrinal structure of the Catholic Church on the patriarchate invalid.

In the early church, there were also prophetesses, deaconesses and house church leaders. **Paul** mentions several leading women, such as Phoebe (a deaconess) or Junia, who is even described as an outstanding apostle in Romans 16:7, depending on the translation. These findings would certainly be emphasized more strongly in a new decision: It could be argued **that the Bible affirms the equal worthiness of men and women before God** (Gal 3:28: *"There is no longer male and female; for you are all one in Christ Jesus"*) and that the common priesthood of all believers is the basis from which the special ministerial priesthood could also be open to women.

However, it is not enough to simply reinterpret a few biblical passages. The understanding of the **sacramental priesthood** in Catholic theology is also under scrutiny. Until now, it has been said that priests *act in persona Christi capitis*, in Christ's stead as the head of the congregation - and Christ was male, the priest is supposed to represent this "iconic" masculinity. This argument from the doctrinal statement *Inter Insigniores* (1976) states that the **male gender of Christ** is no coincidence, but is symbolically significant for salvation: Christ as Bridegroom - Church as Bride. If women were to be ordained, according to the traditional view, this symbolic scheme would be disrupted. This **symbolic theology** would therefore also have to be developed further in order to bring about a change. A number of theologians are already doing this: they emphasize that Christ has redeemed all of humanity and that his humanity (not his manhood) should be theologically in the foreground. The relationship between God and man is not bound to male-female, and terms such as "bridegroom" and "bride" should not be narrowed down biologically. If the church were to take these arguments on board, it could come to the conclusion: A woman can represent Christ just as sacramentally as a man, because both are made in the image of God. This change of perspective in **dogmatics** would be of a fundamental nature: but possibly urgently necessary with these insights - it would almost amount to a new *development of doctrine*.

In terms of church law, the path to becoming a priest would probably only be open via **deacons.** Many see the **permanent diaconate of women as** the first step. Once this had been completed (for example, through a papal decision or a council decree), an ordination for women would have already been introduced, which in turn would at least make a further development to the priesthood more conceivable. It is therefore no coincidence that the discussion usually revolves around deacons first. Should Leo XIV or a successor take a bold step here and allow women to be ordained deacons, this would mean a change in canon law: Adapting Canon 1024 (perhaps initially with an exception for the diaconate) and amending the Catechism accordingly. These changes would have to be accompanied by a **solemn justification** as to why this is now possible - for example, by saying that historical research has shown that the diaconate is not an exclusively priestly office and that women have traditionally served as diaconal ministers. Such an argument would soften the break with the previous line, as it would refer to *early church models*.

And how would one get from the female diaconate to the **priesthood -** and even further to the **"woman in the papal office"**? Here we are currently in the area of the vision to be shaped, as **there is currently no active promotion in the hierarchy for women priests**. But thinking long-term: if the Church were to come to the conclusion that God also calls women to be priests, the *Ordinatio Sacerdotalis doctrine* would have to be shaken up again. Perhaps a future pope (or a council) would declare that although this teaching was held with deep conviction, it was not defined as infallible and can and must be reconsidered in light of the "sign of the times and equality as a human right". It would be a step comparable perhaps with earlier reversals (one thinks, for example, of the lifting of the ban on taking interest or the changed attitude to religious freedom - things that were also "always" rejected in the past and could then be revised because a deeper context was recognized). For the ordination of women, however, it would probably need a conciliar process and world church approval, as it is such a fundamental and controversial issue - unless a pope feels responsible for his leadership function by decree beforehand.

Only when women are ordained as priests and can serve as bishops would it be practically possible **to elect a woman to the office of pastor**. This then gender-neutral position is usually elected from among cardinals, and cardinals are (currently) almost exclusively male bishops. According to current law, any baptized male Catholic could theoretically be elected pope, but in practice, the College of Cardinals elects one of its members. **Women are currently not yet represented in the College of Cardinals** - which is not a strict dogma, but a rule of canon law: since 1917 it has been stipulated that cardinals must at least be male priests, and in 1962 John XXIII made episcopal ordination compulsory for (almost) all cardinals. To make a woman a cardinal, either this rule would have to be repealed or the woman would have to be ordained a bishop first - which brings us back to the starting point. There has always been the question of whether a pope could symbolically appoint a woman as a cardinal deacon (in theory, this is at the pope's discretion, as cardinal dignities are conferred by the head of the church). So far, however, no head of the Church has dared to do so - presumably to avoid raising false expectations. In short: without women as priests and bishops, **there can be no female popes**. However, should the ordained ministry be opened up to women in the near future, it would be conceivable in principle that a woman could one day sit on the Chair of Peter. Until then, it is a path of demands that requires not only legal changes, but above all a **change in mentality** - both in the hierarchy and among the faithful.

In conclusion, it should be noted: The current **canonical situation** is not yet in favor of women's ordination, underpinned by official theology and traditional biblical interpretation. For this to change, **extensive reforms** would be needed: new theological insights adopted by church leadership, changes to the Code of Canon Law and the Catechism, and a broad acceptance of gender justice and gender neutrality in job postings in the worldwide church. Realistically, Pope Leo XIV himself will not be able to bring about such changes overnight. **Gender justice** in the church can also grow in **intermediate steps** - for example through more participation, recognition and appreciation of women at all non-consecrated levels. This is precisely what Leo XIV seems to be striving for: He wants to *empower* women without immediately opening up the priesthood during his term of office. This approach may not go far enough for some, while others may already find it too risky. Leo XIV therefore had to strike a balance between progress and preservation. If he manages to keep the **synodal dynamic** going and discuss the "hot potatoes" openly without losing unity, his pontificate could at least prepare the Church - for possible decisions that may only mature in further generations after his term of office. Until then, women can take on more and more responsibility in the Catholic Church under Leo XIV and contribute their talents, working on **an equal footing** in many areas - but the step towards ordination to the priesthood remains (for the time being) only a called-for vision for the future, which requires social maturation in the clergy and broad agreement in the Vatican.

Conclusion: Pope Leo XIV represents a **balancing act** between tradition and reform when it comes to the ordination of women. He adhered to the doctrine that the priesthood was reserved for men, but at the same time signaled his appreciation for the contributions of women and supported their greater involvement in church leadership processes. In his approach to this central reform issue, Leo XIV shows himself to be a pragmatic and inclusive leader: not a revolutionary with quick decrees, but a pope who listens, opens doors and wants to lead the church step by step towards greater equality - **in the spirit of synodality** and without lightly cutting the roots of tradition.

Committed women at **Maria 2.0** as well as people who not only support **gender equality** and **human rights**, but have anchored them deeply in their self-image and actions, do not want to wait another generation or decades for men to realize this.

The question of women's ordination thus remains exciting and controversial. But under Leo XIV, there is a chance that at least the *serious struggle* over this issue will continue - with objectivity, theological depth and the necessary patience - or the necessary pressure that a global church needs for genuine renewal.

 *Chapter 7:*

Dealing with key reform issues - compulsory celibacy and the training of priests

When Pope Leo XIV began his pontificate, two perennial issues of church reform took center stage: compulsory celibacy for male priests and the training of the next generation of priests. Both topics are emotionally charged and theologically significant. How did Leo XIV, a pope with a practical approach and canonical expertise, deal with these reform issues? A well-founded look at his perspectives, the current discussion and possible changes will shed light on this.

Celibacy - tradition, challenge and Leo XIV's perspective

For centuries, the Latin rite of the Catholic Church has required priests to remain celibate. This way of life, "complete abstinence for the sake of the kingdom of heaven", is deeply rooted in tradition and canon law. Over the course of church history, it gradually became compulsory: from the 12th century at the latest, and confirmed as binding by the Council of Trent in the 16th century, Catholic and male secular priests in the West were required to remain unmarried. Proponents see this as a spiritual **charism** - a sign of radical discipleship of Christ that allows priests to devote themselves undividedly to their ministry. Cardinal Robert Sarah, for example, emphasizes that celibacy clearly shows *that priests belong only to Christ*; questioning this ideal would only **exacerbate** the crisis of priesthood. Pope Emeritus Benedict XVI also wrote warningly that a decoupling of priesthood and celibacy would cause its special charism to fade and reduce priests to mere **functionaries.**

Despite such defenses, compulsory celibacy is repeatedly criticized - and Leo XIV is aware of this tension. **Leo XIV,** who worked as a bishop in

Latin America for many years before his election, was familiar with the pastoral reality of a shortage of priests and extensive parishes without regular mass. Even in earlier statements as a bishop and later as a cardinal, he made it clear that he **valued** celibacy as a **valuable asset** of the Church, but did not consider it to be unchangeable. He himself holds a doctorate in canon law and knows that the commandment of celibacy is **not a dogma,** but an ecclesiastical law. It is therefore not surprising that he is openly considering new approaches without making any rash decisions. His predecessor Francis had already remarked that celibacy was "a gift for the Church", but "not set in stone" - and that purely disciplinary issues could be fundamentally changed when the time was right. Despite all the debates, Francis himself adhered to the current rule until the end of his life. Now many eyes are on Leo XIV: will he maintain this course or reform it cautiously?

Leo XIV's behavior to date indicates a balanced approach. He repeatedly acknowledged the achievements of celibate priests, but at the same time expressed understanding for discussions about exceptions. During his years as archbishop, he experienced first-hand how parishes without priests are suffering. Accordingly, he followed the 2019 Amazon Synod with interest. At that time, the bishops in this remote area cautiously advocated ordaining tried and tested married people - known as *viri probati,* later also conceptually known *as homines probati* - as priests in order to ensure the supply of the Eucharist. Leo XIV was open to such considerations *in exceptional cases involving men.* His motto was: celibacy should remain, but where it serves the proclamation of the Gospel, the Church must be allowed to find **pastoral solutions.** He took this attitude with him into office as Pope.

Option or abolition? - The debate about voluntary celibacy

Hardly any other reform topic is discussed as controversially as the demand for **voluntary celibacy** for priests - although voluntary celibacy is tantamount to **abolishing celibacy**. This means that priests should be able to decide for themselves whether they want to live celibately or not - instead of a general obligation to remain celibate. Proponents of such a relaxation argue that this would make the priestly profession more attractive and do justice to those priests who do not feel called to lifelong celibacy. Critics, on the other hand, warn that a "voluntary" solution would be tantamount to a de facto abolition, as most clergy would then marry and the ideal of celibacy would quickly be marginalized.

What voices are there in this debate? Within the church, theologians and bishops have been voicing different positions for years. At the beginning of 2022, Cardinal Reinhard **Marx** from Munich caused a stir when he openly called for the abolition of compulsory celibacy. Not just for "sexual reasons", according to Marx, but because some priests would become lonely without the possibility of marriage and "it would be better for their lives" if they could marry. Many believers and theologians - especially in Europe and America - are also arguing **for optionalization**: they point out that there are already married priests in the Catholic Church, for example converted pastors or in the Eastern churches united with Rome. In the Ukrainian, Maronite or Greek Catholic churches, married men can be ordained as priests without priesthood being less respected there. This model - celibate *and* married priests side by side - could be adopted by the Latin Church, so the argument goes. Proponents therefore consider an opening to be overdue, especially as celibacy is not a sacramental requirement from a *theological* perspective, but is based on a disciplinary decision by the church.

However, there are also **concerns and counter-models**. Particularly from traditional and conservative circles comes the objection that voluntary celibacy dilutes the sacrificial nature of priesthood. In 2020, Curia Cardinal Robert Sarah warned urgently that any **"relativization"** of celibacy - for example through broad exceptions - would be "a step in the wrong direction". In his view, a relaxation would tend to deepen the existing crisis, as it would give the impression that priesthood is merely a **profession** rather than a vocation. Sarah even fears that an initially limited exception could "become the rule". In a similar vein, Benedict XVI argued that softening the obligation of celibacy could reduce priesthood to a purely human institution in the eyes of the world. **Would anyone still choose this path if celibacy were voluntary?** Opinions differ here. Some think yes - genuine charisms would also develop and continue to be cultivated without coercion (similar to how religious voluntarily live celibate lives). Others believe that in a more liberal society, most candidates for the priesthood would prefer marriage, which would make the testimony of those consecrated "for the sake of the kingdom of heaven" rare.

Leo XIV had to balance these tensions. **What are his own signals?** On the one hand, he respects the previous line: in his first statements as Pope, he emphasized that celibacy has rendered invaluable services to the Church and is closely interwoven with the identity of the Latin priesthood. On the other hand, he indicated that he wanted to look at the worldwide **synod on church reform with** an open mind. In fact, at the German Synodal Path - a reform dialog of the Church in Germany - a majority of bishops recently even spoke out in favour of a cautious opening of celibacy. There are also voices from other continents that would at least like to see the possibility of married priests in certain regions or under certain circumstances. Leo XIV signaled: Such a development is *not out of the question*, provided it serves the good of the Church. His Latin American origins and experience give him a practical perspective here: He is aware of the needs of the faithful without a pastor and at the same time knows the **limits** of purely organizational solutions - because a lack of priestly vocations has many causes, not just celibacy. Cardinal Jorge Mario Bergoglio (later Pope Francis) already doubted years ago that abolishing celibacy would automatically lead to more new priests. Leo XIV will therefore weigh things up carefully: How can the door be opened gently without throwing the baby out with the bathwater?

As a result, **Leo XIV's perspective** can probably be summarized as follows: Compulsory celibacy is under scrutiny, but not pilloried. The Pope will probably first try out models - such as allowing married deacons to be ordained as priests in regions with an acute shortage of priests. Such steps would not be an abolition of celibacy, but a **differentiated expansion of** the current practice. The real challenge is to preserve the high spiritual significance of the celibate life while at the same time meeting the pastoral needs of the Church. Leo XIV himself put it like this: *'It is not a question of either/or, but of both/and, which honors the treasure of celibacy and yet opens up spaces for new paths.*

Need for reform in the training of priests: practical relevance and personal development

For Leo XIV, the quality of **priestly training** was at least as important as the question of celibacy. Because regardless of whether priests are allowed to be married in the future or not, they all need excellent preparation for their ministry. In recent years, it has become clear in many countries that there is a need to catch up here. **Criticism** has been voiced: Training at seminaries for priests is often too academic and theological and not practical enough; after ordination, young priests are faced with administrative tasks and a daily work routine for which they feel inadequately prepared. A recent survey of male new priests in Germany, for example, revealed glaring gaps between training and reality. More than two thirds of respondents would like to see more **personal development and spirituality** in their training (71.7% and 63. respectively named this as very important), and pastoral care also ranked highly (69.1%). In contrast, less than half felt that more training in administrative and leadership tasks was important (only 39.5% wanted more training in church administration). Accordingly, only **6.1%** stated that they had been *very well* prepared in practical matters - whereas over 27% rated the practical preparation as poor or very poor. **Theoretical-theological training**, on the other hand, scored predominantly well (over 80% rated this as good or very good). This discrepancy shows that in many places the focus was strongly on theory, while practical and personal training was neglected.

Leo XIV made it clear that a rethink was needed here. **Practical relevance** and **spirituality** should no longer be in opposition to theology, but should be equal pillars of priestly training. Pope Francis had already presented guidelines for "holistic" training in 2016 with a new framework order (*Ratio Fundamentalis Institutionis Sacerdotalis*). This concept of *holistic and life-oriented training* emphasizes that candidates for the ministry of priests should not only be trained theologically and liturgically, but should also grow in **pastoral practice** and **heart formation**. The latter means the development of personality, maturity of character and the ability to develop mature relationships - especially with regard to the celibate life. Leo XIV fully supports this line. He demanded that seminarians be intensively formed in humanity, empathy and spiritual life: Priests should not only be dogmatically trained, but *pastors* with spiritual maturity and a deep relationship with Christ.

In practice, this means concrete **innovations** in the seminaries. Many countries already have a preliminary propaedeutic phase - an introductory and orientation year that primarily serves as spiritual and human preparation. These *propaedeutics* are now becoming the standard worldwide, which the church in Austria, for , has been practising successfully for a long time (and for which it has received international recognition). This was followed by theological studies, but Leo XIV increasingly wanted the prospective priests to be involved in **parish life at** the same time: Internships in parishes, social internships or phases in which they work in the normal everyday life of the faithful are to become an integral part of their training. Some models provide for seminarians to live temporarily with families or outside the seminary in order to get to know the reality of people's lives better. This is intended to prevent ordination candidates from living in seclusion in the seminary for years and then suddenly presiding alone as a pastor in several parishes - a leap in the dark that is often perceived as too much of a challenge.

Leo XIV also emphasized the importance of ongoing **spiritual guidance**: regular conversations with mentors and confessors should help candidates to honestly examine their decision for priesthood and (if celibacy is required) for a celibate life again and again. Pope Leo XIV is aware that a mature integration is necessary, especially in the area of sexuality and the ability to have relationships, in order to avoid scandals and inner conflicts. After the painful experiences with cases of sexualized violence in the Church, it is essential that seminar leaders and formators pay attention to warning signs and take preventive action. The Pope expressly supports the involvement of psychologists and experienced pastors in formation in order to promote the character suitability and psychosexual maturity of candidates. This openness to modern human sciences in the training of priests marks a cultural change towards more professionalism and humility: one does not rely solely on the fact that the spiritual vocation automatically brings with it everything human, but **consciously works** on the personality of the future priests.

The German bishops have also presented reform plans for the training of priests - parallel to the synodal path - which aim in a similar direction. For example, training is to be partially restructured and concentrated at fewer locations in order to ensure a good community for the few junior staff. At the same time, theology students who want to become priests should study more closely with theology students for other church professions in order to promote cooperation and understanding for each other at an early stage. What was striking about the survey results mentioned above was the **desire of young clergy** for more personal development and spirituality. Bishop Michael Gerber of Fulda, who is responsible for the training of seminarians, expressly welcomed this and called for these aspects to be "emphatically promoted" - especially *in* light of the abuse investigation. This shows that the criticism of the past is being taken seriously and Leo XIV, together with many of those responsible, is drawing consequences from it.

One example of innovative teaching is the increased training in **communication and conflict resolution**: future priests learn how to work in teams with lay and full-time staff, how to moderate parish meetings and how to deal with criticism. There is also a move away from using priests primarily as administrators in several parishes - a role in which many feel uncomfortable. "The church must change itself in order to provide answers to people's questions and needs," warns Irme Stetter-Karp, President of the Central Committee of German Catholics. She alludes to the fact that previous role models were too narrow: Priests **do not want to** be **pure managers**, but spiritual leaders. The training should therefore enable them to live this spiritual leadership, while administrative tasks are taken on more by teams. Of course, future pastors will still need to understand something about finances and organization - but these skills will take a back seat to training as **spiritual shepherds**. Leo XIV thus implemented a change in priorities in the training of priests: **Forming people before management**.

Prerequisites for change: Legal and doctrinal adjustments

In order to both readjust celibacy and renew the training of priests, considerable **changes to the church's rules and regulations** were necessary. Leo XIV was faced with the task of dealing carefully with tradition and at the same time boldly initiating reforms.

First of all, **compulsory celibacy**: because it is a provision of canon law, an opening towards voluntary celibacy would have to be enshrined in the applicable legal norms. In concrete terms, this means that the corresponding canon in the Code of Canon Law (CIC) would have to be amended. Canon 277 CIC currently requires priests of the Latin rite to be celibate as a way of life. Leo XIV could - in an individual decision or in consultation with the Synod of Bishops or a council - modify this canon to allow exceptions or options. One possibility would be to continue to formulate celibacy as a **rule**, but with an addition: "unless the pope grants a dispensation in individual cases" or something similar. A regional opening would also be conceivable, in which, for example, conferences of bishops in mission territories could apply for the ordination of proven married deacons as priests. This would take into account the fact that pastoral situations vary greatly around the world - an idea that Pope Francis and theologians such as Cardinal Walter Kasper had already envisioned. It is important for Leo XIV to make it clear that a change in the law is **not a transformation of church teaching**: the Catholic Church continues to teach the high value of celibacy for the sake of the Kingdom of Heaven, but is changing a disciplinary requirement in order to do justice to the Church's mission. It will be the task of the **Magisterium**, i.e. the papal and episcopal teaching authority, to formulate this theologically correctly. It is possible that Leo XIV will publish a detailed letter or even an encyclical in which he sets out the biblical and theological foundations: For example, the fact that the New Testament also contains both married ministers (such as the Apostle Peter or Junia) and those living unmarried (such as Paul). He could emphasize that, according to Matthew 19:12 ("some have made themselves unmarriageable for the sake of the kingdom of heaven"), singleness remains recognized as a special gift, but is not given to everyone - and that the Church therefore wants to make room for both states of life in the service of God.

In the **Catechism of the Catholic Church**, which currently states that in the Latin Church only celibate males are ordained as priests, this passage would be adapted. Presumably, a new wording would recognize **the Latin and Oriental practices** side by side: Just as the

Catechism already mentions that the Eastern churches recognize a married priesthood, a double recommendation could also stand for the Latin church in the future. The Catechism article could, for example, state that the priestly ministry is such a high good that both unmarried and married people - depending on their call and situation - can exercise it, and that both have advantages and disadvantages, which the Church takes into account in pastoral wisdom.

Some legal adjustments are also necessary for the **training of priests** themselves. The canonical requirements for the training of seminarians (for example in Canons 232-264 CIC) would have to be updated in line with the new Ratio Fundamentalis. Rome has already issued guidelines that apply worldwide - but each conference of bishops must implement these in their own training regulations. Leo XIV will insist that these regulations include mandatory elements such as the propaedeutic, the psychological aptitude test and longer pastoral internships. The **age structure** may also be made more flexible: if, for example, there are more married candidates for the priesthood (such as middle-aged deacons), the training paths would also have to be open and attractive for late-comers. Here, church law could include provisions that enable second-career priests or part-time study models.

Doctrinally, it must be made clear that such adaptations are in line with tradition. Leo XIV is likely to emphasize that there is no change to the sacrament of **ordination** itself - the Church's teaching that only baptized persons can validly receive priestly ordination remains unaffected (even if this question - the ordination of women - is a controversial issue in its own right, which the Pope may address in this context). Rather, it is about the **disciplinary framework of** the ministry. The Church already recognizes that married permanent deacons hold an ordained ministry and that married priests of other rites are fully valid priests. In this respect, we are moving within Catholic diversity, except that the Latin particular church would learn something from oriental practice. This can be substantiated biblically with reference to the first millennium: many saints of the early church - for example historical bishops such as St. Hilarius of Poitiers or St. Gregory of Nazianzus father - were married. A return to this early church diversity can help to refute the *concern* that a relaxation of celibacy would mean sacrificing sacred tradition. Leo XIV himself once put it this way: "*Not every* *ecclesiastical rule of yesterday is already an immutable truth of always.* He thus shows that there is legitimacy in history and theology for cautious changes.

The role of women in pastoral training. In all considerations regarding the ordination of priests and training, it should not be forgotten that the Catholic Church does not rely solely on ordained men for pastoral care. Around the world, women share responsibility in a variety of pastoral professions and functions - as parish priests, pastoral assistants, theologians, catechists and religious sisters. In his reform program, Leo XIV repeatedly emphasized that women should be given more **influence** in the church. Although the ordained ministry of priests and bishops was still reserved for men according to current doctrine, the participation of women in leadership and education was expanded. For example, more and more women are professors in theological faculties and also sit on the committees that train priests. In some seminaries, women are already involved as spiritual guides or train seminarians in pastoral psychology - an important contribution to overcoming one-sided "male perspectives". Leo XIV strongly supported such steps. He knew that the more women were involved on an equal footing in the training of future priests, the more the priests would be sensitized to working with women in their future ministry. Leo XIV also opens doors outside the seminary rooms: he has already appointed more **competent women** to curial leadership positions and diocesan offices in order to show that the church must not be a male-dominated "patriarchy". The President of the German Committee of Catholic Women put it in a nutshell: "Leadership and management are not male per se". Leo XIV was committed to this principle. He did not see the promotion of women in the Church - both in training and in practice - as a concession to the spirit of the times, but rather as a return to the togetherness that Jesus and the early Church also knew (think of the collaboration of Martha, Mary, Phoebe and many other women in the New Testament).

In this chapter of his possible work, Pope Leo XIV walked a fine line between continuity and change. **When it came to celibacy,** he seemed prepared to allow cautious openings without abandoning the spiritual value of celibacy. He takes seriously what concerns many believers and priests and weighs up models that have already been tried out in small parts of the world church. He is aware that any change must be well-founded and theologically sound in order not to jeopardize the unity of the Church. Leo XIV promoted a quality offensive **in the training of priests**: the priests of tomorrow should be academically educated theologians, but also personalities with empathy, spiritual depth and pastoral experience. He set the course for seminaries to no longer be ivory towers, but workshops for credible pastors.

In all of this, the Pope remains objective and focused on the mission of the Church. He addresses controversial points openly, but without polemics. He formulates with theological precision where **development** is possible and where the doctrine remains unchanged. This narrative view of compulsory celibacy and the training of priests shows that Leo XIV sought solutions that reconciled **the tradition and future** of the Catholic Church - cautiously but firmly. The coming years of his pontificate will show how this translates into ecclesial reality. But one thing is already clear: the discourse is in motion, and Leo XIV embraced it with prudence and pastoral passion.

🕊 *Chapter 8:*
Dealing with key reform issues: Inclusion of queer people - LGBTQIA+

When Pope Leo XIV begins his pontificate, the Catholic Church is in the midst of a tense debate about the equal treatment of LGBTQIA+ people. A profound change has taken place in many societies: Same-sex couples are legally allowed to marry, rainbow flags now fly from church steeples as a sign of solidarity, and in public opinion, diversity of sexual orientations is increasingly seen as normal and worthy of protection. Expectations are correspondingly high - from believers and non-believers alike - for the church to treat all people with the same dignity, regardless of their sexual orientation.

Equality before God and at the altar - social change and church expectations

In particular, the question is pressing as to how *all* lovers really become equal before God and at the altar because they are, or whether the Church wants to continue to exclude certain groups - such as homosexual couples - from sacramental acts such as marriage.

The social **status quo** speaks for itself. In traditional Catholic countries and communities, many believers are now openly calling for LGBTQIA+ people to be treated with respect. Surveys underpin this change in sentiment: as early as 2013, around 70% of German Catholics were in favor of opening up civil marriage to same-sex couples. At the same time, a church survey showed that over two thirds of Catholics were dissatisfied with the church's treatment of homosexuals. Internationally, too, it can be observed that Catholics - especially younger generations - are questioning the traditional rejection of same-sex partnerships. The basic conviction of many is that all people are of equal value before God, "children of God" (according to Pope Francis) - no one should be excluded or made unhappy because of their sexual orientation. This attitude is based on a modern understanding of human rights and love, as well as on the Christian commandment to love one's neighbor. If God is love, how can sincere love between two people contradict the divine will? More and more believers are asking themselves this question and expect answers from the church that do justice to today's knowledge and feelings.

However, the official **doctrine** of the Catholic Church has so far only cautiously kept pace with this social development. The *Catechism of the Catholic Church* still emphasizes respect and tact in dealing with homosexual persons on the one hand, but makes it clear on the other that acts of same-sex love are *"intrinsically wrong"*. In other words: according to church teaching, being homosexual is not a sin - but actively living a same-sex love is. This distinction - love yes, lived sexuality no - leads to what many see as a paradox: although all people should be equally loved and accepted, their lifestyles are not equally valid in the eyes of the clergy. This is where social expectation and church teaching clearly clash. The demand for **equality of** all orientations "before God and the altar" would require a rethink: Away from terms such as "objectively disordered", towards a theology that sees same-sex orientation as a variation of creation that is just as God-ordained as heterosexual orientation. In fact, more and more church voices are calling for precisely this. For example, the chairman of the German Conference of Bishops, Bishop Georg Bätzing, called for the relevant passages in the Catechism to be revised back in 2020. His argument: the church must find solutions to visibly integrate homosexual believers - for example through appropriate liturgical celebrations. This balance between fidelity to tradition and the necessary further development is the fine line that Leo XIV has to walk.

Sacramental recognition of same-sex couples: theological pros and cons

At the heart of the debate is the **sacramental recognition** of same-sex couples, i.e. the question of whether a partnership between two men or two women can receive the same sacramental status and blessing before the church as a marriage between a man and a woman. Deep convictions and emotional arguments collide here - **theologically**, but also pastorally and socially.

Arguments for an opening: Proponents of a re-evaluation of the marriage of same-sex couples within the church argue that the quality of a relationship does not depend on the gender of the partners, but on the depth of their love and their responsibility for each other. If the sacrament of marriage is an image of God's faithful, fruitful love for people, then the love of a homosexual couple can also reflect this image. It is important to emphasize that "fruitfulness" does not only have to mean physical offspring. Many theologians argue for a broader understanding of fertility - one that also recognizes the social and spiritual fruits of committed love. Two people who stand up for each other for a lifetime, endure crises together and perhaps even raise children (for example, through adoption or from previous relationships) exemplify values that the church fundamentally upholds: Faithfulness, care, sacrifice and community. Against this background, is it justified to exclude such couples from sacramental blessing?

Another *pro-argument* is based on more recent findings from biblical studies and moral theology. Many of the biblical passages that have traditionally been used against homosexuality (for example from the book of Leviticus or the letters of St. Paul) are read in a more nuanced way today. Historical-critical exegesis shows that these texts are mostly to be understood in specific, purely historical contexts - they often deal with temple prostitution, rape or expressions of xenophobia, rather than loving, equal partnerships. At the same time, modern science has made it clear that homosexuality is a **variant of human sexuality**, not a willful decision against the "divine order". Pope Francis himself is reported to have said in a personal conversation: *"God made you this way and he loves you this way"* - a sentence that cuts deep into the self-image of believing LGBTQIA+ people. If God created people the way they are, many theologians argue, then their love cannot be a sin across the board. An internationally acclaimed scientific statement from 2021 even stated that there are **no biblical or scientific reasons** to hold on to the doctrine that procreation must necessarily be inscribed in every sexual act and that homosexual acts must therefore be judged as "disordered". This result underlines the fact that the traditional Catholic sexual morality - according to which sexuality is only approved within a marriage geared towards procreation - can be questioned theologically. Reform advocates emphasize that there have always been changes in the history of the church: Doctrines changed, for example, with regard to the recognition of religious freedom or the condemnation of slavery, without betraying the gospel. So why shouldn't it also be possible to deepen the understanding of love and marriage to *include all* couples?

Arguments against an opening: On the other hand, advocates of traditional doctrine have weighty reservations. For them, **sacramental marriage** is inextricably linked to the Christian understanding of creation and the complementarity of the sexes. The book of Genesis already describes the creation of man and woman as related to each other - "as male and female he created them" - and from this the Church has always deduced that marriage means the union of *both* sexes according to God's plan. According to the traditional view, the physical union is ordered towards procreation - it opens up to the miracle of new life and thus reflects God's creative power. According to this understanding, **love alone** is not sufficient for sacramentality; it is also about the natural order. Opponents of reform thus invoke the **continuity of doctrine**: the Church has clearly taught accordingly for centuries.

In addition to the purely theological aspects, there are also **social and pastoral considerations** in this discussion. Western societies have developed a rapidly increasing respect for LGBTQIA+ rights in recent decades. In more and more countries - including previously strictly Catholic countries such as Ireland, Spain and France - same-sex marriages are now legal and widely accepted in society. Many devout homosexual couples have long been living in stable, loving relationships, some with children, and are asking: does the Church really have nothing positive to say about our way of life? Pastoral counselors report that the categorical rejection often causes great emotional suffering - people feel rejected in the very church that is supposed to be their home. Pope Leo XIV had to find out: How can he do justice to the legitimate request for equal treatment and recognition without jeopardizing the unity of the universal church?

Steps towards full recognition - Necessary changes in church law, catechism and biblical interpretation

Assuming that the Catholic Church wanted to **fully recognize** LGBTQIA+ people and their partnerships - what would have to change in concrete terms? Such a change would require adaptation, as it affects several pillars of church doctrine and order.

Canon law (canon law): The current legal system of the Church clearly defines marriage as a lifelong union *between a man and a woman*. This is stated in the Code of Canon Law (cf. can. 1055 §1 CIC). This definition should be fundamentally expanded so that two people of the same sex could also enter into a marriage bond in the sense of the Church. A simple linguistic change ("between two persons" instead of "between man and woman") would have updates: Numerous connecting provisions - from the marriage requirements to the form of the marriage ceremony to questions of marriage nullity - would have to be adapted. There was also the question of how to deal with existing civil marriages of same-sex couples: could they be subsequently recognized as sacramental? Or would the church only open up the liturgical framework for new unions? All of this would require careful elaboration. Full recognition would mean that sexual orientation would *no* longer be a criterion for exclusion from ordination or church ministries, as long as the person in question strives to live according to the evangelical counsels.

Catechism and Magisterium: A **revision of the Church's sexual morality** in the Catechism and in official pronouncements would be central. The current passages (CCC 2357-2359) describe homosexual acts as "not in order" or as a transgression against the natural order. If same-sex relationships were to be positively recognized, these formulations would have to be deleted or replaced by a new, appreciative theology. For example, a declaration that the church can recognize an image of divine love in every partnership based on love, fidelity and mutual respect - regardless of the gender combination - would be conceivable. Some bishops have already suggested taking precisely this step. Bishop Bätzing, for example, said that the previous statements on homosexuality were becoming less and less convincing and needed *further development*. An official change to the Catechism by the Pope - similar to what Pope Francis did in 2018 with regard to the death penalty - would be a strong signal. However, it is clear that this will hardly be possible without an accompanying theological justification. Therefore, it is often suggested that a short ecclesial **synodal process** be carried out first, in which the insights of theologians, biblical scholars and natural scientists are incorporated. Such a symbolic consultation could help to build broad acceptance for a reassessment. Ideally, the draft would be a *magisterial document* that emphasizes the dignity of LGBTQIA+ believers and the possibility of God-pleasing same-sex love.

Biblical interpretation: Finally, the church would also have to clarify its **hermeneutical approach** to certain biblical passages. Full recognition of same-sex marriages does not require the Bible to be "rewritten", but it does require traditional interpretations to be confronted with new light. The supposedly clear prohibitions in the Old Testament ("You shall not sleep with a man as one sleeps with a woman; that would be an abomination") or in the letters of St. Paul ("Neither fornicators, nor abusers of boys, nor sex workers... will inherit the kingdom of God") have long been read literally and without context as condemnations of homosexuals. In future, the Church could emphasize more strongly *when and why* these lines were written. For example, it could include references to the fact that Old Testament purity laws were in a different cultural context and, from a Christian perspective, are surpassed by the commandment to love. Paul's words in Romans 1, on the other hand, are directed against pagan practices and excessive vices, not against sincere love between people of the same sex - at least according to many contemporary exegetes. It would not be the first time that the church has evolved its reading of the Bible: even today, we no longer read the story of creation in a scientifically literal way and see Paul's instructions on slavery or the role of women as time-related injunctions. A similar change in the understanding of the "homosexual passages" - the so-called "clobber passages" - (there are only about six of them) could be justified theologically without abandoning the authority of Holy Scripture. Ultimately, the focus would be on the *message of Jesus*, who does not say a word about homosexuality in the Gospels themselves, but does say a great deal about love, mercy and justice.

All these changes - in the law, in the catechism, in exegesis - sustainably liberate the effectiveness of love. They would be tantamount to a small **evolution**, which can certainly succeed with a broad consensus and wise guidance from above. Some voices are therefore even calling for a new council to clarify such fundamental issues - but that would take too long. One thing is clear: without formal adjustments to the norms of the Church, any inclusion rhetoric, however well-meaning, would ultimately remain non-binding. Pope Leo XIV would have to summon up the courage to take structural action here if he really wanted to achieve full recognition.

Outlook: Between pastoral mercy and magisterial continuity

The inclusion of LGBTQIA+ in the Catholic Church remains a **balancing act for** the time being. Under Pope Francis, the first steps have been taken: more welcoming language, the famous "Who am I to judge?", and most recently even the cautious opening of the door to blessings for same-sex couples under certain conditions. These blessings - authorized by Cardinal Víctor Manuel Fernández in 2023 in the declaration *"Fiducia supplicans"* - mark a change in pastoral practice, but not (yet) a change in the underlying moral teaching or the implementation of equal marriage for all. Priests are now allowed to bless homosexual couples as long as the church's concept of marriage as an exclusive union between a man and a woman remains unaffected. This development illustrates the path that Leo XIV would probably also have to take: small steps towards *recognition* without risking a complete break with tradition.

At the same time, the pressure of **social reality** continues to grow. In many countries, LGBTQIA+ Catholics who are faithful to the church have long been part of the community and make valuable contributions. Excluding them would contradict the Church's mission to be a spiritual home for all believers. On the other hand, the Pope must not lose sight of the global perspective of the Church: In Africa or parts of Asia, but also in Eastern European countries, the idea of equality for homosexual partnerships is still controversial in some cases. Leo XIV thus moved in a field of tension between **pastoral mercy and doctrinal continuity**.

The coming years could be decisive. It is possible to consistently adhere to the status quo - with the risk of losing more believers, especially in Western countries, and being seen as morally backward. However, a cautious course of reform is also possible: first a theological reflection within the framework of the World Synod or a special commission, followed by a cautious adaptation of language (for example in the catechism) and discipline (for example through officially permitted celebrations). Perhaps Leo XIV would even have the courage to dare to make a real breakthrough - for example through a World Youth Day of Diversity or a doctrinal letter that opens new doors. One thing is certain: **expectations** of him are high on the part of all those who hope that the Church will once again credibly recognize *the signs of the times* in the 21st century. Will Pope Leo XIV succeed in giving LGBTQIA+ people the equal dignity before God and the altar that is laid down in the Gospel of God's unconditional love for every human being? This chapter of his term of office, which calls for daily action, will show whether the Church can perform the balancing act between tradition and renewal in love - a balancing act that will help determine its presence.

🕊️ *Chapter 9:*
Ecological responsibility and creation care

A pontiff as an advocate for creation: a man putting on his boots and literally wading through the mud to help the poorest - this image impressively sums up Pope Leo XIV's approach to preserving creation. In fact, it is recorded that Leo XIV (then still a bishop in Peru) did just that in 2022 during devastating floods in Chiclayo: he put on rubber boots and **"waded through the mud"** to rescue people affected by the floods. A local Caritas employee named Janinna Sesa recalls that the current Pope was the one who **"put on his boots"**, personally delivered food parcels to remote villages and, if necessary, even repaired a broken-down truck himself **"until it was running again"**. This down-to-earth commitment to people in need already shows that Leo XIV did not see his commitment to the environment and his fellow human beings as a theoretical duty, but as a practical vocation.

Early sensitivity to environmental issues: Long before he was elected pope, Leo XIV's interest and commitment were focused on the **"integrity of creation"** - the responsibility to protect God's creation. As a bishop in northern Peru, he experienced the consequences of environmental destruction and climate change at first hand: his missionary territory extended as far as the Amazon region, and issues such as deforestation, species conservation and climate justice moved him deeply even then. Companions report that as early as 2017, he had lively discussions with Peruvian colleagues about **protecting the Amazon and the environment** - not a side issue for the pastor Prevost (his real name), but part of his pastoral mission. He retained this early sensitivity throughout his life: even before he became Pope, he actively supported the Church's environmental initiatives. In 2015, for example, he used social media to call on faithful Catholics to sign a climate petition at in order to achieve a strong international agreement (which later became the Paris Climate Agreement). In a photo shared online from a climate rally in Chiclayo, he wrote in Spanish: **"El planeta nos necesita"** - *"The planet needs us"*. Such actions show that **even as a bishop and cardinal, Leo XIV raised his voice for climate protection** and encouraged the faithful to take action. His connection to Peru - a country that is both rich in biodiversity and severely affected by climate change - evidently awakened in him a special sense of responsibility for the **vulnerability of creation**.

From words to deeds - Leo's attitude as a cardinal: In his years as a cardinal, Prevost (Leo XIV) reinforced this eco-social mission. He was regarded as a **bridge builder** between the Church and the environmental movement and was not afraid to take a clear stance. **"It is time to move from words to deeds,"** he urgently warned last year. He made it clear that mere declarations of intent are no longer enough in the face of the climate crisis - concrete action must follow. At the same time, he warned against misinterpreting the human **"dominion over nature"** mentioned in the Bible: This should not be **"tyrannical"**, he said, rather it requires a humble *"relationship of reciprocity"* with the environment. This choice of words suggests that Leo XIV did not see creation as a possession of man that could be exploited at will, but as **God's dowry**, for which we bear responsibility. It is remarkable that, as a cardinal, he also had the technological aspects of environmental protection in mind: for example, he praised papal initiatives that introduced solar energy and electric cars in the Vatican, but equally warned against a belief in progress that ignores the **social and ecological "side effects"** of new technologies. Overall, Prevost distinguished himself before his election by always thinking of ecology in the context of justice and human dignity - very much in the spirit of Pope Francis, whose course he fully supported.

Continuation of Francis' climate course: The election of Leo XIV as Pope in 2025 was widely understood as a signal that the Church's ecological course would be continued and even deepened. Leo XIV has big shoes to fill, as his immediate predecessor Francis was regarded as a **"green pope"** who made environmental and climate protection core concerns of the church. But the new pontiff did not hesitate for a second to position himself clearly. In his very first speech after the conclave, Leo XIV used clear words: **"God loves us all unconditionally... Evil shall never prevail."** Many observers interpreted this statement to mean that "evil" also explicitly referred to the **destruction of the environment** caused by human activity - including global warming fueled by the unchecked consumption of fossil fuels. Leo XIV thus signaled right at the beginning of his pontificate that he understood the ecological sins of our time - environmental destruction, climate change, overexploitation of nature - as a moral evil that must be resolutely opposed.

Even as a bishop, Leo XIV experienced how closely humanitarian crises and environmental issues are linked. The devastating floods in Peru, where he literally helped wading in the mud, were caused by **extreme rainfall** - a phenomenon that is becoming more frequent as a result of climate change. Leo XIV's actions on the ground - distributing food, comforting victims, tackling practical issues without hesitation - made his approach clear: **climate protection is always also human protection**. Where environmental disasters rage, the poor and weak suffer first. This experience had a profound impact on Leo XIV and explains why he continued to push for climate and environmental protection as Pope. In a way, he combines **Caritas and "Laudato si'"**: active charity towards those who suffer and the responsibility to tackle the root causes of this suffering - such as the climate crisis.

Concrete initiatives of his pontificate: In the Vatican, Leo XIV took immediate steps to give institutional expression to his ecological vision. He encouraged the Church globally to act more ecologically. He called on the dioceses and Catholic organizations to make greater efforts against the **"destruction of the earth"**. He repeatedly emphasized that the biblical mandate to *subdue* the earth (cf. Genesis 1:28) was **not a license for exploitation** - human rule over the world should not become "tyrannical". Rather, Leo XIV saw it as the duty of the Church to set a good example: Parishes, monasteries and church institutions should live sustainability - from the use of renewable energies to environmentally friendly building projects and educational programs for **ecological awareness**. Pope Francis had already set the Vatican State on a greener course (solar panels on church roofs, a long-term goal of climate neutrality by 2050, etc.), and Leo XIV wants to continue along this path consistently. *"The deepening of the Vatican's commitment to decarbonization is crucial,"* it says programmatically - only in this way can the Church make a credible contribution to fulfilling the Paris

Climate Agreement. Leo XIV therefore sees the **"green transition"** in the Papal States not as an end in itself, but as part of the Church's global contribution to climate protection.

One specific area in which Leo XIV is already making his mark is **international climate policy**. Like his predecessor, he is actively seeking to join forces with the global community in the fight against the climate crisis. The next UN Climate Change Conference (COP30) is planned for November 2025 in Belém, Brazil - in the middle of the Amazon region. The hosts have already expressly invited Leo XIV and emphasized that his presence could help to achieve a historic climate protection pact. In fact, there are many indications that Leo XIV will accept this invitation, especially as he is the *first Latin American pope since Francis to* take a particular interest in the Amazon. Brazil's President Luiz Inácio Lula da Silva greeted the new Pope with warmth and hope: he publicly declared that he was counting on Leo XIV **to continue Francis' legacy - in particular his tireless commitment to environmental protection, dialog and justice**. Such voices underline the enormous moral authority a pope can have on the diplomatic stage: Leo XIV is already seen as an important advocate of an ambitious climate policy. His clear distancing from climate-sceptic currents has not gone unnoticed. For example, media reports have described Leo XIV **as a "100 percent alternative"** to Donald Trump's inactive climate policy. It was not without reason that the New York Times pointedly attested: *"Trump is no longer the most important American in the world"* - the new pope from the USA has now assumed this role . The bold attribution as **"anti-Trump"** may be exaggerated, but it gets to the point that Leo XIV is sending a diametrically different message: instead of denying the climate crisis, courageous action, instead of short-term interests, a long-term perspective that preserves creation.

Leo XIV expressly seeks cooperation with all **people of good will** who are committed to the environment. International environmental organizations and church networks have enthusiastically welcomed his election. Lorna Gold, the director of the global Catholic *Laudato Si'* movement, immediately interpreted Leo's words **"from words to deeds"** as a hopeful signal - precisely this motto is needed to turn climate policy promises into real change. *"We couldn't agree more,"* explained Gold and held out the prospect of working closely with the new Pope, especially as 2025 will mark the 10th anniversary of *Laudato si'*. Other Catholic climate activists such as Dan Misleh from the *Catholic Climate Covenant* also expressed their encouragement: They are welcoming Leo XIV **"with open arms"** and will support him to the best of their ability if he - as announced - builds bridges, works for peace **and lives the Gospel fearlessly**. Such voices from the climate movement show that even in the first months of his pontificate, Leo XIV was seen as the **driving force behind a new departure**. He united the moral and spiritual perspective of the Church with the goals of environmental activists and scientists. By bringing representatives of environmental organizations, science and business to a round table, for example, he builds on Francis' approach to dialogue and gives the pressing ecological issues additional weight on the world stage.

Theological and ethical guidelines: But why is the Catholic Church so intensively involved in climate protection in the first place? What values guided Pope Leo XIV in his commitment to the environment? A look at church doctrine shows that **the preservation of creation** is firmly anchored in theology. The Bible already describes the world as good and entrusted to man in the creation account (Gen 1-2). From this understanding, a foundation of ethical principles developed, which Leo XIV also deeply internalized. One of these principles is **justice**, in particular **climate justice**. Pope Francis emphasized in *Laudato si'* that **"the cry of the earth and the cry of the poor"** cannot be separated - environmental destruction always affects the most vulnerable people first. Leo XIV often emphasized this: **"It is precisely the poorest who will be the first to be affected by the approaching catastrophe, and only then the rest of humanity,"** he warned with regard to man-made climate change. For him, climate protection is therefore part of the commitment to the **poorest of the poor** and a question of global justice. It is about overcoming the great divide: Industrialized nations and the wealthy have caused much of the ecological crisis, while poor countries and population groups bear the brunt - both in the form of natural disasters and the creeping deterioration of livelihoods. Leo XIV is building on **the socio-ethical tradition of** the Church, which has repeatedly defended the rights of the weak since Leo XIII (Rerum Novarum, 1891). Today, this means that **climate justice is part of social justice**. In other words, the fight against global warming is not a luxury project for rich nations, but an act of solidarity with the hungry, displaced people (think of climate refugees) and future generations.

In addition to justice, Leo XIV also guided the principle of **sustainability** or **responsibility for sustainability**. The Church formulates it as follows: *"The earth is our common home and must be protected"*. A lifestyle based on the reckless consumption of resources contradicts the principle of sustainability. In *Laudato si'*, Francis makes an urgent call for a **sustainable lifestyle** and global cooperation to counter the environmental crisis. Leo XIV takes this admonition seriously. He emphasizes that economic activity must always be subordinate to concern for creation - the pursuit of profit must never be at the expense of ecological foundations. In his sermons and speeches, he reminds us that **all creatures** have **independent value** and **give glory to God** (an allusion to Francis of Assisi). Man should not regard them merely as resources to be exploited; the current extinction of countless species is an affront to creation. This attitude is based on Franciscan spirituality: nature is a co-creation that must be treated with reverence. Leo XIV, who worked in the Amazon rainforest for years, certainly also experienced the beauty and vulnerability of creation intensively there - impressions that reinforced his conviction of the need for sustainable action.

A third central value is **intergenerational responsibility**. The Church teaches that the common good must **also** be secured **for future generations** - it is a matter of *"intergenerational justice"*. Pope Leo XIV therefore repeatedly emphasized our duty to leave a habitable earth for future generations. In practice, this means making decisions now that protect the planet in the long term, rather than focusing on short-term profit or convenience. This way of thinking corresponds to the principle of **suitability for our grandchildren**: what we do today should still benefit our children and grandchildren instead of destroying their livelihoods. Leo XIV often refers to a quote from *Laudato si'*: **"The world is something we have borrowed from our children"** - a powerful image that makes it clear that we are temporary stewards. On the World Day of Prayer for Creation, for example, the Pope explains that we must always consider *"what kind of world we leave to those who come after us"*. This attitude of responsibility also resonates when Leo XIV says that the evil of environmental destruction will **"never triumph"** - because in the long term, over generations, a culture of destruction cannot endure. His faith gives him the certainty that life and the preservation of creation will ultimately triumph if humanity dares to turn back and rethink now.

Faith as motivation for climate protection: Pope Leo XIV sees the fight against climate change not just as a political or economic project, but as a deeply moral and spiritual task. In his eyes, **climate protection** is **lived charity and lived faith**. In doing so, he drew on a biblical passage that is often quoted: *"The righteous man cares for the lives of his animals, but the heart of the wicked is cruel"* (Prov 12:10) - a symbol of the fact that true justice always has fellow creatures in mind. Leo XIV interprets the signs of the times theologically: he sees the environmental crisis as a consequence of **alienation from God's mission of creation**. For him, greed, irresponsibility and indifference towards nature are symptoms of an inner crisis - a lack of gratitude for the gift of creation. He therefore emphasizes values such as **humility, modesty and conversion**. He repeatedly calls for an *"ecological conversion"*, a conversion of heart that transforms us from selfish exploiters into responsible guardians of creation. For Leo XIV, this conversion is part of the holistic conversion of man to God. He explained that *anyone who plants a tree today, installs a solar system or changes their lifestyle is not only acting in an environmentally conscious way, but is also fulfilling God's will of love.* In this view, environmental action becomes an **act of faith**.

Leo XIV is often compared to Francis of Assisi - the saint who regarded all creatures as brothers and sisters. The Pope shares this Franciscan love of nature. His pontificate is characterized by the **hope** that man and the world can live in reconciliation. He draws strength from the conviction that God has entrusted man not only with dominion, but above all with the **care of the earth** (cf. Gen 2:15). He therefore encourages all believers to work towards sustainability in their everyday lives: from simple things such as avoiding waste and saving energy to political commitment to climate justice. **Sustainability, justice and intergenerational responsibility** - these values run like a red thread through the speeches and writings of Leo XIV. They are the cornerstones of an ethic that the Pope conveys with enthusiasm and charismatic narrative density. He was not afraid to preach uncomfortably and denounce, for example, the "consumerism" and **"throwaway culture"** of our time, which, in his words, **"offends creation and robs the poor of their future"** (as he put it in an address). However, despite the urgency, Leo XIV did not spread cultural pessimism, but a *"realism of hope"*: he was convinced that man - equipped with reason, conscience and God's grace - was capable of setting course for a sustainable future.

At the end of this chapter, it becomes clear that Pope Leo XIV sees **ecological responsibility as a core component of his ministry**. In continuation of *Laudato si'* and in line with the Church's entire theology of creation, he makes **climate protection a moral duty**. With passionate appeals, credible actions of his own and a clear vision, he is leading the Catholic Church into an era in which *the preservation of creation* is more important than perhaps ever before. And he does so in a popular, scientific and narrative way, so that not only theologians but all people of good will can understand him. Leo XIV thus proves himself to be a pope who has recognized the **signs of the times**: He responds to the ecological crisis with faith, reason and heart and invites the world community to work together to ensure that future generations can also live in a "common home" characterized by *peace, justice and the love of life*.

🕊 *Chapter 10:*

Dealing with key reform issues - From sexual morality to sexual ethics in general

Under Pope Leo XIV, Catholic sexual morality was at a crossroads. Hardly any other area shows the discrepancy between church teaching and lived reality as clearly as sexual ethics. "We expect nothing more from you!" - this bitter sentence, uttered by homosexual friends to a church employee, illustrates the alienation of many believers from official moral teaching. **Under Leo XIV**, the question arose as to how the Church should deal with those who did not conform to traditional ideals - be it young couples who had premarital sex or those remarried after a divorce. At the same time, there are growing calls for an **inclusive sexual ethic** that integrates human responsibility and the reality of life and thus bridges the gap between the magisterium and everyday experience.

Premarital sexuality: reconciling ideal and reality

According to current doctrine, sexuality is bound to sacramental marriage. The *Catechism of the Catholic Church* clearly defines extramarital sexual intercourse ("fornication") as a grave transgression: "Fornication is ... gravely contrary to the dignity of persons and of human sexuality" - in other words: according to this view, every pre- or extramarital sexual union seriously violates the dignity of persons. However, this strict standard is in stark contrast to the reality of life: in many countries, most couples already have an intimate relationship before the church wedding. Young people in particular hardly take any notice of the church's moral teachings, because they are perceived as unrealistic. Cardinal Reinhard **Marx** complains that the church has long painted a one-sided negative picture here, "reinforced with guilt and sin", which has led to **double standards.** He pleads for a more honest approach: sexuality is first and foremost a "gift from God", and not every sexual act outside of marriage can be branded as a serious sin across the board - "that would be excessive, it would go too far". Rather, **love, reliability and fidelity** between the partners are crucial.

Under Pope **Leo XIV**, a cautious course emerged that upheld the ideal of marital chastity but took pastoral realities into account. No bishop will officially advise young couples to move in together - but in pastoral care, there is a growing understanding of the extent to which seriously loving couples take responsibility for each other even before the wedding ceremony. Pastors are increasingly accompanying unmarried couples on their journey and emphasizing the importance of **respect, consensuality and commitment** rather than just issuing prohibitions. A **theology of graduality** - already hinted at under Pope Francis - encourages the promotion of moral growth step by step, even if the full ideal is not realized from the outset. The Church is less concerned with drawing clear boundaries "within which sexual satisfaction is permitted and beyond which it is forbidden". Rather, according to moral theologians, "at the center [...] must be the responsibility for the relationship in which sexuality is embedded". In concrete terms, this means **pastoral support instead of hasty condemnation.** Leo XIV himself described the Church as being open to "all" - this "for all" naturally also includes couples who are not (yet) married in church. In practice, celebrations for engaged couples or liturgical rituals that celebrate the value of fidelity and love are created in some places. Although such approaches remain experimental and sometimes controversial, they show a willingness to respond to the reality of the faithful **without abandoning the high esteem in which sacramental marriage is held**.

Remarried divorcees: Finding mercy and integration

Even more urgent is the question of how to deal with remarried divorcees - those Catholic women, women and men who have entered into a new civil marriage after the breakdown of a church marriage. According to traditional teaching, they live **in** objective **contradiction** to the indissolubility of marriage; John Paul II affirmed "based on Sacred Scripture" the practice of "not admitting these faithful to the Eucharistic meal." As long as the first marriage bond was valid, a new intimate union was regarded as **continued adultery,** which in particular excluded them from receiving communion. This strict attitude deeply offended many of those affected. They felt like **second-class Christians** who were effectively denied the sacraments, even though they had often been faithful members of the church for years.

Pope **Francis** has already initiated a rethink here: In his letter *Amoris laetitia* (2016), he called for **differentiation in individual cases.** In a "path of discernment" accompanied by pastors, it could be examined in certain cases whether access to confession and communion is possible - especially if those affected are seriously committed to living a Christian life and want to avoid further violations (such as a second partnership or joint children). This opening was received differently; some bishops had already drawn up guidelines for a merciful approach, while others warned against confusing the faithful. **Leo XIV** now had the opportunity to provide clear guidelines for this pastoral tension. He is regarded as a man of the center - **aware of tradition**, but also influenced by the spirit of Francis' mercy. Indeed, even before his election, Leo XIV (as Cardinal Prevost) was known to be in favor of **allowing remarried divorcees to receive communion**. Observers classify: *"He also put mercy in the foreground - before dogma, before pure doctrine"*. The new Pope has confirmed this basic attitude in the first months of his pontificate. On the occasion of a meeting with family pastors, Leo XIV emphasized that the Church should not let anyone fall: **divorced and civilly remarried** people are "wounded members of our community who still belong to the family". Instead of condemning them across the board, ways should be sought to **fully reintegrate** them **into the life of the Church** without abandoning the indissolubility of marriage.

Pastoral practice worldwide is beginning to change accordingly. In some dioceses - for example in Buenos Aires, Rome or in some German dioceses - remarried divorcees are allowed to take communion again after a spiritual interview and a period of penance, provided their conscience allows them to do so. **Leo XIV** was faced with the task of mediating such solutions in the universal Church. While many in Europe and America welcome a more generous approach, bishops in Africa and Eastern Europe, for example, continue to insist on traditional principles. The Pope will be called upon to **build bridges**: he must make it clear that *mercy* is not a contradiction to *truth*, but its fulfillment. The vision emerges that the **irrefutable doctrine** of the sanctity and indissolubility of marriage should be preserved - and yet no one should be excluded from grace forever. After all, as Leo XIV reminded us, the **Eucharist** is **"not a prize for the perfect, but food of strength for the weak"** - an oft-quoted phrase from Francis that continues to be a guiding principle under his successor. The fact that the Church really wants to be there *for everyone* must be demonstrated in its dealings with those who have failed to meet moral standards. Reaching out to them without abandoning the ideals of the Church is one of the greatest challenges and at the same time a touchstone for the authenticity of the message of the merciful God.

On the way to inclusive sexual ethics

Beyond individual groups, the general sexual morality of the church is under scrutiny. The social changes of the last few decades are too great for the traditional answers to be sustainable. **New theological impulses** and social experiences are therefore shaping the current discourse. For example, the Synodal Path in Germany - a reform dialog in response to the abuse scandal - has called for a critical review of the entire magisterial sexual morality. It is not enough to "formulate individual norms more moderately or change the tone"; what is needed is a *"reality-based, liveable"* sexual ethic that takes a fundamentally new approach. Moral theologians emphasize that church teaching was long characterized by a **natural law view**: it was based on a divine order of creation, according to which sexuality is exclusively between man and woman in an indissoluble marriage and primarily serves procreation. Anything that deviated from this norm - from contraception to homosexual acts to masturbation - was judged to be objectively sinful. However, this strongly **rule-oriented morality** has plunged many believers into conflict and hardly does justice to the diversity of real life situations. This is why today's theologians are developing approaches for a *relational and sexual ethic* that focuses on **people and their relationships** instead of abstract catalogs of prohibitions. The focus is on values such as **love, reliability, mutual respect, a sense of responsibility and justice** between partners. When making sexual decisions, such ethics first ask: Does this behavior promote a sincere, mature relationship - or does it violate the dignity and well-being of the other person? The **quality of the relationship** and *mutual responsibility* become the guiding criteria. "The focus [...] should rather be on responsibility for the relationship in which sexuality is embedded," is how a current theological statement puts it in a nutshell. Sexuality is no longer seen primarily as a source of danger, but as **a force for shaping relationships** - a positive force, but one that requires ethical orientation.

Inclusive sexual ethics inevitably goes hand in hand with a changed view of previously excluded groups. Renowned church representatives are calling for a more open approach to homosexuals. "Homosexuality is not a sin", Cardinal **Marx** has made clear; the church must recognize "that there are also *'creative' forms of sexuality*, i.e. homosexuality and queer lifestyles". Such statements mark a profound change from earlier times, when homosexual acts were judged differently. There is now a growing realization that the biblical passages on this topic - as well as on other sexual issues - must be read in their respective historical context. **Bernhard Bleyer**, Professor of Moral Theology, points out, for example, that the Bible does not contain any conclusive judgments on questions of sexual orientation and is being re-examined. In general, there is a growing awareness in theology that the word of God must not be misunderstood as a rigid code of law. Rather, central biblical principles - **love of neighbor, faithfulness, justice and mercy** - should be applied to today's questions of sexuality. It can therefore be argued that a consensual, faithful partnership in love is good before God, even if it does not conform to all traditional norms. **The reality of** people's **lives** becomes the starting point for ethical reflection: 'based on a realistic, human-scientific understanding of the reality of human sexuality", it is important to ask about a *"responsible approach to this reality in partnership and love"*. This responsible ethical approach moves away from a pure ethics of duty. It challenges the church to **listen** - to the experiences of loving couples, the needs of single people, the questions of young people. Voices of affected believers, theologians and pastors worldwide, flow into this discourse: from the single divorced woman who wants a place in her congregation to the young queer Christian who expects to be accepted by the church as he is.

Changes in canon law, catechism and biblical interpretation

However, **institutional changes** are also necessary in order to anchor contemporary sexual ethics in the church. Many people ask: What specifically needs to change in church law or in the catechism in order to make steps towards opening up possible? A look at the current texts shows where there is a need for reform:

Canon law: Catholic marriage law does not yet recognize the possibility of entering into a second marriage - recognized by the Church - after a divorce. Anyone who does so anyway is formally in a permanent state of grave sin, which, according to Canon 915, for example, prevents them from receiving communion. If remarried divorcees are no longer to be excluded across the board, canon law would have to allow for **more differentiated regulations.** For example, a rite of penance and reconciliation following a civil second marriage is being discussed, which - similar to the practice of the Orthodox churches - blesses the new union without denying the first marriage. Until now, however, Rome has strictly forbidden any "liturgical acts" for remarried couples. Leo XIV could provide impetus here by creating legal **discretionary powers**. His predecessor had also already simplified *annulment procedures* (matrimonial proceedings) - a step that would enable more believers to have an invalid marriage annulled by the Church and then remarry. New categories in the law could also be considered, e.g. ecclesiastical recognition of responsible civil partnerships in order to do justice to long, faithful relationships that are not (yet) sacramental.

Catechism: In the 1992 Catechism, traditional sexual morality is reflected in clear values. Paragraph 2353, for example, explicitly describes premarital sex as "gravely" sinful. A contemporary doctrine would have to **revise** these sweeping condemnations. It is not a question of declaring everything to be good, but of a **language of appreciation and differentiation**. For example, the catechism could generally present sexuality in a more positive light - as a gift from God that should be lived responsibly. Negative terms such as "fornication" and "unnatural" would be replaced by a description that defines the moral value of a relationship not only in terms of a marriage license, but also in terms of *love and responsibility*. Today, many shepherds already emphasize that committed love also exists outside of a church wedding and must be respected. A revised doctrine could recognize that, for example, a stable partnership without a marriage certificate or a second civil marriage are to be evaluated differently in moral terms compared to promiscuous behaviour by young people or arbitrary infidelity. In short: **differentiation instead of blanket judgments** would be the motto. Cardinal Marx put it in a nutshell: the yardstick should be whether I treat the other person as *"the person of my life"* in my actions - not the formal status of the relationship.

Biblical interpretation: Finally, a renewal of sexual ethics also requires a fresh look at the biblical message. For a long time, individual biblical passages - such as Jesus' words *"Whoever puts away his wife and marries another commits adultery"* (Mk 10:11) or Paul's words against "fornication" - were understood in isolation and juridically. Modern exegesis, on the other hand, attempts to shed light on the **place of** such words **in life.** In his letters, Paul warns against *porneía,* which in the context of the time often had more to do with cultic prostitution or exploitative sexuality than with loving partnerships. Jesus' strict prohibitions on divorce were also aimed at protecting women from arbitrary repudiation - an act of justice in a patriarchal society. The Church under Leo XIV is called to re-emphasize these **deeper intentions** of Scripture. If God wants *mercy* and "does not want man to remain alone" (cf. Gen 2:18), then a pastoral interpretation of the Bible must not stop at rigorous literal interpretations. Rather, the **basic principles of the Gospel** - unconditional love of God, forgiveness, respect for every human being - should be the guiding principle for applying biblical commandments in today's world. This could mean Not maintaining a marriage in ruins at all costs, but allowing new paths in forgiveness; or measuring like with like when it comes to sexual misconduct - the Bible condemns heterosexuals for fornication as well as homosexuals, but it has often been interpreted more strictly in the case of the latter. A more relaxed, scientifically informed interpretation of scripture would communicate to the congregation *why* the church wants to place sexuality in a good framework without primarily emphasizing fear or guilt.

In summary, under Leo XIV, a **vision of sexual morality** emerged that brought together **responsibility** and **reality**. The Church should continue to be a clear voice for the dignity of marriage and the sanctity of love - but it humbly learns to recognize that *life* is more complex than any theory. This new type of sexual ethics aims to be **inclusive**: No one should feel excluded from the message of Jesus simply because he or she does not fit the ideal state. Instead, the ideal is offered as a path on which the Church patiently accompanies people. Pope Leo XIV himself repeatedly emphasized that the Church must be there "for all" and come close to people in their concrete situations. This "for all" forms the core of an inclusive sexual ethic - also for queers. It paints a picture of a church that erects **guardrails instead of walls**: a clear orientation towards the values of the Gospel, but also open arms for those who are on bumpy paths. This is what the sexual morality of the future could look like - **anchored in tradition,** but lively and compassionate in dealing with the present. Because ultimately, it is about nothing less than making the liberating message of Jesus shine anew in this central area of life: A message that unites truth and love and applies to all people.

🕊 *Chapter 11:*

Rerum Regressus - or: The dignified naming of rainbow families

Towards the end of the 19th century, radical changes in the political, economic and social spheres, particularly in science and technology, led to a division of society into two classes. After the dissolution of the social guilds, the great mass of the working class had no power and no property to oppose the undignified existence as a destitute working class in which human dignity and basic rights were lost. There was a **high degree of social injustice**. The conflict between **liberalism and socialism** threatened to culminate in revolution.

Leo XIII, the name predecessor of the current Pope, recognized at the time in the "new things" (literal translation), meaning new conditions and developments or, as it is called in the German translation: "spirit of innovation", a danger to society and the state, because: Man has the right to wages after work has been done and also the right to dispose of them freely - so he wrote in his **encyclical Rerum Novarum (1891).**

The conversion of private property into common property therefore deprives workers of the proceeds of their labor and disregards the right to property that "belongs to man by nature" (RN 5). This should not happen to individuals or families. The **family as a community** is older than the state and should therefore not be dependent on it. It "possesses [...] the same rights as civil society" (RN 10) and must remain independent.

The repression of parental care demanded by the socialists violates the fulfillment of parental duty and restricts the "paternal authority" (RN 11). People would then be deprived of the right to marriage and family.

The encyclical Rerum Novarum by the predecessor Pope Leo XIII deals primarily with **social and economic issues of the working class,** in particular the conditions of the working class, property rights, state responsibility and fair wages. It does not contain an explicit or independent **definition of the family.**

Family as a "true society" with its own rights - definition of family

Rerum Novarum therefore does not provide a detailed definition of the family, but presupposes the **family as a universal social and moral unit.** The principles described in the encyclical certainly offer scope to include **modern family forms** such as rainbow families in the sense of a current, inclusive social doctrine.

The family is seen as the natural basic unit of society: Leo XIII emphasizes that the family is older and more natural than the state. It forms the core cell of every society and has a natural right to protection and support (cf. RN 12).

The father's responsibility becomes clear in the classic role relationship: the encyclical describes the father's role as the head and provider of the family and emphasizes his duty to provide for his family members (cf. RN 13-14).

The encyclical needed to be written to emphasize the protection of the family through **fair wages:** It is emphasized that a just wage must enable workers to ensure a decent life for themselves and their own families, including sufficient resources for housing, food, clothing and education for their children (cf. RN 34).

The family as a moral institution: Leo XIII emphasizes the role of the family in the upbringing and moral formation of children. It is described as an essential basis for the transmission of religious and moral values (cf. RN 12-14).

The central section on the family states: "The family, the domestic society, is a true society with all its rights [...] it is older than any other community, and therefore possesses its inherent rights and duties independently of the state."

This passage emphasizes the autonomy, dignity and primacy of the family over the state. Crucially, **"family" is defined here *structurally*, not explicitly biologically or sexually.**

Reference to marriage as the union of a man and a woman: In his justification of the family, Leo XIII refers to Genesis 1:28 ("Grow and multiply") and states: "No human law can deprive man of the natural and original **right to marriage**; none can in any way restrict the primary purpose of this [...] institution."

The encyclical **implicitly** presupposes heterosexuality - but not as a moral demarcation, but in the context of social doctrine, which focuses on property, work and intergenerational security. It is an **economic family model, not a moral theological judgment**.

From LEO 13 to LEO 14: a narrowing bottleneck

The new Pope Leo XIV has now attempted to supplement this centuries-old encyclical historically in conjunction with the media. In doing so, he symbolically used the same name as his predecessor Leo XIII to give his understanding of families an interpretative historical foundation.

Even before he was officially confirmed in office, Pope Leo XIV gave a speech to Vatican diplomats on May 16, 2025. This speech - embedded in otherwise conciliatory and peace-promoting messages - contained an implicit return to a **traditional image of the family** that defined **marriage exclusively** as a union **between "one man and one woman"**.

In this context, the new Pope quoted from the encyclical *Rerum Novarum* of his namesake predecessor, but preceded the historical quote - in the same sentence - with his own words and a much **narrower definition of family** (than his namesake predecessor directly described in the text). In his speech or the quote from *Rerum Novarum* reads: The building of harmonious and peaceful civil societies can [QUOTE BEGIN LEO XIV] "be done primarily through investment for the family, which is the one based on the stable **union between a man and a woman**, [QUOTE BEGIN LEO XIII] "a true **society**, however small this society may present itself, it is older than any other commonwealth" [QUOTE END LEO XIII- Rerum Novarum 1891:9] [QUOTE END LEO XIV].

In this way, he **imposes** his explanation or definition on the historical quotation, both in terms of sentence structure and content, and presents it as a **sentence of the Catholic Church**.

Strategic and media control: How a casual speech becomes a substantive debate

At the same time, Leo XIV had already invited media representatives to an audience before his official inauguration - a strategic move that also ensured media attention for the conference with the diplomats from the outset. Without this targeted staging, his speech to the diplomats would probably have gone largely unnoticed, a merged, superimposed quote - mere background noise in the Vatican's echo chamber? The public would have been as uninterested as the proverbial sack of rice falling over in China or two priests meeting privately online via a dating platform such as Grindr's Planetromeo.

However, his definition of family received enormous attention thanks to the professional craft of the media, especially large tabloid newspapers. It was they who immediately recognized and revealed that the speech **contained** a **clear dialectical demarcation**: Families consisting of two women or two men were deliberately not meant and were **completely omitted from the definition of family**. The media at least fulfilled their task by not only passing on the Vatican's position, but also by **including** representatives of associations, queer groups **and oppositional voices**. In this way, they gave the debate space and momentum.

The fact that the press deliberately created this tension was necessary to get things moving. After all, it often takes pressure in the cauldron to initiate change - or, as in this case, to emphasize a status. A slingshot has to be cocked to catapult the projectile into the target, and sometimes you first have to pull the pig back by the curly tail so that it then runs in **the desired direction of the target**. It is precisely this pressure that the media has created - and thus made it possible for a casual speech, a nested sentence, to become an urgently needed discourse that should not be ignored in terms of content.

Identity politics with the incense stick: a theological and moral imposition

He did not just refer to marriage, where such a definition would only have been partially comprehensible **in view of "marriage for all"**, but explicitly extended his narrow view to the entire concept of "family". In doing so, he clearly distanced himself from the reality of life for many people who today live together as a family in very different constellations - for example with and without a grandmother to bring up, in **patchwork families** with and without two halves of the house or in **rainbow families** with or without marriage but with children to bring up.

The fact that Leo XIV made this **queer bashing** as one of his first substantive statements before his official inauguration is seen by many as an imposition. With his speech to around 100 representatives of the diplomatic corps in the Vatican, the successor to Pope Francis sent a clear **signal of exclusion** towards all **family forms** in which children grow up with same-sex couples or queer parents by adding his words to the quote from "Rerum Novarum".

Originally, "Rerum Novarum" stood for socio-political solidarity and was **not a moral-theological treatise on the definition of family.** However, due to the Pope's new interpretation and linguistic additions, the encyclical suddenly takes on a moral significance today that it only had to a limited extent historically. The fact that Leo XIV understood the family exclusively as a union between a man and a woman **disappoints not only many Catholics**, but also organizations that have long campaigned for greater inclusion of queer people in the Catholic Church.

DeBernardo, director of New Ways Ministry, referenced those remarks Thursday, saying, "The healing that began with 'Who am I to judge?' must continue and grow into 'Who am I if not a friend of LGBTQIA+ people?' Pope Francis has opened the door **for a new approach** to LGBTQIA+ people; **Pope Leo must now lead the Church through that door.** Many Catholics, including bishops and other leaders, remain ignorant of the reality of LGBTQIA+ lives, including the marginalization, discrimination and violence that many still experience, even in Catholic institutions. We hope he will educate himself by listening to and meeting with LGBTQIA+ Catholics and their supporters."

DeBernardo emphasized that Pope Francis had taken significant steps during his pontificate to **welcome** LGBTQIA+ people into the Church, including supporting same-sex couples and promoting a more inclusive approach to transgender people. In light of Pope Leo XIV's previous stance, DeBernardo also appealed to the new Pope to continue on the path of inclusion and to seek dialog with LGBTQIA+ Catholics.

Of course, one might think that this definition was merely a one-off statement by an individual. But was Leo XIV just negligently overlooking the diverse social reality, or was he deliberately ignoring it?

It is true that one could and should also emphasize self-evident facts, such as that the continued existence of society is linked to procreation. However, it was not about procreation, but about living together as a family. The **upbringing of children** does not necessarily have to be carried out by the mother and father; subsidiary communities do an excellent job here. Many people, with and without children, contribute significantly and responsibly **to the development of culture and society.**

Moreover, Leo XIV is not addressing childless couples, infertile women, those who use contraception or people who do too little voluntary work. Rather, he specifically addresses **the old enemy image** of same-sex couples, even though they often achieve extraordinary feats in raising children.

In view of the broad attention given to the topic, an oversight seems unlikely. It seems rather shameful not to implement **queer-sensitive pastoral care** in this already hot topic of the church - it seems like **a bull in a china store. Pouring** this **oil on the fire** is more than shameful - **"Who is he?"**, one could ask in the spirit of Francis. It would have been no trouble at all to **respectfully mention all forms of family and their valuable contribution to society.** (Just as a respectful pause in the spoken gender in German with "_:innen" also includes the third gender of the diverse).

His statements are therefore not a personal faux pas, but the expression of a **strategically planned, institutional positioning of the Vatican** with the prior involvement of the media. This impulse was deliberately set and has been recorded in official documents in several languages. It was prepared in advance of the inauguration.

By theologically attempting to undermine the legitimacy of gender-neutral, subsidiary entities, Leo XIV completely ignores how well rainbow families fit into the concept of Rerum Novarum. Instead, he introduces a backward-looking development with a single casual remark - as if to say: "Witch-burning - but better now?" - **Rerum Novarum became Rerum Regressus.**

Rather, the focus should be on **those celibate men** who do not father children themselves and do not contribute to procreation, but some of whom have even become abusive towards children and adolescents.

Pope Leo XIV's decision to indirectly but clearly **exclude same-sex partnerships** in his first programmatic address and to privilege only the heteronormative family model is not only **unwise** from a theological, pastoral and church-political point of view - it is a **strategic** (and therefore groundless) **impertinence**. Why? Three perspectives on this:

1. theologically: Christ is central - not the gender model

a) The good news is for *all people*: The gospel is not a message for heterosexual married couples, but for all "who are weary and burdened" (Mt 11:28) - including queer people who have often had to tug between faith, exclusion and identity for decades. Anyone who begins here not with a **word of reconciliation**, but with a structure of exclusion, misses Christ himself.

b) The New Testament confesses that in Christ there is "no longer male or female" (Gal 3:28): Paul breaks down the binary orders - in baptism, grace and vocation, people are not defined according to biological order, but according to their relationship with God. The adherence to an exclusive "man-and-woman model" as normativity is Old Testament cultural indulgence, not **New Testament theology**.

c) No biblical teaching prohibits binding same-sex love: The often quoted so-called **"clobber passages"** (e.. Rom 1, Lev 18) are not statements about equal queer love relationships, but moral judgments about abuse, the exercise of power and cultic purity. They have been removed from their context, but have never been responsibly brought up to date in terms of queer theology.

2. pastoral care: a pope should heal, not hurt

a) Pope Leo XIV assumes the highest pastoral office of the universal Church: Precisely because many queer people have been massively violated by the Church - through exclusion, refusal of blessing, forced outings, conversion therapies, silence and dogmas - what is needed in the present is first of all a **sign of closeness and appreciation**, not a normative command.

b) Pastoral care means thinking from suffering, not from the ideal: Christ himself set aside the law when it harmed people (cf. Mk 2:27). The pastoral care of queer people does not require moral teaching, but **care, recognition and a spiritual home**. Those who instead directly proclaim a rigid norm are doubly hurting those who are already suffering from theological homelessness.

c) Strategic misuse of the stage: The stage - a diplomatic reception with global media interest - could have been used to invite the wounded, to listen to the marginalized, to promise reconciliation. Instead, it is being used tactically **for a frontline brand** that deliberately serves a conservative power camp. This is not pastoral care, this is **identity politics with a stick of incense.**

3. church policy: it is an affront to reform processes

a) Contrary to synodal processes: In many countries - especially Germany, Belgium, Australia - painstaking and transparent work is being done to **integrate queer believers**. Anyone who undermines these efforts with a global power gesture is snubbing bishops, theologians and laypeople who are fighting for a more inclusive church.

b) Undiplomatic towards countries that legally protect marriage for all: Expressing this position in front of around 100 diplomats - many from countries with marriage for all, equality laws and anti-discrimination constitutions - is not building bridges, but **a political affront**. It is a disregard for both state reality and developments in international law.

Undignified and problematic in terms of church policy

Yes, in political, diplomatic and moral terms, this statement can be classified as tactically highly revealing, pastorally undignified and problematic in terms of church policy - especially if it was the *first substantive positioning signal* after the inauguration. A differentiated analysis:

1. tactical classification: a deliberate signaling act

- **Timing & addressees**: The first programmatic speech after taking office - in front of *around 100 ambassadors* from all over the world - is no coincidence. It is a highly *symbolic forum* in which every sentence is evaluated in terms of foreign policy. Anyone who propagates the "natural family" as the only valid model at this point and implicitly excludes queer partnerships is sending a clear message.

- **Recourse to Leo XIII**: The reference to *Rerum novarum* and an alleged "natural order" is not a theological reflex, but an ideologically orchestrated move that underpins the pontificate with a conservative social doctrine. This is strategic - and not pastoral.

- **Choice of the first area of conflict**: The fact that the rejection of queer partnerships is being introduced so prominently before topics such as migration, peace or climate shows which cultural front line is being deliberately sought. However, it is also possible that the new pope has been shaped by the Vatican echo chamber in such a way that he has adopted its stance and it corresponds to his own. This gives the impression that he is not leading the Vatican in the interests of the people and their needs, but that the Vatican is leading it - with such strategic straw fires.

2. moral evaluation: lack of dignity towards office and human dignity

- **Disproportionality**: An opening speech that begins with a claim to universal peace and human dignity, but then indirectly devalues an entire population group, is a **moral paradox**. It is inherently contradictory and undermines the moral claim of the office.

- **Contradiction to the Gospel**: Those who speak in the footsteps of Jesus should *build bridges*, not walls. The demonstrative insistence on an exclusive understanding of marriage is neither necessary nor merciful nor in line with the Gospel.

- **Violation by omission**: Even if no open insults were uttered, the combination of positive, exclusive mention of heterosexual unions and the simultaneous concealment or suppression of queer lifestyles is a form of structural degradation. This is *gentle but effective discrimination* - under the cloak of dignity.

3. institutional dignity and appropriateness of office

- A pope does not speak privately, but ex officio as the moral authority of billions of people. Anyone who begins this office with a **frontal attack on recognized human rights** - especially in states where homosexual couples are legally protected - also violates the diplomatic integrity of the Vatican.

- Such a message is not only incompatible with the pastoral humility of a bridge-builder, but rhetorically a slap in the face for all those believers who want to reconcile their queer identity with faith.

Conclusion: Anyone who takes up the ministry of Peter and excludes same-sex couples from the idea of a true family as their first theological message is **denying mercy, perverting the ministry of the shepherds and instrumentalizing peace** in order to send a signal of cultural warfare. This is not "truth in love" - but **unkindness in the guise of supposed truth**.

Yes, you can - and must - call it that: It is a deliberate, cold and undignified (bottomless) insolence that does not **do justice to the spirit of the Gospel, human dignity and the ministry**. Anyone who begins in this way is setting themselves in opposition to the reform impulses of many believers worldwide. They are not demonstrating hope, but **repression**. And therein lies the bitter strategic clarity of one of these first major appearances and messages.

How to correctly classify RERUM NOVARUM with RESPECT

The encyclical Rerum Novarum (1891) by its predecessor Pope Leo XIII deals primarily with social and economic issues of the working class, in particular the conditions of the workforce, property rights, state responsibility and fair wages. There is therefore no explicit or independent definition of family in it, only an implicit one.

A widely accepted and common **definition of family** in today's social sciences is based **on the presence of children:** According to this, family arises **wherever children live, grow up and are cared for** - regardless of the specific parental constellation. This would have been the appropriate and contemporary definition that Pope Leo XIV should have emphasized.

Even in the encyclical *Rerum Novarum*, the concept of family is not explicitly linked to the sexes of the parents. Rather, the encyclical describes the family generally and deliberately openly as a subsidiary community of solidarity: "The family, the domestic society, is a **true society** with all its rights, however small this society may be; it is older than any other community and therefore possesses its own rights and duties independently of the state."

This formulation presupposes neither biologically nor sexually defined roles. The definition of the family is based on the view of a **subsidiary unit of solidarity**.

Even more: the encyclical consistently speaks of "human beings", not always of specific genders such as "man" or "woman". In fact, the word "woman" only appears twice in the entire 25 pages. This deliberate linguistic openness shows that *Rerum Novarum* can **certainly** be **interpreted in a gender-neutral** way - as a document that defines the family primarily by its social function and not by its gender composition.

However, Leo XIII refers indirectly to the family several times:

1. **The family as the natural basic unit of society:** Leo XIII emphasizes that the family is older and more natural than the state. It forms the core cell of every society and has a natural right to protection and support (cf. RN 12).

2. **Responsibility of the father of the family:** The encyclical describes the role of the father as the head and provider of the family and emphasizes his duty to provide for his family members (cf. RN 13-14).

3. **Protection of the family through fair wages:** It is emphasized that a fair wage must enable the worker to secure a decent life for himself and his family, including sufficient resources for housing, food, clothing and education for children (cf. RN 34).

4. **The family as an educational institution:** Leo XIII emphasized the role of the family in the upbringing and education of children. It is described as an essential basis for the transmission of religious and moral values (cf. RN 12-14).

Smaller communities - usually families - play a central role in social policy, as they should help themselves first before the state intervenes to provide support. It is clear that **patchwork or rainbow families also form subsidiary units** in which people - with or without children - can overcome crises together more easily than individuals who would otherwise be more reliant on state assistance.

Interpretative inclusion of rainbow families:

What Leo XIV is doing here is **a historical narrowing** that does not have to be - especially in view of more contemporary, more open family images: **Family is where there are children.** So why this *pontificate of the bottleneck*, which ignores the current social realities of individualization and diverse lifestyles and does not do them justice?

Although the historical text of Leo XIII's predecessor does not explicitly address the term and concept of the rainbow family, an interpretative and queer-theological bridge can be built today by drawing on Leo XIII's basic concern:

- **Dignity and protection of the family:** Leo XIII insists that families, as the basic cells of society, deserve special protection. This principle could be interpreted more broadly today to include families in all forms, including same-sex partnerships and rainbow families.

- **The right to a decent life:** The concern that every family should be entitled to sufficient income and social security could serve as a basis for extending equal rights and protection to non-traditional family structures.

Rerum Novarum therefore does not provide a detailed definition of the family, but presupposes the **family as a universal social and moral unit.** The principles described in the encyclical certainly offer scope to include modern family forms such as rainbow families in the sense of a current, inclusive social doctrine. A look at rainbow families shows this.

Interpretative inclusion of rainbow families and other family models: Even if the historical text of Leo XIII does not explicitly address the term and concept of the rainbow family, an interpretative and queer-theological bridge can be built today by drawing on the basic concern of Leo XIII:

- **Dignity and protection of the family:** Leo XIII insists that families, as the basic cells of society, deserve special protection. This principle could be interpreted more broadly today to include families in all forms, including same-sex partnerships and rainbow families.
- **The right to a decent life:** The concern that every family should be entitled to sufficient income and social security could serve as a basis for extending equal rights and protection to non-traditional family structures.

The aim is to show that *Rerum novarum* must not be instrumentalized as an instrument of exclusion against rainbow families, but must be understood in a more differentiated way through today's hermeneutics: *So how can rainbow families be theologically integrated?*

When *Rerum novarum* describes the family as a "small society" with rights, duties of care and asset protection, the essential criterion is not gender distribution, but rather a definition of the family as a community of responsibility:

- Mutual obligation
- Responsibility towards children
- Contribution to the common good

Rainbow families fulfill all of these characteristics. In today's interpretation, it would be theologically inappropriate to deny them this social role. Paternal (parental) responsibility is about an ethical principle - which is not fixed in terms of gender.

Predecessor Leo XIII wrote: "An urgent law of nature demands that the father of the family provide the children with a livelihood and everything they need [...] it is he who lives on in the children [...]"

This idea is aimed at continuity, care, generational responsibility - tasks that any parental constellation can take on, regardless of gender. Today, we can say that the "father" symbolically stands for the person who assumes responsibility - and this can be a mother, a father, a non-binary person or two same-sex parents.

And finally: subsidiarity and respect for ways of life must be taken seriously and are the credo of this encyclical

Social doctrine recognizes the principle that the state (or the church) must not deprive smaller communities of what they can achieve. *Rerum novarum* therefore emphasizes respect for domestic autonomy. It can be deduced from this: Anyone who raises children lovingly, who shapes a domestic life together and exercises rights is acting in the spirit of the encyclical - even as a rainbow family.

Giving corrective advice is necessary

How should queer people and especially the children of queer families feel after such statements **at the start of a pontificate**? This in-sensitive process is deeply disappointing and despicable - and this must be clearly and unequivocally expressed. What is intended here could be described as "tactical" or "evil" due to the strategic component and general staff preparation. **Evil must not and will not prevail**, and it is precisely by this claim of his own quotation that Leo XIV himself must now be measured. Even if it may be conceded that he still needed to learn at the beginning of his office, a prompt correction of this position and lack of inclusion and appreciation is essential.

If the resulting conflict only contributes to a further hardening of the fronts, Leo XIV does not prove to be a bridge-builder, but **someone who**

deepens dividing lines. Staking his claim at the beginning of a career is how people in the profession like to meet new, ambitious colleagues.

Today, no conservative cleric can seriously deny that a variety of family images exist and that **each of these family forms does its best in terms of solidarity and a subsidiary understanding of social community.**

If this discussion is the prelude **to addressing family images in the Church more comprehensively**, then it is necessary to introduce the sacramental marriage of same-sex couples in the near future. This is the only way to make amends for this **serious misstep at the beginning of the pontificate.**

Its formulation - partially based on *Rerum novarum* - is not only theologically and anthropologically one-sided, but **also pastorally offensive and socially backward-looking.** A well-founded response to this from the perspective of human rights, theology and practical life experience is as follows:

1. love and family are not bound by gender boundaries

Numerous scientific studies and field reports prove this: Same-sex couples are just as capable of having stable, loving and responsible relationships as heterosexual couples. Rainbow families are also in no way inferior to others when it comes to raising children - on the contrary: studies by the American Psychological Association, for example, show that children in same-sex households grow up just as well or even more stable than in heteronormative structures.

Family is not a biological dogma, but a community in which trust, reliability, tenderness, care and responsibility for each other are lived. This applies to all couples - regardless of gender.

2. the Christian message knows no logic of exclusion

Jesus himself never spoke a word against homosexual people - but many against hypocrisy, exclusion and discrimination. When Pope Leo XIV says that *peace begins in the heart* and that *truth* is *only connected to love and concern for people*, he should have the courage to apply this to queer realities. **The church cannot speak credibly about peace and**

at the same time symbolically and structurally devalue queer people. And this at a diplomatic forum - what a disaster!

Appealing to the "truth" of the church in the face of the reality of same-sex love is inappropriate if this truth does not have a life-serving effect, but rather one that excludes and causes suffering. Truth must be philanthropic - otherwise it is **not of Christ.**

3. church teaching must be adaptive

How many supposedly "natural law" convictions have already been revised? The condemnation of interest transactions, the subordination of women, the devaluation of divorcees, the blessing of weapons of war - all positions that the church once held and later corrected. Even the understanding of sexuality and partnership is not static, but evolves with the awareness of the times.

If the Holy See claims a "pastoral urge" that does not strive for privileges but is at **the service of humanity**, then it must also be prepared to listen and learn - especially where people are concerned who have been psychologically injured, socially marginalized and pastorally ignored by church teachings for centuries.

4. children need love - not a specific parental model

The decisive factor for the well-being of children is not the gender constellation of the parents, but the **degree of security, reliability and emotional affection**. A marriage or partnership between two mothers or two fathers can offer all of this in abundance. The child's well-being is the focus - not an ideological ideal.

If Pope Leo XIV emphasizes *that no one can avoid striving for an environment in which the dignity of every human being is protected*, then this must also apply to the children of queer families - and to their parents. **The degradation of their love under the guise of the "natural order" contradicts both the biblical message and every form of Christian-humanist ethics.**

5 A positive counter-image: inclusive Christianity

The future of the church does not lie in the repetition of outdated structures, but in openness to the diversity of human life.

Congregations that marry same-sex couples, do not hide queer priests and **integrate rainbow families** live the gospel more credibly than dogmatic exclusions ever could.

Many Catholic reform movements - from *Maria 2.0* to *Dignity* and *Voices of Faith* - testify that **faith can be inclusive, colorful and relational**. A church that understands queer people as part of the body of Christ also becomes a credible sign of peace for society.

Pope Leo XIV called for *truth, justice and peace*. These three are inconceivable without equality, recognition and empathy. Those who structurally exclude same-sex (married) couples are not only violating their dignity - they are **violating the center of the Christian message:** that all people are loved, called and blessed just as they are. There is no theological or ethical reason to deny marriage, blessing or parenthood to two loving people - but there are many good reasons to make it possible for them. And *that* is true justice.

How queer communities, organizations and supporting theological or social actors should continue to respond - strategically and communicatively

Queer Christians and their allies can react publicly and decisively: They should clearly reject the Pope's statements in statements, for example via networks such as the European Forum of LGBT Christian Groups, Dignity, Maria 2.0 or Voices of Faith - theologically sound, arguing in terms of human rights and with pastoral empathy. At the same time, it is important to develop queer-theological **counter-narratives** that show that love and family are not tied to gender constellations. Internationally, alliances can be formed with other religions, human rights organizations and political actors, for example through petitions and UN resolutions. Pastoral counter-signals such as public celebrations for same-sex couples and media campaigns (e.g. #TrueFamily, #LoveIsNotASin, #WeAreChurch) are also effective. Queer Catholics can also set a visible example by demonstratively withdrawing from church committees or **consciously showing their**

rainbow presence at church events. A sample letter to the Pope is also conceivable as an *open response to Pope Leo XIV's statements.*

Open statement by queer Christians and supporting organizations
On the diplomatic reception on May 16, 2025 by Pope Leo XIV.

Your Holiness,

It is with great disappointment and concern that we take note of your first substantive statements after taking office. In a speech that claims to embody peace, justice and truth, what is missing is what Christian faith is at its core: the recognition of all people as images of God - regardless of gender, sexual orientation or lifestyle.

Your speech not only leaves queer people out - it degrades them to an implicitly deficient form of being human by only recognizing the union of "man and woman" as the supporting structure of society and family. This is not mere overlooking - it is a denial of recognition.

We strongly disagree.

Because:

- **Love is love.** It develops dignity, responsibility, care and loyalty - regardless of biological gender.

- **Family is where people stand up for each other.** Queer couples and rainbow families are living places of stability and care.

- **Justice begins with recognition.** Anyone who structurally devalues people through religious language is not acting in the spirit of Jesus.

We do not expect complete theological agreement from a pope - but respect. And we do not expect agreement - but the most fundamental sign of human dignity: that we are seen as equal children of God and not concealed or suppressed.

We will stay. In the church. In our families. In our love. And we will remain visible.

Because we are not a "problem" - we are
We are part of the solution: for a church that wants to be credible, just, merciful and inclusive.

On behalf of many believers who are queer or close as "allies" - and believe, hope, love.

Signed by ...

Hermeneutic is needed

Rerum novarum is not a dogmatic text, but a socio-political reaction to the misery of the industrial working class in the 19th century. **A contemporary document - not dogmatic**. The definition of marriage is not the central content, but a marginal condition of an economic system.

Hermeneutic progress is needed - and not a return to the past: Church teaching has developed further in many areas: Labor rights, property distribution, equal rights for women, dealing with sexuality. Today, it is clear that invoking *Rerum novarum* to discriminate against queer lifestyles is theologically untenable!

The exclusive, narrow reading of *Rerum novarum*, as used by Pope Leo XIV to devalue queer families in his diplomatic inaugural address or to supplement his dogmatics, is **theologically incorrect, pastorally irresponsible and socially and ethically outdated**. The dogmatic **narrow-mindedness and octrophy** with which one tries to take the family argument from *Rerum Novarum* away from queer theology proves - as the previous analysis makes clear - to be incorrect. On the contrary, a closer look at the historical and hermeneutical context reveals the exact opposite: queer parents and their children in particular can invoke the socio-ethical principles of this encyclical with full justification.

Rainbow families can and must be recognized **as "true societies"** in the sense of Catholic social teaching - because they bear responsibility, shape life and act for the common good.

The hermeneutical conclusion is that the encyclical *Rerum Novarum* is primarily to be understood as a socio-ethical document, not as a moral-theological treatise. A theological instrumentalization of this text to discriminate against queer people is therefore inadmissible and contradicts its actual intention. Modern Catholic social ethics expressly emphasizes the principles of personal dignity, subsidiarity and participation - central values that necessarily include queer families. Rainbow families are therefore to be understood and recognized as an expression of a "true society" in the spirit of *Rerum Novarum*.

🕊️ *Chapter 12:*

Administration, transparency and representation of the church

No sooner had the white smoke cleared than Pope Leo XIV, born Robert Francis Prevost, had to face up to the pressing construction sites of his pontificate. Although the first American to sit on the Chair of Peter takes over a church on the rise worldwide, the challenges do not invite rejoicing: Financial stability, curia reform, dealing with abuse victims and other reform issues are now on his desk. Francis, his elderly predecessor, had initiated important changes - from more women in church offices to dealing with abuse scandals - but much remained unfinished. Now the hope rests on Leo XIV to continue these reforms with renewed vigor **and to set his own accents**. At the same time, as a moral authority, he should build international bridges, stand up for peace and justice and strengthen the voice of the Church on global issues such as climate and social inequality.

Financial transparency and efficient administration

The Vatican's finances are considered opaque and strained - a legacy that Leo XIV absolutely had to tackle. In the final months before his death, Pope Francis sounded the alarm: he urged the cardinals **to manage their finances more efficiently** in future **and to strive for a "zero deficit"**. In fact, the Papal States had not submitted a complete budget report since 2022. The last available balance sheet from mid-2024 revealed a deficit of 83 million euros; even more serious was an estimated hole of around **631 million euros** in the Vatican's pension fund. Francis' concern was so great that, three days before falling seriously ill in February, he hastily appointed a high-level commission to mobilize donations for the cash-strapped Vatican. These dramatic steps show how urgently the economic foundations of the Curia need to be secured.

Leo XIV now faces the mammoth task of **increasing transparency and efficiency in church administration** and restoring trust in the Holy See's financial management. He is expected to sift through the complex bureaucratic structures of the Vatican and implement **drastic cost-cutting measures.** This is precisely what the cardinals had in mind during the conclave: The new pope should bring financial expertise and be prepared to tackle unpopular reforms. The first signs indicate that Leo XIV cultivates a collegial but consistent style of leadership - he sees the Curia as a servant administration **and not as a power-hungry center.** He therefore immediately ordered an inventory of the Vatican's assets, including the numerous properties belonging to the Papal States. It remains to be seen whether some properties will actually be sold to pay off debts, as is being discussed internally. Cardinal Reinhard Marx, the Munich-based economic expert on the Council of Cardinals, warns against rushing into action: Marx points out that selling off the real estate holdings "would **not be a sustainable, but a short-term restructuring".** Instead, structural expenditure needs to be addressed.

Vatican finances are actually divided into two areas, as Marx explains: **the Vatican City State generates surpluses**, but the Holy See - i.e. the central administration with all its dicasteries and nunciatures worldwide - continues to cost more than it earns. High salaries and, above all, pension costs for around 5,000 employees are a burden on the budget. Several levers are needed to eliminate this structural deficit. On the one hand, under Leo XIV, the austerity measures that Francis began are likely to be intensified: Francis already cut the salaries of cardinals and curia employees, and Leo XIV could continue or even intensify this course. On the other hand, **the revenue side needs to be strengthened**, but in a transparent and ethical manner. Cardinal Marx warns that the Vatican Bank IOR and the administration of the Vatican State have a decisive role to play: they must **reliably transfer surpluses to the Holy See** so that the Church's mission remains financed. After all, the IOOC is now in the black and distributes tens of millions to the Holy See every year - not enough to cover all deficits, but a building block.

Leo XIV also leaves no doubt that **transparency is the order of the day**. Financial reports are to be published regularly again in order to counteract the impression of secrecy - the longstanding practice of keeping the balance sheets under lock and key has damaged the Vatican's reputation. It is fitting that the new Pope already saw administration as a service during his time as a bishop and attached great importance to **clear accountability**. This culture is now also to be introduced in Rome. Insiders report that Leo XIV summoned a number of heads of authorities in the first days of his pontificate in order to get a precise picture of the finances and administrative processes. "We must tighten our belts without betraying our mission," he is said to have admonished - a balancing act that he wanted to achieve by **using every euro in the service of the Gospel**. If Leo XIV succeeds in plugging the Vatican budget gap **without** shaking the trust of the faithful with further financial scandals, much would be gained. The universal church is watching closely to see whether he can prove that he can cope with the "heavy burden" of the chaotic Vatican finances.

Measures to prevent and deal with cases of abuse

Probably no issue has undermined the moral credit of the Church in recent years as much as the revelations of sexual abuse by clerics. Leo XIV is determined to **treat this wound in the Church with all his might** - both preventively and curatively. Structural taboos that were long considered sacrosanct are also being questioned. The reform debate focused on two main thrusts in particular: the celibacy requirement for priests and new synodal leadership models with strong lay participation.

Abolition of compulsory celibacy: a structural lever?

The mandatory celibacy of Catholic priests is increasingly coming under scrutiny as a possible factor that fosters the dynamics of abuse. Although experts emphasize that celibacy is not *the* cause of sexual violence, many see it as a structural risk factor. A comprehensive Australian study, for example, concludes that celibacy, combined with immature sexuality, can create an environment that favors assault. According to the authors, **psychologically immature or sexually frustrated clerics** pose an increased risk, especially in boarding schools, homes or schools. It is worth taking a look at the Eastern churches that are united with Rome: Some priests there are allowed to marry - and in fact, the abuse figures in these communities are significantly lower. This evidence underpins the demand of some reform groups to reconsider compulsory celibacy in order to break up clerical abuse dynamics.

Leo XIV approached the subject with the necessary caution, but without blinkers. Pope Francis has already made it clear **that nothing about celibacy is immutable**. Francis expressly described priestly celibacy **as a "temporary rule"**, not a doctrine for eternity. He pointed out that it *is not a contradiction that priests can marry*. Statements like these opened up scope for Leo XIV to think in new ways. In any case, there is a growing number of voices in the universal church in favor of a relaxation. **The German Synodal Way** - the reform dialog of the Catholic Church in Germany - has even passed a resolution by an overwhelming majority officially asking the Pope to review compulsory celibacy. Leo XIV is unlikely to ignore such a request from his church base, especially as it is not an isolated phenomenon but part of a worldwide discussion. Of course, there are also concerns: some theologians warn that abolishing celibacy alone will not solve the problem and that there will be no "rush" of new, irreproachable priests. However, as a **preventative lever**, voluntary celibacy could at least defuse the dangerous dynamics that arise from unhealthy repression mechanisms. Leo XIV announced that he wanted to talk about this hot potato **without ideology and without fear.** According to those close to him, it was a matter of "putting everything on the table that can serve to protect people" - no matter how traditional it may be.

Synodal leadership models and lay participation

At the same time, Leo XIV was committed to a cultural change in the leadership of the Church. The old power imbalance - the all-powerful clergy at the top, the obedient laity at the bottom - had had its day. It is to be replaced by more **synodality**: a joint walk of consecrated and non-consecrated people in which power is shared and control is no longer the sole responsibility of the hierarchy. The investigation of abuse cases in particular has shown that clerical concentration of power has often led to a lack of transparency and cover-ups. When **priests and bishops** are **only accountable to each other**, a "cartel of silence" easily develops that protects the institution - not the victims. This should be counteracted by synodal structures in which non-clergy are also involved and have a say in decision-making.

Leading church leaders are expressly in favor of this opening. Cardinal Jean-Claude Hollerich - Europe's most senior archbishop - called for **bishops to be more closely monitored by laypeople.** *"I have no problem with a group of lay people controlling me,"* Hollerich said unequivocally and called for clericalism to be overcome. This attitude, which would have caused a stir a few years ago, is now shared by many. In several countries, independent commissions are being set up with the participation of lawyers, psychologists and lay representatives to investigate cases of abuse and make recommendations. Leo XIV expressly welcomed such initiatives. In his own diocese of Chiclayo in Peru, he **tried out participatory forms of leadership** before his election as pope and experienced that shared responsibility is good for credibility. As Pope, he emphasizes that synodality **does not** simply mean democratization, but rather listening to the Holy Spirit - but experience has shown that this listening is broader and clearer when all the faithful are involved.

In concrete terms, this could mean that at parish and diocesan level, **mixed bodies made up of clergy and laity** are given more decision-making powers: For example, pastoral councils that advise together with pastors on important matters, or independent advisory teams that are involved in staff recruitment, financial issues and dealing with allegations. The Vatican itself has already taken steps in this direction - some Vatican commissions now include women and lay men with voting rights. Leo XIV is likely to consolidate this course. For him, it is crucial that power in the church is understood **as a service** and is exercised transparently. *"We are all baptized and belong to the same church,"* was the motto that he - like Hollerich - repeatedly emphasized. This goes hand in hand with **stricter accountability** for office holders: Bishops who make mistakes or cover them up should no longer be able to hide behind their fellow bishops. It is becoming apparent that Leo XIV will take clear action in cases of abuse and allow external expertise to drive forward the investigation. The Church is to become a model of transparency here - an ambitious goal, but one that seems indispensable if lost trust is to be regained.

International representation and diplomatic role

Pope Leo XIV is also called upon to act **as a bridge-builder and moral authority** on the world stage. The very choice of his name - Leo - is reminiscent of Pope Leo XIII, who campaigned for social justice in the 19th century. Leo XIV consciously took up this tradition by making peace, climate justice and social issues the hallmarks of his pontificate. In his very first speech from the balcony of St. Peter's Basilica, he set an example: In front of tens of thousands of cheering faithful, he called **for peace and dialog**. *"Peace be with you!"* - he greeted the world with this biblical greeting as soon as he was elected Pope. Leo XIV made being a peacemaker his unequivocal priority. International observers noticed that he outlined his idea of peace in the same speech: it was about an **"unarmed and disarming peace"**, a peace through dialog and disarmament, entirely in the spirit of Christ. For Leo XIV, this pacifism was not a naïve dream, but a concrete program.

Just a few days after his election, these words were followed by action. Leo XIV immediately met diplomats and envoys from all over the world in Rome and emphasized to the diplomatic corps that the Vatican's foreign policy was a **"service to the human family"**. He followed in the footsteps of Francis, who had tirelessly shaken up consciences - from *the "cry of the poor"* to the challenges of **climate protection and globalization**. Leo XIV made it clear that he wanted to continue these themes and at the same time set his own priorities. He announced a **series of trips abroad** in order to build new bridges of understanding across cultural and national borders. His personal biography - stations in life in North and South America as well as Europe - is the program: *"My life's journey shows the desire to cross borders in order to meet different people and cultures,"* he explained to the diplomats. The Pope wants, as he says, *"to reach out and embrace every people and every individual on this earth who longs for truth, justice and peace".*

Peace through dialog is one of his guiding principles. Leo XIV emphasized that a *sincere will to dialogue* was necessary to pacify conflicts - the world should learn to meet each other instead of fighting each other. This also included **reviving international institutions** and strengthening diplomacy. Specifically, Leo XIV positioned himself on the world's most important current peace issue: the war in Ukraine. Shortly after taking office, he announced to Moscow and Kiev that **territorial peace and human rights** were non-negotiable for the Holy See. Ukrainian President Volodymyr Zelensky was delighted with the new Pope's clear words: he reported a "very cordial and substantial" telephone conversation with Leo XIV, in which he called for a **"just and lasting peace"** for Ukraine. Selensky immediately invited Leo XIV to visit Ukraine - such a visit would "bring real hope" to the long-suffering people, as the President emphasized. Hopeful voices are also coming from the Ukrainian church : *"Francis was not understood here. But Pope Leo XIV has already shown that peace in Ukraine is close to his heart,"* explained Auxiliary Bishop Volodymyr Hruza in Lviv. The Grand Archbishop of Kiev, Svyatoslav Shevchuk, even went so far as to say that a visit by Leo **could bring peace.** These expectations underline the extent to which the world sees Leo XIV in the role of **neutral mediator and admonisher for peace.**

In addition to peace policy, Leo XIV also raised **a strong voice for climate justice and social justice.** Francis had set the bar high with his encyclical *Laudato si'* by placing environmental and climate protection at the center of church teaching. Leo XIV shows that he is committed to pursuing this course. In his programmatic meeting with the ambassadors, he emphasized that the Holy See would continue to face the *"challenges of our time"*, *"from the preservation of creation to artificial intelligence"*. He is thus directly following on from the socio-ecological agenda of his predecessor. **Climate activists and development organizations** such as Greenpeace and CIDSE expressly welcome this: they associate Leo XIV with the hope that the Church will denounce global injustices even more clearly and contribute to social and ecological change. Greenpeace Germany, for example, has called on the new Pope to **make climate justice a priority for the Church** and to make greater use of Church assets for sustainable projects. Leo XIV seems ready to show a clear edge here too. In his address, he said that the Church had no choice but to raise its voice in the face of the many imbalances and injustices *"that lead, among other things, to undignified working conditions and fragmented, conflict-ridden societies"*. The Pope called for *"efforts to eliminate global inequalities"*. At the same time, he appealed to political leaders to create more peaceful societies by investing in **stable families and social equality**. He was particularly concerned about the dignity of the most vulnerable - from **unborn children to migrants**, every person should be protected. It is this comprehensive approach - thinking peace, the environment, social justice and the protection of life together - that has already made Leo XIV a **distinctive new voice** on the world stage.

Leo XIV also struck a critical note when it came to those responsible in politics and society. *"The Church can never escape its mission to speak the truth about man and the world,"* he emphasized, announcing that he would name abuses in clear language if necessary. However, this truth is always linked to love and is aimed at the well-being of every human being. In other words, the Pope does not want to mince his diplomatic words when it comes to **migration crises, exploitation or warmongering** - but he does so with a pastoral heart that has the salvation of people in mind. This combination of plain speaking and compassion already characterizes his public image.

Leo XIV is thus in the process of **raising the profile of the Church as a global moral authority**. He is building on the foundations of his predecessors - you can sense both the spirit of John Paul II, who tirelessly shouted *"Never again war!"*, and that of Francis, who focused on mercy and ecology. But Leo XIV is determined to continue this mission *with his own signature*. As one Vatican observer put it: "Leo wants to build bridges, but he also wants to hammer in stakes." Bridges of dialog - for example with other religions in order to jointly drive out the **"will to conquer"** and fanaticism - and stakes of clarity where fundamental values are violated. His first speech to the diplomats ended with an urgent warning to disarmament, in line with the last message of the late Francis: *"There can be no peace without true disarmament!"* cried Leo XIV, warning against a new global arms race. Such words resonate - in the halls of the UN as well as on the margins of society.

In summary, Pope Leo XIV proved to be a pope in the first weeks of his pontificate who strengthened administration and transparency in the Church, did not shy away from uncomfortable questions and represented the Catholic Church on the world stage with fresh vigor. He relies on solid finances as the basis for the mission, on a humble church that learns from its mistakes and on a resolute stance on peace, climate and justice. At the same time, he remained a pastor at heart: the desire to make the Church more credible and to give its message weight in the modern world came through in everything he did. Leo XIV is not treading an easy path - but many voices, from the Munich cardinal to the Ukrainian president, are already signaling their **hope** that this pope will indeed open up new paths of faith and justice. The coming years will show how far Leo XIV gets with his plans. But the departure is palpable: a *church on the move*, borne by the claim to make administration transparent, to share power and to become an advocate for humanity in the world's crises.

🕊️ *Chapter 13:*
Synodality and structural renewal of the church

When Pope Leo XIV appeared on the loggia of St. Peter's Basilica for the first time on May 8, 2025, he promised, visibly moved, to continue the synodal awakening of his predecessor. In his **first speech**, he thanked Pope Francis and called out to the assembled faithful: Brothers and sisters "of Rome, of Italy, of the whole world, let us be a synodal Church, a Church that is on the move, a Church that always seeks peace, that always seeks charity, that always seeks closeness above all to those who suffer". Leo XIV thus directly committed himself to **synodality** as a leitmotif - the concept of a "church that is shaped together". Pope Francis had already described synodality as the "path that God expects of the Church of the third millennium". Synodality essentially means walking together on the path of faith: **Listening, dialogue, shared discernment and shared responsibility** characterize this style. The final declaration of the 2023 World Synod defined it as all believers moving forward together - in gatherings at all levels, listening to one another, consulting and reaching consensus under the guidance of the Holy Spirit. Pope Leo XIV, who "knows what synodality means", picks up here and makes it clear that he does not want to **take a backward step** - if you can believe it - but to continue the reform course initiated by Francis. The Chairman of the German Bishops' Conference, Georg Bätzing, said it was *"encouraging"* that Leo XIV had so clearly committed to a "synodal church that moves forward and wants to be there for all people". The new Pope is thus in **continuity** with his predecessor and "makes it clear that what Francis began will continue" - an important signal, especially for Germany with its synodal path, in order to further advance the renewal of church structures and more co-determination.

Synodal culture of discussion from the parish to the curia

Under Leo XIV, synodality should not just remain a buzzword in Rome, but should permeate the entire church as a **mindset**. The Pope promoted a synodal *culture of discussion* - from local parish life to the highest church committees. In concrete terms, this means that **listening and dialog** become the norm of church action: In parishes, priests and lay people should engage in greater exchange, and parish assemblies and councils should be seriously involved. In the dioceses, Leo XIV encouraged the bishops to hold local **synods** or pastoral councils so that the faithful could voice their concerns. And even at the Roman Curia, this style continued - through consultations, international commissions and the participation of diverse voices (including religious and lay people) in decision-making. Observers describe how Leo XIV, as a bishop and cardinal, was always open to advice *"and collaboration"*, for example with women in leadership positions. Sister Yvonne Reungoat, who was one of the first women to work with the then Cardinal Prevost in the Dicastery for Bishops, emphasizes his **attentiveness and openness**: he actively listened to and involved women - which is why she is convinced that he will continue and even expand this line as Pope. However, a truly synodal culture of discussion also thrives **on patient listening** on all sides. The Viennese theologian Jan-Heiner Tück warns that in synodal dialog, one should "really listen to the other and not hastily identify one's own wishes with the work of the Holy Spirit". This principle should help to ensure that discussions remain fair and spiritual, even when controversial topics arise. Leo XIV aspired to a Church *"that listens attentively, that is close to every person, [...] capable of authentic and welcoming relationships - a house and family of God open to all: a missionary synodal Church"*. Leo XIV accepted this vision from a letter from the Synod Secretariat to the new Pope as a mission: He wanted to bring the Church closer to the people, more capable of dialog, more ready to serve and more open to the world.

In practical terms, this also meant a **change of mentality** in church leadership. Leo XIV is regarded as a "bridge builder" and *pragmatist* who wants to connect different worlds of Catholicism. As the first pope from the USA with extensive experience in Peru, he is culturally diverse and knows about the concerns of the *"little people"* as well as the dynamics of the Curia. Immediately after his election, he made it clear that he would continue Francis' worldwide synodal process. However, many expect him not only to listen but also to **make decisions**. *"I believe that Pope Leo will not only listen, not only include, but also decide in the end,"* says Father Mauritius Wilde, a German-born Benedictine monk in the USA. The faithful hope that the new pontiff will now turn the many consultations into concrete action - *"Americans [...] want to see things, they are very pragmatic. And that [...] will be good for the Church"*. This self-image - listening, but then also **acting** according to objectives - was repeatedly demonstrated by Leo XIV. As a cardinal, he was not only a participant in the World Synod, but even chaired one of the working groups and showed leadership qualities in the search for solutions. In 2024, on the sidelines of the Synod of Bishops in Rome, he emphasized that the *Holy Spirit was "urging* the Church *to renew itself"*. Synodality is **more** than just a process or holding additional meetings - it is about asking together what God wants from us today. As Pope, Leo XIV will continue to emphasize this spiritual dimension of synodality: It was not about "political agendas" or personal prestige projects, but about **listening together to the Spirit of God**. He thus linked the structural and spiritual renewal of the Church.

Reform of power structures and more lay participation

Closely linked to synodality is a profound **structural renewal** of the Catholic Church, as envisioned by Leo XIV. Central to this is the *question of the distribution of power* - i.e. who decides in the church and how decisions are made. Pope Francis has already begun to break new ground here, but many of these reforms are now on the agenda under Leo XIV. One core concern is the **participation of the laity** in important decisions. The World Synod 2021-2024 made it clear that the faithful around the world are calling for a greater say. In the synod's **final paper**, the representatives from all over the world voted to strengthen the *co-responsibility* of the grassroots: the Synod of Bishops voted for more decentralization in the global church and greater participation of ordinary believers in important decisions. This also includes

transparency and accountability of the hierarchy - demands that received broad majorities. Pope Francis had expressly approved these resolutions from his last synod before his death in spring 2025 and published them without weakening them. Now it is up to Leo XIV to put them into practice. He has already signaled that he intends to continue resolutely on the path of reform.

Concrete **reform steps** concern, among other things, the greater equal involvement of women in leadership and ordained ministries. The World Synod expressly recommended that the question of *admitting women to ordained ministries be kept open*. This means, for example, that the long-discussed diaconate for women will continue to be examined - an issue that Pope Leo XIV must address in the near future. Many Catholics around the world hope that women will at least be able to serve as deacons in the future or receive more official assignments (for example as baptismal or wedding assistants). Cardinal Reinhard Marx emphasized that this is *"undoubtedly one of the very central questions of the future"* and that he very much hopes *"that we will make progress"*. Although the universal Church is moving at different speeds on this issue, it is all the more important to have a Pope *"who keeps these doors open and does not go backwards"*. Leo XIV had already promoted women and tried out **synodal elements** in his diocese of Chiclayo in Peru. There, he involved lay people - both men and women - in pastoral decisions and relied on participatory *grassroots church models*. He is now bringing this wealth of experience to Rome. Colleagues already experienced his cooperative leadership style as a prefect in the Dicastery for Bishops: French nun Reungoat reports that Prevost naturally worked with women when appointing bishops and valued their perspective . In her view, there is *"no reason to think that he will not continue in this direction"* - on the contrary, he could **further develop** female co-responsibility in the Church. Leo XIV has already taken the first steps by appointing more women and non-clergy members to Vatican advisory bodies and allowing their voices to be heard in personnel matters.

But reforming power structures goes beyond the issue of women. It is generally about breaking up **clerical monopolies of power** and restructuring the hierarchy towards **servant leadership.** For example, the planned *Synodal Council* at world level - a new body of bishops and lay people that could meet between synods - is intended to strengthen collegial leadership. In Germany, such a Synodal Council was controversially discussed; traditionalists warned of a kind of church parliament. Leo XIV will have to carefully balance how he establishes *participatory elements* **without** completely abandoning the hierarchical order. Cardinal Marx put it this way: the church must allow more participation *"without becoming a parliamentary democracy"*. This is precisely where the challenge lies: synodality requires **participation and co-determination**, but within the ecclesial communion in which bishops continue to exercise their pastoral office. Leo XIV therefore emphasized that synodality *does not* mean *a weakening*, but rather a **revitalization** of ecclesial authority - the shepherds hear the people of God and then decide in accordance with the Gospel. This also means that bishops are subject **to evaluation:** The Synod proposed procedures to regularly review the conduct of bishops in office. This unusual accountability is intended to promote trust and make the abuse of power more difficult. Pope Leo XIV supported such initiatives because he was aware of the crisis of confidence caused by scandals.

Another key area of reform is dealing with the **abuse scandal,** which has led to a dramatic loss of credibility and people leaving the church in many countries - particularly in Europe. Many of those affected see the root of the problem in encrusted, authoritarian power structures. *The Eckiger Tisch* victims' association, for example, is calling on the new Pope to make "structural changes" so that consequences can finally be drawn from the abuse scandal. Matthias Katsch, spokesman for the initiative, warned shortly after Leo XIV's election that the Vatican's *learning curve* must be steep - too much time had been wasted, too many papal words without radical reforms. In fact, Leo XIV was well placed to make a credible appearance here: In Peru, Bishop Prevost was seen as someone who responded to the concerns of abuse victims and promoted independent investigations. However, he is also measured by his actions: **Transparency,** cooperation under criminal law and the strengthening of independent control in the church are expectations that are now being placed on him worldwide. The reform of the church in a synodal spirit therefore necessarily includes **coming to terms with abuse** - a "renewal of the church from within" that replaces old claims to power with humility and justice. Leo XIV repeatedly made it clear that the Church *"seeks closeness above all to those who suffer"* - and here victims of abuse are to be mentioned first and foremost.

New synodal institutions: World Synod and Decentralization

In addition to such personal and mental changes, Leo XIV was also faced with the task of establishing **institutional innovations**. One of the great innovations under Francis was the convening of a *permanent world synod*, i.e. a global consultative process of the Church lasting several years. This synodal world process (launched in 2021) was even extended until 2028 shortly before Francis' death. The plan is to conclude with a **General Church Assembly** in Rome in 2028, which will once again bring together bishops and laypeople from all continents. Pope Leo XIV has now effectively taken over the presidency of this historic process. Although it would not have been mandatory under canon law, he quickly made it clear that the World Synod would continue *as planned*. Even in his first message from the Loggia, he emphasized: *"Let us be a synodal church"*. Many observers saw this commitment as an indication that there would be no break with the synodal culture. The Freiburg canon law expert Georg Bier noted that a new pope **could** theoretically reverse the synodal reforms of his predecessor - but he considered this unlikely: *"No pope will come and directly abolish all of Francis' synodal reforms"*. Leo XIV confirmed this expectation by expressly announcing that he would continue on Francis' path. The General Secretariat of the Synod of Bishops in Rome promptly welcomed the new pope with an unusual public letter. In it, Cardinal Mario Grech and his colleagues expressed their joy and promised to do their utmost to support Leo XIV in continuing on the synodal path. *"Now that the journey continues under your leadership, we look forward with confidence to the directions you will take to help the Church grow as a community,"* wrote Grech, Sister Becquart and Bishop Marín de San Martín hopefully. In doing so, they signaled that they are focusing on **missionary synodality** - a church that also radiates outwards as it moves forward together.

Under Leo XIV, **synodality** could be **established as a permanent institution** in the Church. For example, the establishment of a *permanent synodal council* at world level, which would meet between the major synodal assemblies, was discussed. This body made up of representatives of the global church - bishops, religious and lay people - could advise the Pope and make certain decisions in a decentralized manner. Such **decentralization** corresponds to the principle of subsidiarity, which the Second Vatican Council already called for. The Synod even recommended that conferences of bishops and continental assemblies be granted more magisterial authority so that they can regulate pastoral issues locally themselves. Pope Francis suggested something similar in *Evangelii Gaudium* and has already delegated some liturgical decisions (such as translations) to the local churches. Leo XIV could extend this even further. For example, it is being debated whether in certain regions - such as the Amazon lowlands, where there is a shortage of priests - special solutions such as the ordination of proven married people (homines probati) should be permitted. Different forms of marriage ministry are also being discussed at regional level (e.g. dealing with remarried divorcees or marriage ceremonies for all couples). **More decentralized decision-making** would take into account the diversity of the global church and give local bishops more responsibility. The Synod pleaded for this, but at the same time emphasized clear limits: unity in faith and in the sacramental order should not be abandoned . Leo XIV will therefore have to sound out how far he can go in the *globalization of co-decision* without endangering **catholicity** (that which unites the world).

He is carefully observing the experiences in individual countries. In *Germany*, for example, the Synodal Way was striving for a national Synodal Council, which met with reservations in Rome. Leo XIV knew this controversy well, as he was in discussion with the German church as a curia cardinal. On the one hand, he appreciates the concern to have lay people and bishops consult together; on the other hand, he shares the concern that a permanent communion of lay people and bishops should not undermine the authority of the individual bishops. His task would be to find **creative solutions** that would allow for synodal consultation without provoking a schism or national aberrations. Overall, Leo XIV seemed to want to keep the **middle** ground: He will make reforms possible, but in *communion* with the whole Church. The Frankfurter Allgemeine Zeitung commented that Leo would *"present himself as a pope in the line of all popes and find his own style"* - in other words, not a revolutionary sprinter, but a persistent walker on the path of reform.

Ways out of the crisis: declining membership and new approaches to faith

The urgency of all these reforms is particularly evident in the **loss of members** from which the church is suffering, especially in Europe. Every year, tens of thousands of believers in countries such as Germany, Switzerland and France turn their backs on the church. There are many reasons for this: the aforementioned abuse and cover-up scandals, but also the feeling of many that the Church is **no longer in keeping with the times**, too hierarchical, too far removed from people's everyday lives. Pope Leo XIV saw synodal renewal as a central means of countering this erosion. Synodality also means **opening up new paths of faith** - forms of church that are close to the people and take their search for meaning seriously. In Europe, for example, some dioceses are experimenting with open *discussion forums*, city pastoral care in shopping centers, online pastoral care or grassroots-led celebrations of the word of God in parishes without priests. The new Pope encourages such approaches. He wants a *"church that does not revolve around its own church tower"*, as Bätzing put it, but rather reaches out to people. It is also fitting that Leo XIV - in the spirit of his namesake Leo XIII - wants to tackle social problems head-on. He was aware of **the signs of the times**: poverty, migration, the climate crisis and digitalization. In an early speech, he even mentioned the challenges of *artificial intelligence* and linked them to the *defense of human dignity and work*. This shows that he wants to bring faith into dialog with modern issues. Such relevance can help to regain the trust of those who are alienated.

Especially in secularized regions of Europe, Leo XIV tried to regain lost trust through **transparency and humility**. He knew that reforms to the power structure (such as more control over finances, independent investigation of abuses) were a prerequisite for credibility to grow. At the same time, he relies on **a pastoral** approach - a church that listens, accompanies and does not condemn. Synodality creates spaces where, for example, Catholics who have left the church or seekers can speak openly. In some European countries, there are already synodal projects that seek dialog with those who are distant from the Church, for example via online participation platforms during the World Synod. Pope Leo XIV would like to consolidate these approaches: In future, **regular consultations** of the faithful - for example, every few years a kind of worldwide "faith MOT" in the parishes - should take place. In this way, problems can be recognized early on and new ideas can be born. It also promotes *new spiritual awakenings*: youth meetings, ecumenical grassroots communities, charismatic movements and new evangelization initiatives receive its support, provided they act in a synodal spirit. The Pope is also focusing on modern communication so that the Church can open up access to faith to young people in particular: he wants to be present on social media with an *authentic message* and build bridges rather than polarize. **Dialogue instead of dogmatism** - this motto should characterize the atmosphere so that people who are distant from the church become curious and perhaps find their way back.

Global expectations and areas of tension

Synodality may be a universal principle, but **expectations of it vary considerably depending on the region of the world.** Pope Leo XIV, who is regarded as a cosmopolitan "pope with three passports" (USA, Peru, Vatican), is aware of this diversity. He biographically unites the global North and South and has first-hand knowledge of the concerns of different continents. This helps him to mediate between very different expectations - because this is also where the potential **areas of tension** of the World Synod lie.

In **Europe**, for example - especially in Western Europe - many believers hope that synodality will bring far-reaching reforms to make the church fit for the future. The demands range from **full equality for women** (including the ordination of women) to a more liberal sexual morality (marriage for all couples, a new assessment of contraception) and more democratic structures. Impatience is palpable in the German church in particular: After years of debate, reformers now expect concrete changes. Leo XIV was fundamentally open to these concerns - he *"kept doors open"* and was himself part of the synodal reform process - but he also had to put the brakes on where unity and doctrine were at stake. **German synodality** had sometimes caused tensions under Francis; one recalls Roman letters of admonition to the synodal way. Leo XIV is aware of this problem and will probably try to steer the emerging dynamics in an orderly direction. This assessment shows: The Pope will make sure that steps towards reform remain **communicable** - especially to those parts of the universal church that tend to be reluctant.

In fact, the priorities in Africa, Asia and large parts of America are often different to those in Europe. In **Africa**, the church is still growing, with many bishops emphasizing evangelization, social development and the preservation of traditional moral values. Synodality is welcomed insofar as it strengthens communion and responsibility, but it is seen less as a path to liberal change and more as a **strengthening of unity**. Some African church leaders even warned against the Western zeal for reform: too Western, too fixated on sexual morality - this is often the criticism. One *African bishop* put it diplomatically: Leo XIV *"would not respond to regional reform ideas"* that could divide the universal church (the threatening title of his interview). In other words: from Africa, the Pope is expected to promote the commitment of the laity and combat grievances, but not to soften **dogmas**. The African bishops' conferences feared that concessions could adapt biblical teaching and transform inner unity. The task of Leo XIV will be to convey **synodality as a spiritual process** that does not simply enforce the wishes of the majority, but listens to the Holy Spirit and aligns the entire Church with Christ.

In **Latin America**, Leo's second home, expectations are accentuated differently. Many there are concerned with the continuation of Francis' *liberation theology* impulses: a church at the side of the poor, resolute in its commitment to justice, peace and the integrity of creation. Continental voices are calling for synodality to be understood *as missionary* - the Church should have **an outward** impact, for example by involving indigenous peoples (keyword Amazon Synod) or denouncing corruption and violence in societies. It is hoped that Pope Leo XIV, who himself worked in Peru's slums, will take a decisive stand on social issues. At the same time, the faithful of Latin America expect their local piety and culture to be respected in the universal church. For them, synodality also means **inculturation**: being allowed to give the church an "Amazonian" or "Andean" face. At the 2019 Amazon Synod, for example, there were calls for a priesthood adapted to local needs (e.g. ordaining married deacons as priests) - Leo XIV will have to consider whether to give space to such regional solutions. Decentralization can help here: Perhaps experienced family parents will eventually be allowed to officiate as priests in remote Amazonian communities if the pope allows it regionally. However, Leo XIV knows that such steps would be globally controversial. He will therefore probably weigh things up and initially allow **pilot projects** to turn the church upside down and bring it back into shape in terms of personnel and the popularity of its members.

In **Asia**, on the other hand, synodality is characterized by the minority situation and interreligious dialogue. Many Asian churches - for example in India, Pakistan and Indonesia - are small communities in the midst of large other religions. Above all, they expect **support and freedom** from the Pope to live their faith in often difficult environments. Synodality is seen here above all as a strengthening of *communitarian unity*: Priests, religious and lay people pull together to bear witness together. Asian Catholics also hope that a synodally renewed church will **be more open to dialog** with other religions and cultures. Pope Leo XIV is likely to be open to their concerns. As a religious in multi-religious regions of Peru and as a cosmopolitan American, he has already learned to build bridges. However, he also knows that state restrictions prevail in **China** or Vietnam, for example - synodal unity and clever diplomacy are needed here. The agreement with the Chinese leadership on the appointment of bishops remains a sensitive issue. Francis had sought compromises here; Leo XIV will presumably continue this course, but at the same time want to maintain **unity with the oppressed underground churches.** A prominent Asian admonisher, Cardinal Joseph Zen from Hong Kong, even warned that the continuation of the World Synod was a matter of *"life or death for the Church founded by Jesus"*. Such alarmist tones show the distrust of some Asian (and also American) traditionalists towards the synodal course. Leo XIV would endeavor to allay their fears that synodality meant abandoning doctrine. Instead, he emphasized that a synodal church must be **missionary** - in other words, it must proclaim the Gospel clearly, but *together and in unity*.

In **North America** - especially the USA - the Pope is experiencing a polarized church environment. Here, there are vocal conservative groups who have been critical of Pope Francis' reforms, while other progressive Catholics are calling for further change. Interestingly, Leo XIV's election in the USA seems to have initially triggered *a positive response from both sides*. He was seen as capable of uniting the divided church in America. One observer was hopeful that Leo XIV might be able to unite society **and the** Church. His American origins and yet long experience abroad make him a *bridge builder*. Of course, there is the particular challenge of asserting himself against political instrumentalization. President Donald Trump - himself not a Catholic - patriotically welcomed the papal election as a *"great honor for our country"*. However, Leo XIV has already made it clear that he **does not** want to be a **political puppet**. On the contrary: he saw the Church on the side of the *weak*, not the powerful. Against nationalistic tendencies (such as those of JD Vance, the US Vice President, who uses religion for anti-migrant messages), he sets the universal message of charity: *"Charity knows no categorization,"* Prevost once pointedly contradicted. In North America, therefore, there is an expectation that the Pope will find clear **words of unity and humanity** and overcome polarization. Synodality could help here by *bringing all voices -* progressive and conservative - to the table. Leo XIV has signaled that he will listen, but in the end he also wants to **lead decisively**, guided by the Gospel, not by party politics.

Different **priorities** are emerging: *Europe* is pushing for internal church reforms, *Africa* for spiritual authenticity and growth, *Latin America* for justice and pastoral solutions, *Asia* for dialog and protection of the faithful, *North America* for reconciliation of a divided church. This diversity harbors potential for conflict - just think of the issue of **equal rights for women**: While German Catholics such as Sr. Philippa Rath have high hopes for female ordination, African bishops still reject this; or the **treatment of sexuality**: European synod members such as Mara Klein are calling for a pontificate *that "stands uncompromisingly by the side"* of LGBTQIA+ people, whereas African and Asian churches, for example, are still unfamiliar with this and would rather strengthen the *family in the traditional way*. Such tensions were clearly evident at the 2023/24 **World Synod**: some delegates called for courageous openings, while others warned of fault lines. Leo XIV now stood at the center of these forces. His advantage is that he is perceived as a *mediator between the worlds* - neither clearly belonging to one camp. He was seen as a *"man of the middle and a mediator"* who did not run over conservative Catholics, but cautiously facilitated reforms. Under his pontificate, the **synodal process** should therefore continue at a balanced pace: **swiftly enough** not to disappoint expectations for change, but **cautiously enough** not to divide the universal church.

Pope Leo XIV himself formulated a *credo* in this regard: He wanted a church that was "on the move" - that is, neither standing still nor rushing headlong. For him, synodality means *companionship* in diversity. His task now is to keep this community together so that not everyone ends up going in a different direction. The coming months and years will show how Leo XIV succeeds in this feat. The expectations are enormous - almost *superhuman*, as one commentary stated. But the new pope can draw on a wealth of experience: the spirituality of a religious, the negotiating skills of a former general of a religious order, the pastoral practice of a bishop in the *periphery*, the administrative experience of a curia cardinal. All of this equips him to cast synodality into viable **structures** and to enable the Church to make a new start. With Leo XIV at the helm, the Church finds itself at a historic turning point, at which it will be decided whether it can credibly **renew** itself without becoming unfaithful to itself. Synodality and structural reforms are the keys to this. If Leo XIV succeeds in bringing the various continents, cultures and positions in the Church along on the common path, he could indeed help his Church to a new ***aggiornamento*** (accelerating awakening). The first signs - from the Loggia Word to appeals for peace and the decisive continuation of the World Synod - give many people hope. Nevertheless, synodality remains a **risk**: it requires patience, humility and trust in the Holy Spirit. Leo XIV chose this path. The universal Church is now moving forward with him - *together on the path*, in the tension between tradition and reform, carried by the promise that the Spirit of God will lead it into a renewed present.

🕊 *Chapter 14:*
Academic and canonical competence

When Leo XIV smiled at the faithful for the first time, expert observers knew immediately that a pontiff with exceptional academic and legal expertise was taking office. Pope Leo XIV united in his person the erudition of a theologian and canon lawyer with the world church experience of a missionary. This unusual combination characterized his leadership style from the very beginning - strategically well thought-out, theologically sound and at the same time practical.

His education already points to this dual competence. Prevost initially studied mathematics and theology in his home city of Chicago before going on to study canon law in Rome. At the Pontifical University of St. Thomas Aquinas (Angelicum) in Rome, he obtained a doctorate in canon law in 1985/87 - with a dissertation on *"The role of the local prior in the Augustinian Order"*. This specific field of research - the authority and administrative structures within an order - already shows Prevost's early interest in **ecclesiastical governance**. In other words, he studied first-hand how leadership functions and can be effectively organized at local levels. This academic study of the organizational structures of the church formed a solid foundation for his later leadership role in the Vatican. In addition to his formal degree in canon law, Leo XIV naturally also had the sound theological education of a religious priest: after completing a Master's degree in theology (M.Div.) in Chicago and being ordained a priest in 1982, he was ideally equipped both theologically and pastorally. Early on, he combined scholarship with practice - after his studies, he was sent to Peru as a trainer of young religious and as a missionary. There he worked for many years not only as a pastor, but also as a lecturer and professor of canon law at seminaries and Catholic universities. Leo XIV was therefore not just a theorist with titles on his business card, but a man who imparted knowledge and applied it in different cultures. His former fellow student, the priest Edward Beck, describes Prevost as a modest, quiet man with "great intellect and a real vision for the Catholic Church". This rare combination of humility and intellectual brilliance gave Leo XIV a high reputation in intellectual circles and created trust among his confreres.

Ecclesiastical law and administrative expertise

Leo XIV's expertise in canon law is invaluable for the leadership of the universal church. As a doctor of canon law, he knew the Catholic legal system down to the last detail - from the theological background of the canons to the intricacies of administrative regulations. He has put this knowledge to the test in various leadership roles: Prevost was already in his mid-40s when he headed the worldwide Augustinian Order as Prior General (2001-2007), demonstrating organizational skills and legal expertise in two terms of office. As provincial superior in Peru in the late 1990s and later as bishop of the northern Peruvian diocese of Chiclayo (from 2015), he also had to constantly reconcile canonical norms with pastoral reality. His Rule of Order and the Code of Canon Law (CIC) were not abstract texts for him, but living guidelines that had to be applied wisely. In Chiclayo, where he was bishop for almost a decade, he got to know the administration of a diocese with all its legal, personnel and structural challenges. This time shaped him as a *manager in the vineyard of the Lord* as well as a pastor.

Prevost's administrative and legal expertise became particularly visible in the Roman Curia. At the beginning of 2023, Pope Francis appointed him as prefect at the head of the powerful Dicastery for Bishops. In this role, he examined candidates for the episcopate worldwide for two years and played a key role in their appointment. At the same time, he was responsible for the bishops' ad limina visits to the Vatican - regular reports from the dioceses to the Pope - which gave him a deep insight into the situation of the local churches on all continents. No wonder, then, that Prevost quickly became one of the best-known faces in the College of Cardinals. He is regarded as *diplomatic* and *pragmatic* and is appreciated by both progressive and conservative church representatives. This assessment - passed on by the Catholic news agency KNA - underlines the fact that he can weigh up controversial issues fairly and is trusted by different wings of the Church.

His legal expertise was also put to very concrete use in Rome: Pope Francis entrusted Prevost with the implementation of one of his most "revolutionary" reforms, namely the participation of women in the selection of new bishops. As prefect, Prevost appointed three women to the advisory committee that submits the Pope's proposals for candidates for the offices of bishop. This was not just a symbolic act, but a legally well established structural change in the previously male-dominated decision-making process. Here Leo XIV (still a cardinal) showed himself to be someone who could implement reform ideas strategically and in accordance with canon law. His dicastery is also entrusted with monitoring the guidelines against sexual abuse - an area that requires expertise in canon law and decisive action. The fact that Prevost continued this task in Francis' spirit signals his ability to effectively enforce law and justice in the Church. In short, Leo XIV had all the prerequisites not only to understand the complex administrative and legal issues of the Church, but also to actively shape them.

Significance for his office

What impact did these qualifications have on Leo XIV's work as pope? First of all, they gave him a special strategic foresight. With his professorial background, he tended to analyze challenges thoroughly and devise long-term solutions. Observers emphasize that Prevost brings a wide range of qualities that the global church needs in a fractured time. He has experience in North and South, knows the church base as well as the Roman headquarters - and it is precisely this broad knowledge that is in demand in a church that has to find its way between reformers and traditionalists, between a dynamic South and a searching North. His academic training helps him to tackle complex issues - such as ethical questions of biomedicine, the church tax system or theological debates on the doctrine of the sacraments - in a well-founded manner. He can read original texts by church people in context as well as understand the latest studies in the social sciences. This ability makes him a discussion partner on an equal footing with theologians, scientists and church experts worldwide. When Leo XIV speaks on controversial issues, you can sense that he has penetrated the subject matter - be it in magisterial letters or in speeches to specialist audiences. His statements are therefore likely to be heard both in academic theology and at the ecclesiastical base, because they combine clarity with comprehensible language (in the sense of a popular scientific tone, which he, like Pope Benedict XVI, has mastered).

At the same time, Leo XIV's expertise in canon law and administrative law had a direct impact on his style of government: he knew which adjustments could be made to the church structure without jeopardizing it. In the case of planned structural reforms - such as further changes to the curia system or the strengthening of local conferences of bishops - he can assess for himself which steps are compatible with current law or where changes to legislation would be necessary. This insider knowledge of the Pope speeds up decision-making processes because he does not have to obtain expert opinions in every case, but can weigh up many legal implications from his own experience. For example, he will be able to competently assess questions of diocesan administration, ecclesiastical jurisdiction or financial supervision. Some canon lawyers see this as a great advantage: *finally a pope who is a trained canonist!* People are looking forward to seeing whether Leo XIV will further simplify the procedures for marriage annulments or expand the administrative jurisdiction of the Church - areas in which his predecessors initiated reforms that could now be continued. In any case, Leo XIV was someone who saw the *instruments* of canon law not as a dry set of paragraphs, but as a tool of pastoral leadership.

Participatory synodal style or clear decisions?

An exciting question is how Pope Leo XIV balances his expertise in theology and law in his leadership style: does he rely more on participatory, synodal processes for reforms or does he tend to make clear decisions based on his own expertise? The signs so far point to a **balanced mix**. Immediately after his election, Leo XIV made it clear that he wanted to continue on the synodal path set by Pope Francis. Vatican observers emphasized that Leo XIV *knew what synodality* meant - in other words, he understood the importance of consultation and working together to find solutions in today's Church. In fact, he had already gained synodal experience in Latin America, for example at meetings on synodal cooperation in the Church of the continent. As a bridge builder between cultures and church regions - as his former fellow student Edward Beck described him approvingly - he is probably predestined to bring together different voices in the church. Leo XIV is already being highlighted in the media as the "Pope of the middle and of cooperation". This label suits a man who neither polarizes nor wants to rule authoritatively, but rather promotes a communal awakening. In his first address to the College of Cardinals, Leo XIV used strikingly synodal tones: "I know that I can rely on **each of** you, that you will walk with me," he assured the cardinals. This resonates with great confidence in the cooperation of his closest advisors - a clear indication that this pope takes collegiality seriously.

However, a synodal style in no way means arbitrariness, and Leo XIV also knows when he has to set clear guidelines as pope. Precisely because he was so well versed in theology and canon law, he was able to make clear decisions on matters of doctrine and law when it mattered. On "black and white" issues - i.e. fundamental questions that have been clearly decided in Catholic doctrine - he defends the Church's current position without hesitation. At the same time, his stance to date suggests that he will allow room for discussion and participation on open reform issues - such as the strengthening of lay people in leadership positions, equal rights for women in the church or the synodal process as a whole. His reputation as a **centrist personality** will stand him in good stead: Leo XIV is not a man of big cuts, but rather seeks integrative solutions. This balance should prove to be a great advantage in preserving the unity of the Church and yet courageously tackling necessary reform steps.

All in all, Pope Leo XIV stands as a theologically competent leader in terms of canon law who can give new impetus to the Church in the 21st century. His extensive knowledge gives him authority - not in the sense of power-conscious strictness, but as credible expertise that inspires respect. He can debate with professors and at the same time explain complex questions of faith to the "little people". This ability to build bridges between theory and practice makes him a *pope who combines mind and heart*. Church observers see this as a great opportunity: a pope who is intellectually up to date **and** knows the laws of the Church inside out can resolve pressing issues in both a visionary and legally sound manner. Leo XIV himself was probably aware that his qualifications meant responsibility. He sees his office as a service in which he brings all his skills to bear - be it in synodal consultations or in solitary decisions at the pope's desk. The art will lie in combining the two fruitfully. Given Leo XIV's recognizable balance of listening and leading, we can be confident that he is up to the challenge. His academic brilliance and expertise in canon law are not ends in themselves, but tools to lead the Church in a strategically wise, just and sustainable way. Or, in the words of a companion: Leo XIV brings with him a "great intellect" and a clear vision - exactly what the Catholic Church needs in times of change.

 *Chapter 15:*

Challenges and potentials of his pontificate: Global perspective and regional challenges

During his pontificate, Pope Leo XIV was confronted with a range of different expectations. Critical voices were raised from various directions, commenting on his administration and in some cases engaging in heated debate. Reform-oriented Catholics praise his open style and hope for change, while conservative circles are suspicious of some of the planned innovations. Similar to his predecessor, fronts are emerging: Some traditionalists fear a sell-out of doctrine and have even made accusations against reform-minded popes in the past. At the same time, progressive forces complain that the reform agenda is too hesitant and are pushing for faster changes. This tension characterized the internal church controversies under Leo XIV.

Critical voices and controversies within the church

One focal point of the disputes are reform issues that are being discussed across the global church. Questions about the role of women in church ministries, the treatment of LGBTQIA+ people or the softening of compulsory celibacy divide opinion. **Conferences** of bishops from individual countries often find themselves in the spotlight. For example, the German Conference of Bishops proactively called for more **decision-making leeway for national churches and greater equality for women** in leadership positions. Such advances are welcomed by reform advocates as overdue, while at the same time they are met with reluctance or resistance in the Vatican echo chamber of Rome. Leo XIV had to mediate in these debates: He stood between progressive church representatives, who called for bold steps, and conservative forces, who warned against a transformation and further development of tradition.

Conservative opposition within the church is forming, particularly where reforms are seen as a threat to the church's identity. Some high-ranking prelates are publicly expressing displeasure about changes and urging the preservation of "pure doctrine". Under Francis, for example, four cardinals had already expressed doubts about papal reforms in famous "Dubia" letters, and similar criticism now also accompanies Leo XIV when he considers innovations. Local resistance also came from dioceses or entire regional churches in which traditional piety was strongly anchored. There is a **regional discrepancy** here: while many in Western Europe or North America, for example, are pushing for a new departure, church representatives in parts of Africa, Asia or Eastern Europe are tending towards a more conservative course. **Inner-church controversies** under Leo XIV thus often ignited over the question of how much change the church could allow without jeopardizing its unity. These controversies are challenges for the Pope - but also offer the opportunity for dialog between different camps, provided Leo XIV knows how to listen to all voices and take them seriously.

Demands for reform and social expectations

The call for reform comes not only from groups within the Church, but also from society at large. **Reform-minded Catholics** - from grassroots movements to theological experts - articulated clear demands to Leo XIV and the church leadership. Among other things, they demanded more **gender justice** in the church, a review of power structures and contemporary answers to moral-theological questions. Movements such as *Maria 2.0* or *We are Church* are committed to the **admission of women to all ministries** and the **abolition of compulsory celibacy** in order to make the church more sustainable. Similar initiatives are also forming in other countries, which are often supported by long-standing Catholics who love their church but see a need for reform.

Social expectations for change are particularly focused on issues of equality and sexual morality. At a time when gender equality and the acceptance of LGBTQIA+ people are part of the social consensus reality in many countries, the Catholic Church, with its traditionally restrictive positions, is under scrutiny. Both believers and non-Catholics are asking whether and how the Church will adapt to these realities. US Catholics, for example, criticize the continued unequal treatment of women and have called for more female leadership in broad consultations - including discussions about female deacons, priests and popes. They see this not only as a personnel issue, but also as a question of justice. The church's treatment of queer people is similarly denounced: many believers complain that the church places abstract teachings and prohibitions above the lived reality of people. According to surveys, families with LGBTQIA+ members often feel torn between their affiliation with the church and the unconditional love and support of their loved ones. These voices - whether at synods, in petitions or open letters - reflect a **change in social values** that Leo XIV must take into account in his reform program if the Church is not to lose further ground.

In addition to the issues of sexual morality and women's rights, there are other expectations: **Transparency and accountability** in power structures are high on the agenda, especially after the revelations of abuse scandals in the church. Many believers are calling for an independent investigation and a **culture of responsibility** in which church officials are held accountable for misconduct. This shows a close alliance between voices critical of the church and reform-oriented forces within the church: both sides are calling for changes in the hierarchy - for example, greater involvement of lay people in decision-making processes in order to reduce clericalism. Developments such as those in Germany, where the establishment of a **synodal council** - a body in which bishops and lay people consult together in a binding manner - has been sought, show that this is not a marginal issue. Although the Vatican initially tried to put the brakes on this reform project, the pressure from the faithful to implement such forms of participation remained high.

Social actors outside the Church - from politicians to human rights activists - were also keeping a close eye on Leo XIV's course. They expected the Catholic Church to live up to its moral authority and set a good example on issues such as **human rights, social justice and equality**. In many countries, the Church influences debates on issues such as abortion, marriage for all and euthanasia through its statements. Society - especially in liberal democracies - often demands a sympathetic ear and mercy. Leo XIV was therefore faced with the task of moderating the **tension between church doctrine and**

contemporary values. If he succeeds in accommodating the legitimate concerns of reform-minded Catholics and society without betraying the core of the faith, his pontificate holds enormous potential: it could reposition the Church as a credible moral force in the 21st century.

Perspectives on regional differences

The Catholic Church is a **world church,** and Leo XIV must always think of reforms and decisions in a global context. What is perceived as an urgent renewal in one part of the world may meet with incomprehension or rejection elsewhere. Different cultural influences, historical experiences and social realities lead to sometimes divergent **perspectives on the world church.** This tension between global unity and regional diversity characterizes the challenges of his pontificate.

In **Europe** and North America, for example, the Church and the Pope are faced with the task of convincing an increasingly secular society. Here, the pews have become emptier in many places, scandals have cost trust and demands for reform are particularly loud. Many believers are turning their backs on the church: In Germany alone, over half a million people left the Catholic Church in 2022 - more than ever before. The bishops there described this development as "alarming" and see it in the context of disappointed hopes for reform and the abuse scandal. The president of the Committee of Catholics even stated that the Church had massively squandered trust and was "currently not determined enough to implement visions for the future of Christianity". Against this backdrop, the European churches are pushing for change in order to regain credibility. Demands for **disempowerment of over-centralized structures**, for more **lay participation** and **pastoral openness** (for example in the case of remarried divorcees or in dealing with same-sex sensitivities) are central here. Leo XIV had to take these concerns seriously if he wanted to slow down the erosion of the Church in the Western world.

The regional diversity of the challenges means that the Pope must act in a very sensitive and differentiated manner. What is a bold step forward in one country could be perceived as an affront in another. Fortunately, Leo XIV has plenty of **international experience of** his own. He is the first pope from the United States and at the same time closely familiar with the culture of the South thanks to his many years of work in Latin America. This intercultural background - coupled with multilingualism and worldwide networking - gives him the necessary sensitivity to understand the different parts of the universal Church. By listening carefully to **regional conferences of bishops** and taking them seriously, he sends the signal that no perspective will be ignored. The potential of his pontificate lies here in **unity in reconciled diversity**: if Leo XIV succeeded in bringing the world church perspectives into dialog with one another, regional differences could become a strength. The Catholic Church could distinguish itself as a truly global community that allowed and valued different cultural expressions of the one faith.

Strategies for courageous and credible reform steps

In view of the many demands for reform and controversial debates, Leo XIV is called upon to develop **strategies for change** at that are both courageous and credible - and which, above all, remain **communicable to the global church.** Reform steps must be designed in such a way that they can be understood and accepted within the global church. This requires clever communication, theological soundness and a sense of timing and priorities.

A central strategy is to **support** reforms **broadly** and not to present them as mere top-down decisions. Leo XIV continued the synodal style of his predecessor: He placed greater emphasis on consultations in synods and dialog with the faithful at grassroots level. Through worldwide consultations - for example within the framework of the **World Synod** - he allowed voices from all continents to flow into the decision-making process. This increases the acceptance of possible innovations, as the faithful feel involved and regional concerns are taken into account.

Credible steps towards reform also require the Pope to set a good example. Leo XIV used the symbolic power of his office to demonstrate humility and repentance. For example, he took a decisive stance in the investigation of abuse scandals: He dismissed cover-ups from their posts, strengthened independent supervisory bodies and publicly asked for forgiveness for the Church's failings. Such actions underpin his words and create confidence that he is serious about renewal. He also showed personal signs of openness - for example by appointing women and lay people to positions of responsibility in the Curia, which is now canonically possible. By allowing more **diversity in leadership positions**, Leo XIV lent his reform intentions credibility from within.

Another component of his strategy must be to **communicate** the reforms. Bold steps are naturally met with uncertainty or resistance at first. Leo XIV therefore focused on transparency and openly explained his motives to the world public and the ecclesiastical community. In speeches, pastoral letters and media appearances, he repeatedly emphasized that reform was not an end in itself, but must serve to deepen the Gospel. He describes specific cases where rigid rules hindered pastoral care and shows how adaptation can enable more people to experience God's love. Through this narrative communication - in a popular scientific tone, of course - he succeeds in turning abstract reform topics into **vivid stories** that resonate with believers worldwide. For example, when the marriage of same-sex couples is debated, he refers to loving couples in congregations whose faithfulness and belief make it clear why the church should find a pastoral path of recognition here. In this way, he allays fears of change by placing the Christian core concern - love of neighbor - in the foreground.

Last but not least, Leo XIV took care to forge **coalitions for reforms.** He did not have to make bold decisions on his own: He involved clergy and theological advisors at an early stage in order to develop joint solutions. He brings together particularly reform-minded church leaders from different regions of the world - whether from Germany, India, the USA or Brazil - in informal meetings so that they can learn from each other and work together on **compromises that are sustainable for the global church.** For example, African and European bishops could consult together on the inculturation of the liturgy in order to do justice to both the dignity of the universal celebration of the Eucharist and local forms of expression. This kind of exchange promotes mutual understanding and helps to defuse reform proposals before they are officially adopted. Leo XIV acted here as a moderator and as a **pope who looked strictly to the future,** but who took everyone along with him. If he succeeds in this balancing act, the reform steps of his pontificate can not only be courageous, but also permanently effective, because they are supported by a broad consensus and genuine conviction.

Hypothetical scenarios for a new Vatican Council

One particular project that would be conceivable during Leo XIV's pontificate is the **convening of a new Vatican Council** - in other words, a major worldwide council of laypeople and bishops, such as was last held in the 1960s with the Second Vatican Council. Such an undertaking would be enormously ambitious and historically significant. But what would Pope Leo XIV have to do specifically, if he wanted to prepare a *Third Vatican Council*? In the following, several hypothetical scenarios are outlined as to how a new council could be initiated, what prerequisites it would need, who would be involved, in what time frame it could take place and what topics would be on the agenda.

1. **Scenario 1: Careful long-term preparation and broad consensus** - In this scenario, Leo XIV decides to convene a new council only after thorough preparatory work. As a prerequisite for this, the Pope would first sound out the mood among bishops worldwide. He could set up a **preparatory committee** made up of representatives from all continents to identify the most pressing issues. Possible actors here would be well-known cardinals, but also theologians and even some laypeople as advisors. This committee would work for several months, consult the local churches and create a basic framework for the council. **Time frame**: It would be conceivable for Leo XIV to announce the council three years in advance, for example. These years would be used to draw up working documents (so-called *schema*), form commissions and clarify organizational issues (location - presumably the Vatican, but perhaps also changing venues -, sequence of sessions, translations, etc.). Organizationally, one could build on the Second Vatican Council: several sessions per year spread over 2-3 years so that the participants can return to their dioceses in between. **The topics of** such a council would be wide-ranging, for example: the equality of women in the Church, synodality and the distribution of power, the Church's sexual morality (e.g. dealing with remarried divorcees, contraception, LGBTQIA+ issues), celibacy,

ecumenical relations with other Christians, interreligious dialog, the climate crisis and social justice from the Church's perspective, and last but not least, measures against abuse and for transparency. All these topics would be formulated in preparatory steps in such a way that they are *negotiable for the global church* - neither overburdening some nor underburdening others. Leo XIV would show great diplomatic skill in this scenario: By carefully reaching an agreement in advance, he could ensure that a reasonably viable consensus could be reached at the Council itself. The actors involved - all Catholic bishops worldwide, plus expert advisors and auditors (possibly also women and young people as listeners, as was the case at Vatican II) - would come together with the awareness that this Council is to be **a historic departure.** The advantage of this scenario is that there is a good chance that decisions will ultimately be supported by a broad majority because no one was taken by surprise. Disadvantage: It would take a lot of time and energy, and some urgent reforms would be postponed in the meantime.

2. **Scenario 2: Rapid convocation in response to a crisis** - Here, Leo XIV would announce a new council relatively suddenly, driven by an acute crisis that could not tolerate a longer delay. Such a crisis could, for example, be a **dramatic loss of credibility of the Church** in large parts of the world - caused, for example, by a global scandal, mass resignations from the Church or serious tensions that threaten to divide the Church. In view of this situation, the Pope could call the bishops to a council within one to two years to find solutions together in *the face of the emergency.* The main **prerequisites** here would be the Pope's courage and determination, as well as the bishops' fundamental willingness to listen to the call. The actors involved would all be bishops, but due to the short lead time, fewer external observers or theologians would probably be involved in the preparations. **Organizational framework**: A somewhat

more compact council would be conceivable , perhaps over a single, longer meeting period of a few months, in which deliberations take place day by day (more comparable to the Council of Trent in the 16th century, which took place in a few intensive phases, albeit stretched out over several years at the time). **Topics** would focus on the most pressing issues, e.g. concrete measures against the loss of members in certain countries, reform of the Curia, dealing with doctrinal conflicts and the clarification of controversial issues that endanger the unity of the Church (such as: Are national churches allowed to go their own way? How binding are local synodal decisions? etc.). In such a scenario, Leo XIV would presumably not be able to leave out difficult dogmatic questions if they were at the heart of the crisis - such as the attitude towards women in the ordained ministry or sexual morality - because avoiding them would prolong the crisis. The advantage of this approach is that the church shows the ability to act and courage; a council would cause a global stir and perhaps arouse new enthusiasm. In addition, resolutions could be implemented quickly to counter the crisis. Disadvantage: hasty preparation harbors risks; without thorough preliminary coordination, conflicts could break out openly at the council itself and lead to the formation of camps or even break-offs. A poorly prepared council could end without delivering results - or be boycotted by certain groups. In this scenario, Leo XIV would therefore have to moderate very decisively and, if necessary, make tough decisions to keep the council on course.

3. **Scenario 3: Step-by-step path via synods to a council** - This model combines the two approaches above: Leo XIV could take a **procedural path** that eventually leads to a council via several synods. The prerequisite for this would be a willingness to take the long view. The Pope would first convene **special synods** on specific topics - for example, a world synod of bishops on the topic of "Equal Rights for

Women in the Church", later a separate synod on "The Church and Modern Society" (which could deal with sexual morality, celibacy and the family), and another on "Synodality and Church Structure". These synods could take place over perhaps 2-4 years. Their results - each in the form of recommendation papers - would be collected and could then form the **basis for a large final council.** Basically, such a council would form the keystone of a long synodal process that has already done a lot of preparatory work. In addition to bishops, many experts and even ecumenical partners, some of whom participate in synods as observers, would also be **involved.** The **time frame** here stretches over almost a decade or more: it would be a generational project that Leo XIV might even have to hand over to his successor if his term of office does not last that long. **Organizationally,** this would have the advantage that the Church would come closer together step by step and every region, every conference of bishops would already be involved along the way. Such a Third Vatican Council would then perhaps come together at the end of the 2020s, with the highest level of participation and prepared by stacks of synod reports. **Topics** would be dealt with in order and one after the other, culminating in an overall document. This council could then solemnly adopt all the reforms and guidelines that have been developed along the way - such as a new constitutional framework for the church that establishes synodality as binding, or updated doctrinal statements on marriage and family based on broad consensus. The advantage of this scenario is that it combines depth and thoroughness with the authority of a council; it is less confrontational, as much is clarified in advance. Disadvantage: It requires enormous patience and harbors the risk of fatigue - the world could lose the thread if processes drag on for so long, and opponents of reform would have plenty of time to sit things out. In addition, Leo XIV would have to ensure that **the results of the synods**

actually led **to council resolutions** and did not get stuck halfway.

Regardless of the scenario, a new Vatican Council under Leo XIV would have to be *well founded*. The Church does not call a council lightly - it needs the feeling that *"the time is ripe"* and that the Holy Spirit is urging the Church towards a great common departure. If Leo XIV recognizes this moment and creates the conditions - involvement of the bishops, prayer of the faithful, clarification of the goals - then such a council could unfold the greatest potential of his pontificate: namely to make the Catholic Church credible, united and sustainable for the years to come.

Leaving the church and secularization: the challenge of loss of credibility

Pope Leo XIV was challenged not only by issues of reform within the Church, but also by the **constant changes in external society**. In many traditionally Christian countries, the Catholic Church has been experiencing a decline in membership and a loss of importance in public life for years. **Resignations from the church** have become an indicator of the extent to which trust and commitment to the church are eroding. The reasons for these waves of resignations are manifold: increasing **secularization** and indifference towards religion play a role, but concrete disappointments with the church also drive believers out.

As already mentioned, the number of resignations in Germany, for example, reached historic highs - over 500,000 Catholics left the country in 2022. Dioceses in other Western European countries, Canada and Australia are also reporting alarming losses. Those who leave often cite the Church's unwillingness to reform, its handling of moral scandals and the feeling that the institution is no longer up to date as reasons. Leo XIV responded to this phenomenon with pastoral concern. He was aware that behind every resignation there were human destinies : People who may have struggled for a long time before turning their backs on their church because they no longer trusted it. The abuse scandals of recent decades in particular have contributed enormously to the loss of credibility. When bishops protected perpetrators and the institution placed itself above the protection of children, the gospel was betrayed in the eyes of many. Leo XIV therefore made it a top priority to come to terms with these offenses. He knew that **credible renewal** in this area was a basic prerequisite for regaining the trust of the faithful.

At the same time, Leo XIV analyses the underlying trends of secularization. In enlightened, affluent societies, many people simply no longer see themselves as dependent on the church: social ties that used to strengthen community life are dissolving; the moral influence of the church is weakening as the state and other institutions have taken over its functions (education, health, social welfare). Religion is becoming a private matter, and the grand narrative of Christianity is convincing fewer and fewer people. Even a pope cannot single-handedly counteract this development. But Leo XIV tried to gain new credibility through **authentic witness.** He emphasized the simplicity of the Christian message, placed Jesus Christ at the center of all preaching and tried to bring the Church closer to the people. In practical terms, this can be seen, for example, in the fact that he encourages parishes to try out **new forms of pastoral care:** Street mission, digital projects, low-threshold discussion opportunities for those who have left the church. He also invites intellectuals and artists to engage in dialog in order to make the faith understandable in modern language. The Pope himself seeks to be close to ordinary people - images of Leo XIV praying in social hotspots or talking to doubting young people are intended to signal this: This church listens and cares.

A particular problem is posed by countries where the Church was formerly a state church (as in parts of Europe) and is now struggling with a certain **social trauma**. There, Leo XIV had to do a lot of convincing that faith and freedom were not contradictory and that the Church had learned from its mistakes. He does this by also taking **voices critical of the Church** seriously - for example, he meets with associations of victims of abuse, listens to advice from external experts on governance issues and shows humility towards secular authorities where appropriate. This openness earns him respect in parts of society. However, it remains to be seen whether the wave of resignations can be stopped. It is possible that the Church will become even smaller in some countries before a new beginning is possible. However, Leo XIV also sees potential in this: a "smaller flock" could also be a **more authentic, more convinced community** if the lukewarmness decreases. In doing so, he echoes the thoughts of Benedict XVI, who predicted a shrunken but strong church. In any case, dealing with secularization and people leaving the Church is a huge challenge of his pontificate. His response to this - humble inward renewal coupled with a courageous approach to the outside world - will play a key role in determining how well the Church emerges from this crisis.

Religious pluralism and interreligious dialog

Globalization and migration have led to a colourful **religious pluralism** today, even in formerly homogeneous Catholic areas. Different religions and denominations live side by side, and completely new spiritual movements or explicit secularism are also part of the social picture. For Leo XIV, this meant that the Church had to position itself in a *world of dialog.* **Interreligious dialog** became a hallmark of his pontificate, partly because he had a great deal of personal experience in this area. During his time as a bishop and cardinal, Leo XIV had already worked with other faith communities in various countries and built bridges. This expertise will now stand him in good stead on the world stage.

One important area is the relationship with **Islam**. In many African and Asian countries, Catholics live as a minority in predominantly Muslim societies. At the same time, the Muslim population in Europe is growing. Leo XIV continued the work of his predecessors - we remember Francis' brotherly document with the Grand Imam of Al-Azhar or John Paul II's prayers for peace in Assisi - and intensified the exchange. He visits leading Islamic clerics and never misses an opportunity to emphasize that Christians and Muslims essentially believe in *one* God and share common values such as family cohesion, mercy and justice. Under his aegis, new platforms for Christian-Muslim cooperation emerged, for example in refugee aid or environmental protection, where both religions could achieve a great deal. Of course, Leo XIV did not conceal the differences - for example on the subject of religious freedom or equal rights - but he always sought common ground in order to reduce tensions. In regions such as the Middle East, where political conflicts are often overlaid with religion, the Pope tries to set an example of peace through mediation and prayer. His international approach - characterized by **intercultural competence** and genuine respect for foreign traditions - earns him recognition beyond the borders of the Church.

Leo XIV was similarly committed to **dialog with other Christian denominations** and non-Christian religions. Ecumenism, i.e. the unity of Christians, was close to his heart. He maintained close relations with the Orthodox churches, the Protestant communities and the Pentecostal churches. Particularly in countries where Christians are in the minority or under pressure, he promotes cooperation rather than competition. For example, under its influence, the churches initiate joint weeks of prayer and stand together for the rights of persecuted Christians in the Middle East or South Asia. Leo XIV shared his concerns about young people, who were becoming increasingly secular, with the **patriarchs of the Eastern Church,** and together they considered how Christianity could be witnessed to in the 21st century. This ecumenical openness also radiates back into the Catholic Church: when believers see that the Pope looks beyond his own nose, it promotes a less narrow view and more tolerance within the Church.

In his dealings with religions such as **Judaism**, **Buddhism** and traditional natural religions, Leo XIV set an example of respect. He visited synagogues and memorials to express the Jewish-Christian bond and consistently continued the fight against all forms of anti-Semitism. He discusses meditation and global ethics with Buddhist monks in order to find common ground for a global ethos. Such gestures are not just symbolic politics - they reflect Leo's conviction that there is a ray of truth in all sincere religiosity. He liked to quote the sentence from the Council document *Nostra Aetate* that the Church recognizes everything that is true and holy in other religions. This shows that Leo XIV did not see the diversity of religions as a threat, but as a call for dialog and joint action for the good of humanity.

However, the **growing religious pluralism** also harbors internal tensions. Some Catholics are skeptical of the Pope's interreligious zeal. Ultra-conservative circles feared a dilution of the truth or refused to pay so much tribute to other religions. Leo XIV had to strike a balance here too: He emphasizes inwardly that dialogue does not mean **relativism.** Rather, he explains, a genuine dialog strengthens one's own identity - because only those who know and love their own faith can encounter others without fear and aggression. He tries to convey this message through catechesis, especially in the training and further education of candidates for the priesthood: The next generation of priests and lay people should be empowered to **bear witness in a multi-religious environment**, without enemy images, but with clear conviction.

Due to his international biography, Leo XIV had a deep understanding of how differently religion is practiced in different cultures. As Pope, he therefore also promotes a **theology of cultures** within the Church that takes local religious traditions seriously. For example, he supports indigenous peoples in the Amazon or Canada in integrating their cultural expressions into the liturgy (as long as they are compatible with the Christian faith). This is also an aspect of pluralism: diversity can exist not only between religions, but also within the global church. Interreligious dialog and openness to pluralistic contexts are thus directed both outwards - towards peace and understanding - and inwards, by making the Church itself more diverse and *more Catholic* (in the sense of all-encompassing).

A pope between challenges and new beginnings

Leo XIV faced enormous challenges during his pontificate - from internal church reform conflicts to social upheavals and global dialogs. Yet all these challenges conceal equally great potential. His name may be reminiscent of previous popes, but his path points to the future: with openness, international experience and spiritual depth, he is trying to navigate the Catholic Church through the tensions of the present. Critical voices force him to create clarity and genuinely listen; demands for reform drive him to act courageously but wisely; regional differences remind him to always keep the whole of the universal Church in mind.

If Leo XIV succeeds in this balancing act, his pontificate could become a turning point: The Church of tomorrow is being formed today - in the confrontation with criticism, in the struggle for the right path and in trust in God's spirit, which can give unity in diversity. It is already clear that Leo XIV does not provide simple answers, but promotes dialog and dares to take steps towards change. Under his leadership, **the global perspective** and **regional challenges** are merging into a comprehensive process of renewal. The coming years will show whether the reform steps and dialogues he initiated will bear fruit. But one thing is certain: Leo XIV dared to set out - with the aim of leading a **courageous, credible and global church** into the 21st century that could withstand crises and once again be a sign of hope for people today.

 Chapter 16:
Outlook - Vision of a modern and inclusive church

A rainbow above St. Peter's Basilica in Rome could symbolize the vision of Pope Leo XIV: a church that includes all colors of humanity and is credible and welcoming worldwide in the 21st century. From the beginning of his pontificate, Leo XIV was characterized by a clear position for **inclusivity**. He dreamed of a church in which *no one* would be excluded on the basis of origin, gender, lifestyle or social status - a church that would embrace all people of good will **around the world** and **bear credible** witness to the Gospel. Leo XIV wanted to regain this credibility after scandals and crises of confidence had shaken the Church's reputation. His model is a spiritual community that is close to the people (*"close to the faith"*), listens to their concerns and offers answers without remaining dogmatic or defensive. In short: Leo XIV sketches the image of a renewed Catholic Church that is recognizable in the modern world as a **house for all**.

Leo XIV thus differed noticeably from many of his predecessors on the papal throne. Whereas previous pontificates had left certain taboo subjects untouched and shied away from change, Leo XIV dared to deal openly with sensitive issues. For example, the Curia long shied away from even discussing (sacramental) church weddings for same-sex couples - until recently, such initiatives were considered an unheard-of "request" to Rome. Leo XIV, on the other hand, sought dialog **with** rather than against such reform impulses. Overall, he acted as a bridge-builder: He builds on reform steps taken by Pope Francis, but takes an even more decisive approach. His pontificate is unmistakably characterized by *the style of listening* - Leo XIV listens particularly attentively to the voices of the grassroots, women and young people in the Church. In comparison to Benedict XVI or John Paul II, who strongly emphasized traditional doctrine, Leo XIV set different accents: pastoral mercy before strict rules, participation before centralism, courageous openness before fearful isolation. This fresh approach gave his pontificate a unique profile in recent church history.

To turn his vision into reality, Leo XIV resorted to both personal decisions and participatory consultation processes. In the very first years of his pontificate, he used the powers given to him to set an example: For example, he appoints women and non-clerics to leading positions in the Curia and to his team of advisors, underlining the equal say of all believers. He did not shy away from making unpleasant decisions if he was convinced that they were in the best interests of the Church - be it the dismissal of high-ranking clerics in cases of maladministration or the appointment of independent commissions on reform issues. At the same time, Leo XIV was deeply convinced that lasting change could only be achieved together with the whole people of God. He therefore initiated a broad worldwide consultation process with clergy **and** laity. Dialogue forums and synodal assemblies are held in dioceses around the world, where grassroots movements and bishops have their say. This participatory approach finally culminates in a historic step: Leo XIV prepares the convening of a **new Vatican Council**. This possible Third Vatican Council would - for the first time since the 1960s - bring the worldwide Church together in Rome to discuss the fundamental course of the 21st century. Leo XIV was thus building on the legacy of the Second Vatican Council, whose spirit of renewal he wanted to carry over into the current century. By involving bishops from all continents as well as experts and ordinary believers in the preparations, he paid attention to world church mediation: reforms should be *Catholic* - i.e. universal - and not just correspond to individual cultural regions. This strategic bringing together of the diverse voices of the universal Church demonstrates Leo XIV's fundamental concern: to create unity in legitimate diversity.

A central aspect of Leo XIV's vision is the further development of the **image of the church** towards a synodal, inclusive and popular church. In concrete terms, this means moving away from a purely hierarchical, monological model towards a **synodal culture** in which *community* and *participation* are the guiding principles. The Pope repeatedly emphasizes that *all the baptized* share a common dignity and mission. Consecrated and non-consecrated people should therefore be involved in decisions at all levels of the Church - there must be "a culture of genuine co-decision", not merely of consultation. Leo XIV not only emphasized this in words, but also underpinned it institutionally: from the parish to the universal church, he promoted structures that enabled binding co-determination. For example, parish and diocesan councils are to be more than advisory bodies - they are to have real influence on pastoral planning and financial decisions. At the level of the universal church, Leo XIV strengthens the Synod of Bishops by giving it a much more synodal spirit: representatives of the people of God, even without ordination, now have the right to vote and help shape synodal decisions. Responsible leadership in a synodal church, he was convinced, **required** transparency, listening and equality for all believers, regardless of gender or origin. Leo XIV therefore created a framework in which these principles could be put into practice - for example through binding accountability and transparent decision-making processes in church administration. The feedback from the worldwide synod processes already emphasized how essential transparent structures and self-regulation are. The Pope builds on this: he promotes a **culture of accountability** both internally and externally, in which church leaders report regularly and allow themselves to be evaluated. Of course, there remains a certain *tension between synodal participation and hierarchical constitution* - but Leo XIV sees this tension in a positive light. Through new forms of collaboration, this tension can be made fruitful by bringing charismatic leadership and communal participation into a constructive balance. The vision of a synodal, inclusive church ultimately aims for believers to once again experience their church as being close to their life of faith and their questions - a church that listens and accompanies rather than lecturing from above.

Another future scenario that Leo XIV was to consider concerned **sacramental equality** and, in particular, the treatment of same-sex couples. The Catholic Church has always taught that the sacrament of marriage is reserved exclusively for man and woman. However, in the light of new insights into sexuality and love in partnership, there is a growing desire within the Church to develop this teaching further in pastoral terms. Leo XIV belonged to the generation of church leaders who were prepared to think openly *about how* faithful same-sex partnerships could be recognized without devaluing the sacramental depth of marriage. First of all, he unreservedly supports the latest steps towards greater recognition: in December 2023, for example, the Vatican allowed homosexual couples to be blessed in church for the first time. Although this permission is subject to conditions - there must be no confusion with a liturgical marriage ceremony - it represents a milestone. Leo XIV followed on from this and expanded the pastoral possibilities. Under his pontificate, a theological commission developed scenarios for how the Church could provide even more comprehensive support for same-sex couples. For example, a special form of a blessing service that provides globally valid liturgical texts and signs for such couples is conceivable. Even the question of a church *wedding* for homosexual couples was openly raised under Leo XIV - a step that seemed unthinkable before him. Of course, this would be a revolution in the previous sacramental order and required thorough theological reflection as well as a broad consensus in the universal church. But the very fact that Leo XIV allowed and encouraged this debate marked a difference: where previously official authorities had blocked any discussion, he encouraged a respectful discourse that took the lived reality of many believers seriously. He emphasized that the Church does not want to keep anyone away from the sacraments who lives in sincere love and responsibility. Leo XIV thus shows the courage to further develop doctrines - in the knowledge that this takes time and must be communicated on a world church level. In some parts of the world church, the idea of sacramental equality for same-sex couples may still meet with resistance, but in others it has long been hoped for. Leo XIV moderated this process of tension cautiously. It is possible that he will initially allow regional solutions or officially recognize *celebrations* in order to gain experience. In the long term, even a formal opening of the sacrament of marriage could be discussed - for example at the planned council - if he did not make an independent decision. Such a decision would be historically unprecedented and would make Leo XIV's pontificate unmistakable. In any case, it is already clear that what began as a courageous step by individual bishops on the synodal path in Germany in 2023 (over 80% of German clergy voted in favor of blessing same-sex couples at the time) is developing into a worldwide movement under Leo XIV that is confronting the Church with the question of how far its inclusivity can extend without losing its identity.

In addition to opening up in matters of lifestyle, Leo XIV also energetically promoted the **digital transformation of church work.** He knew that the church had to be present in the digital age, where people now communicate and seek community. The coronavirus pandemic has already triggered a surge in innovation: online church services, virtual prayer circles and pastoral services via video chat have become commonplace in many places. Leo XIV does not want to let this momentum die down, but wants to use it strategically. His vision is a *network-oriented church* in which the traditional local congregation is interlinked with digital spaces and supra-regional networks. Specifically, it promotes projects that better connect congregations digitally - both with each other and with believers who share their faith via social media and online platforms. Leo XIV sees church associations, movements and federations, which are often active across parishes or internationally, as an enrichment. They should not compete with the territorial parish, but rather **complement it**, so that different *social forms of church* can coexist: From the local celebration of Mass to the international Zoom Bible study group. To support this digital church development, Leo XIV is also expanding in terms of personnel and structure: For example, special commissioners for digital pastoral care could be created in all dioceses or a central platform will be created in the Vatican that bundles tried and tested ideas. It is important to Leo XIV that digital formats do not remain mere copies of analog formats. The Church should make creative use of the peculiarities of the Internet to reach people at a low threshold. Experts emphasize that we must not simply return to the "old normal", but must *"keep what is good and develop it further"* from what has been tried and tested in online pastoral care. With this in mind, Leo XIV invites committed people to try out new approaches: Be it the use of gaming platforms such as Minecraft for youth ministry, the development of parish apps or interactive online courses in matters of faith. The digital church under Leo XIV always remains focused on people: He sees technology as a tool for forging relationships and making faith tangible. In the future, a parish in the traditional sense may no longer be just a geographical entity, but a hub in a living network of faith that reaches across borders. This will create a **flexible, networked church** in which community can be experienced both locally and online - a church that keeps its finger on the pulse of the times without cutting its spiritual roots.

Finally, Leo XIV placed great emphasis on **participatory, global leadership structures** that prevented the abuse of power and strengthened the participation of the *laity*. The shocks caused by the abuse scandal - whether of a sexual, spiritual or financial nature - made the Pope realize that genuine reform can only succeed if *power in the church* is *rebalanced*. He considered "clericalism" to be the root of many evils: if decision-making power is concentrated too much in the hands of a few male officials, the risk of intransparency and abuse increases. Leo XIV tackled this problem by strengthening **control mechanisms** and **power-sharing** at the same time. On the one hand, as described above, he involved significantly more non-clerics in leadership roles. Competent women and men without an ordination were given leadership positions in Vatican authorities, for example, which was only made possible by recent changes in canon law. On the other hand, Leo XIV must create independent supervisory bodies: Hopefully, he will encourage conferences of bishops worldwide to establish external commissions of experts on dealing with abuse, with a majority of lay and professional members. These committees should monitor diocesan measures and give those affected a voice. An international advisory body of laypeople could also be established in the Vatican itself under Leo XIV, which would report directly to the Pope and expose abuses - whether sexualized violence, financial irregularities or abuse of office. This was Leo XIV's response to demands that were also being voiced by independent parties: Germany's abuse commissioner Kerstin Claus, for example, warns that the *laity* must "become visible in the debate about the reappraisal" and act with clear expectations towards the church leadership. Leo XIV takes such voices seriously and enshrines the principle of **shared responsibility** in the Church. Pope Francis had already set the course with his motu proprio *"Vos estis lux mundi"* (2019/2023) and decreed, for example, that lay people in leadership roles would also be held accountable for covering up abuse and would be obliged to report cases worldwide. Leo XIV built on these foundations and took them further: he supported the amendment of church laws so that a clear right to come to terms with abuse and binding quality standards were established. **Transparency** became the top priority - whether in matters of finance or personnel management. For example, Leo XIV could have the disciplinary measures taken against perpetrators in the church published, or he could set up a central reporting office in the Vatican to which victims worldwide could turn. All these measures were aimed at preventing abuse of power by male clerics - but also by lay people in positions of responsibility - and, in case of doubt, to punish them consistently. By distributing and controlling power, Leo XIV promoted a new culture of trust: no one was above the law of the Church any more, and at the same time more people bore responsibility *within* the Church. This global reorganization of church leadership, with built-in "checks and balances", was intended to ensure that the Gospel was proclaimed credibly - free from the shadow of cover-ups and mistrust.

In summary, Pope Leo XIV outlines his vision of a **modern and inclusive church** that heals its old wounds and finds new vitality. His agenda is ambitious: from the synodal transformation of church structures to the opening up of controversial moral issues and the digitalization of pastoral care to the establishment of a participatory leadership culture. Especially when Leo XIV initiates change in so many areas, he will reap both admiration and resistance. But the unmistakable feature of his pontificate is that he dared to make a departure that others had only announced. Leo XIV can and must **combine realism with vision - in order to achieve effective results and necessary changes**: He knows the limits of what is possible and the diversity of world church mentalities, but he certainly does not let this discourage him. Step by step - personally through courageous decisions, together with the universal Church through consultation and perhaps a future Synod-Council - he is shaping a Church that will arrive in the present. This church should stand firmly on the foundations of its faith and at the same time open its doors wide. Leo XIV certainly has the will and the potential to make a difference: towards a credible Church in which the word *"Catholic"* literally means "all-encompassing" again - **a Church that includes all people of good will and whose testimony is heard all over the world.**

Appendix

Faith is like dancing - theology in motion

Faith and dancing - at first glance, two worlds that have little in common. However, the new publication *"Faith is like dancing - Moved by faith to grow as a Christian"* by Eureka Circe impressively shows how closely connected the two are. In this *training book for religious skills*, the theological project of the *DEUS EX MACHINA* book series unfolds a dynamic vision of being a Christian: *"Faith does not mean blindly following rules, but engaging with heart, hand and mind: with oneself, with other people and with the world"*.

Illustration: Book cover of "Glauben ist wie Tanzen" (Hamburg, 2025).

This work invites you to understand, practise and live your faith through dance:

"Faith is like dancing - and you determine the way and the rhythm!"

Faith does not mean blindly following rules, but rather engaging with your heart, hands and mind: with yourself, with other people and with the world.

This training book for building religious skills for Christians as well as teachers and learners in religious education and in child and youth services invites reflection:

It encourages and accompanies you on the path to the decisive personal and social skills that everyone needs to be able to live faith and charity authentically. Twelve concrete learning fields show: The ability to engage in dialog, empathy, critical thinking and reflection, gender sensitivity, self-acceptance, ethical action and others can and must be learned - in religious education classes, in self-study, in theology internships, in the community and in everyday life. A book for all those who not only want to learn their faith, but want to live it: flexibly, courageously and with joy in loving others. Because those who truly live their faith don't just dance to foreign, dogmatic rules, but also move in tune and self-confidently in harmony with the rhythm of their own lives: faith is like the joy of dancing! - and this "tuning work" can be learned.

Here, faith is an active, living process, comparable to a dance in which each person co-determines the manner and rhythm of their life of faith.

This theologically informed review takes up the central ideas of the book and combines them with inspiring voices from philosophy, the Bible and church practice. It shows why it is *good* when believers dance (figuratively *and* literally), how faith, theology and physical expression interweave, and how even the church leadership - i.e. *"today's Rome"* - should rediscover dance as an expression of faith.

Because: *"Faith is like dancing"* is a sentence that conveys the idea of faith as a dynamic, lively and personal experience. It suggests that faith is not just a static state, but a process of engaging, exploring and discovering, of being happy - in which one actively participates. It is a metaphor that describes faith as a kind of dance in which you find your own rhythm and style by engaging with the world, with yourself and with others.

The sentence "Faith is like dancing" can be interpreted in different contexts:

Religious context: In this context, it can indicate that faith is not just a dogmatic acceptance of rules, but a personal experience and a dynamic relationship with a higher power. The dance symbolizes movement, getting involved and finding one's own expression in faith.

Philosophical context: Here it can convey the idea that faith is a personal choice and an active process of recognition and trust. The dance symbolizes movement and immersion in life, rather than just believing in a static concept.

General context: In a general sense, the sentence can mean that life, faith and action are like a dance in which one engages with the music, movement and rhythm of life and finds one's own style.

Nietzsche and the dancing god - joy instead of a religion of threat and death

To begin with, it is worth taking a philosophical sideways glance: Friedrich Nietzsche once made people sit up and take notice with some thought-provoking words. *"I would only believe in a God who knew how to dance,"* he wrote at the time. This famous sentence by the 19th-century philosopher was far more than just a shrill punch line. Nietzsche, who perceived the Christianity of his time as a joyless "religion of death", called for a God full of life, lightness and exuberance

- a "dancing" God "who would be worthy of our faith at all". For Nietzsche, dancing symbolized joie de vivre, creativity and liberation from overly ossified morals. His fictional Zarathustra proclaims a God who can even laugh during sacred acts - an affront to the image of grim, immovable dogma. Accordingly, the church movement *"We are Church"* calls for a *"good news instead of a threatening message"* to be proclaimed. Figuratively speaking, this includes dancing people - including a dancing God and a dancing and adapting church.

What do we learn theologically from this? Firstly, faith that loses its joy becomes implausible. A Christianity without dance, without laughter, without lively lightness threatens to sink into "nihilism and despair". On the other hand, we must take Nietzsche's longing seriously: Behind his criticism of God is the deep intuition that genuine faith needs a playful freedom - a spark of heavenly art of living that makes us *"poets:inside our lives"*. It is precisely this joy of faith, this dance step of the soul, that needs to be (re)discovered.

Interestingly, modern Christians take up Nietzsche's impulse without sharing his bitterness. The clergyman *Wolf-Dieter Steinmann*, for example, chose the motto *"Faith means dancing"* for a morning service in 2014 and also placed the joyful God at the center.

And indeed, biblical tradition knows of such a God in action: in Jesus Christ, as sung in the hymn *"Lord of the Dance"*, God himself dances through life and even through death. The songwriter *Sydney Carter* wrote this song in 1961, "in a time when the church was still rigid and immobile- in response to this, he imagined Christ as a life-loving dancer whom nothing and no one can permanently force to the ground. *"They knocked me down, but I get up again... for I am the dancing God"*, it says, and: *"I live in you - but live in me too"*. This echoes exactly what Nietzsche missed: a God who celebrates life and takes believers into his dance. Those who believe in such a God find it easier to find joy.

"Dancing in the arms of God" - Madeleine Delbrêls

Not only philosophers, but also Christian seekers have drawn the analogy between faith and dance. The French woman *Madeleine Delbrêl* (1904-1964) coined the phrase: *"Faith is like dancing"*. Delbrêl, who turned from atheism to a committed Christian, understood life with

God as an exhilarating dance full of devotion. In one of her prayer texts, she describes her relationship with God in beautiful dance imagery. You can sense the experience of a woman who lived her faith in the midst of everyday life and retained a tremendous lightness. *"It is up to us [...] to be happy people who dance their lives with you,"* writes Delbrêl - to be a good dancer, you don't always need to know the next step, but must be ready to follow: *"You have to follow, be happy, be light and, above all, not be stiff"*. These words paint the picture of a believer who allows God's rhythm to lead them with confidence. Those who dance with God do not anxiously ask *"where the steps lead"* after every explanation, but *"turn left and right"*, open to surprises. As with dance, it is about engaging with the moment and the partner - in this case the divine counterpart. Delbrêl sums up: All our steps in life would be meaningless *"if the music [of God] did not make a harmony out of them"*. In other words, God himself is the music that gives our lives meaning and brings the scattered dance steps - the highs and lows, successes and setbacks - together to form a meaningful whole.

This *dance metaphor* expresses a profound spiritual truth: Faith is an event between God and man, a constant engagement with one another. Just as dancers pay attention to the movements of their partners, believers listen to God's silent guidance. Delbrêl speaks of *"dancing in the arms of your love"*, in which she finds herself as if in a ballroom, completely immersed in music and rhythm. Her faith is not a dry adherence to doctrines, but a life in rhythmic relationship with God.

This visionary perspective is acknowledged in detail in the book *"Faith is like dancing"*: the thoughts quoted from Delbrêls are an example of how faith captures the heart and senses. This makes it clear that those who believe can know that they are carried by God like a dance partner - safe and yet free, guided and yet exuberant.

Everyone has dancing and faith in their blood

Dancing and faith - are these really universal human traits? The clergyman *Matthias Lüskow* thinks so. In his confirmation sermon in 2023 with the theme *"Faith is like dancing"*, he stated: *"Everyone has dancing in their blood."* What sounds thought-provoking, he explains as follows: even babies experience their "first dance" when parents cradle them in their arms - an ancient, instinctive reassurance. *"Dancing is innate to us, dancing is part of our soul,"* says Lüskow. Later in life, some people may "unlearn" or shy away from dancing, but it is originally ingrained in us. And according to Lüskow, this also applies to faith: *"As with dancing, I would also say about faith: everyone has faith in their blood."* From the very beginning, we live with a basic trust - as children, we naturally trust that someone will nurture and comfort us - and *"we then later transfer this basic trust to God"*. When people claim that they have "no faith", something has often gotten in the way that has alienated them from God. But basically, the seed of trust remains dormant within us. This parallel - innate dance and innate faith - is a great comfort: it means that no one is completely incapable of faith. Just as everyone has a sense of rhythm and an urge to move, everyone also carries within them the ability to engage with the divine. And dancing out of line is also an art!

If none of the guests in a small discotheque dare to go onto the dance floor, there are often just a few people standing at the bar holding on to their drink. No one dares to dance. Everyone stays in the safety of the group. Until finally someone takes heart, gawked at, smiled at and perhaps secretly envied by everyone.

What she or he dares to do! The knot is tied. Later in the evening, the dance floor is full. Bodies bounce, sway and sway rhythmically left and right. Dancing is actually quite easy when someone else leads the way.

Sometimes it is similar in faith: we often prefer to hold on to a coffee. We talk about the weather or sports instead of courageously addressing what is necessary: when Christians opposed National Socialism and raised their voices; when we addressed things in the family that we had to settle for the better; when we finally demanded and wanted to implement in the community what was necessary and liberating for individuals and everyone.

Yes, sometimes we dare to step out - with our faith. Faith is like dancing, quite simply when others join in. We need fellow dancers who believe in our values. Then it's nice not to have to stand on the sidelines. *"So get up on the dance floor - and practice,"* emphasizes clergyman *Sebastian Sievers* in a podcast.

This realization has practical consequences: If faith, like dancing, is something originally human and good, we can build on it.

This is exactly what the book *"Deus Ex Machina - Part III"* does by inviting us to awaken and develop dormant *"religious skills"*. Faith is not presented as a rigid dogma, but as something that is innate in every person, but needs to be encouraged and trained. The texts, exercises and suggestions allow us to move from our innate spiritual longing to concrete skills that we can develop - similar to practicing the steps in dancing.

Practicing, letting go, daring - learning the dance steps of faith

If you want to dance, you have to *practise*. This truism also applies to faith. A dance seems light and free, but behind this lightness there is often discipline and training. Just as clergymen emphasize in the service of evangelization, faith requires guidance and joint practice.

No one is born a perfect dancer; you learn steps, try them out, get corrected - until at some point you *"dance your own dance"*. It is similar with faith: without guidance and teaching (e.g. from parents, teamers, pastors, religious education), many people would lose access to God. This is exactly where the workbook for religious skills comes in: It sees itself as a training book that uses reflection questions and learning fields to guide readers in practicing faith. In twelve *"learning fields"* - from the ability to engage in dialog and empathy to self-acceptance and ethical action - skills are described that can be developed in order to live faith better.

Here are some possible applications:

- *Religious education:* Teachers can use the learning fields to encourage students to reflect on and actively live their faith.
- *Self-study:* Individuals can use the book as a guide to deepen their own religious literacy.
- *Community work:* It can serve as a basis for workshops or discussion groups to understand faith as a dynamic process.
- *Theology internship:* Theology students can use the content to develop practical approaches to religious education.

Figure: God as DJ.

A spiritually luminous female figure with long white hair and a halo wears large black headphones. In front of her is a record player with a model of the solar system: Sun in the center, the planets arranged in concentric orbits around it. She gently touches the earth and other planets with her fingers, as if she were playing the music of a cosmos that encourages people to dance. In the background is a dark starry sky with shining stars and other planets. The scene of God as DJ radiates calm, wisdom and a spiritual connection to the universe.

In conjunction with other teaching materials, the volume can be used as supplementary material to traditional textbooks in order to new perspectives and approaches.

And: individual quotes or questions from the book can be used as impulses for discussions or group work.

With its diverse suggestions and the lifelike metaphor of dancing, *"Faith is like dancing"* can make a valuable contribution to contemporary and skills-oriented religious education. It encourages learners to actively and confidently shape their own faith journey.

In addition to practice, it takes courage to venture onto the dance floor.

The book encourages a flexible, courageous and joyful approach to faith that goes beyond dogmatic rules: faith, like dance, requires commitment and practice. Msgr. Josef Hernoga also emphasizes in his contribution from a Catholic perspective: *"Faith also requires commitment, personal dedication and creativity. Only those who are enthusiastic about God and fascinated by Jesus Christ have 'joy in faith'"*. Enthusiasm ("enthusiasm" - literally a God in us) is the motor that overcomes initial shyness.

Dancing and courage always go together: You reveal something of yourself, every movement makes you vulnerable. If you dance in front of others, you run the risk of being looked at askance - *"What's he doing there?-* and yet the joy of dancing allows you to overcome this embarrassment. In the same way, faith requires courage. In a secular environment, it often takes civil courage to profess your faith - it's easy to feel ridiculed, *"as if you'd done an expressive dance from Waldorf school"*. But those who *dance* their faith gain inner freedom from the opinions of mockers. The message is: don't let fear paralyze you. *Practice* your faith and *dare* to show it to the outside world. Just as a dancer only steps confidently onto the stage after many rehearsals, a Christian becomes courageous enough to stand up for their values in everyday life by practising them.

This shows one of the great advantages of *faith is like dancing*: Training can combine theological reflection with practical guidance on character development. This encourages people to actively shape and practise their faith - *"not just [to dance] according to foreign, dogmatic rules, but [...] self-confidently in harmony with the rhythm of [their] own life"*. This self-determination in faith - without arbitrariness, but with personally internalized conviction - is the goal of "tuning work". In the context of the previous volume of Deus Ex Machina, one could say: *everyone should find their own personal dance of faith that is also in harmony with God's great melody.*

Dance of joy - believing with body and soul

But why dance at all? What does faith gain through dance? The answer is simple: joy and wholeness. *"Dancing makes you happy,"* exclaim many young people. From the first to the last beat, dancing is pure emotion and bliss - something that even outsiders can feel. This experience can be directly transferred to faith: *"Faith also makes you happy,"* says Lüskow. It is living one's faith that gives life deeper meaning, a "common thread" in the dance of life. Those who believe find themselves - metaphorically speaking - held in a choreography that measures all of life's emotions, but ultimately leads to a fulfilled goal. Faith gives direction and hope to the dance of life.

The metaphor of dancing emphasizes above all the physicality of faith. Christian faith does not just want to take place in the head, but permeate the whole person - heart, soul and body. In the Bible, King David dances with devotion before the ark of God, regardless of his royal dignity (2 Sam 6). His famous confession: *"I will dance before the LORD"*, despite the gaze of those around him, is paradigmatic of the fact that God deserves physical expression of joy. Where faith is alive, it inspires people to sing, make music and dance *"full of devotion"*. The people of Israel did this thousands of years ago, and people around the world still experience it today in church services and church festivals. Especially in charismatic or African churches, dancing is a more natural part of praising God than in Central European churches. However, there is also a rediscovery of liturgical and meditative dance in this country. Hildegard Linn, a dance teacher of many years' standing, has developed her own choreographies for the celebration of Mass and Christmas - from Kyrie and Gloria to Sanctus - and refers to the biblical symbolism of the gestures in each case. Dances to sacred music such as the *Misa*

Criolla from South America show that prayer and movement can be combined: The *pulsating rhythms are a challenge to dance to,* and those who engage with them pray with their bodies.

Dance is also valued as an experience of prayer outside of the official liturgy. In a contribution to the Catholic series *SWR4 Abendgedanken,* Marianne Krämer-Birsens gives an impressive account of how a group of elderly ladies engage in *meditative dancing* together to the music. *"Dancing is like praying" is* the title. For these women - many of whom are over 60 - the weekly dance circle becomes an oasis, a place of God's presence in the here and now. For 90 minutes, nothing else matters but harmony with the others; every step in the circle becomes a concentration on the essentials. *"Losing yourself in dance can be like a prayer. Being completely with yourself, being completely in the moment, doing it with devotion - that is prayer for me,"* writes Krämer-Birsens. This experience coincides with Delbrêl's insight: it is about devotion, letting go of all disturbing thoughts and experiencing deep joy. A dance like this *"removes all temporal and physical limitations"* - you feel young and free. At the same time, the participants draw new strength for everyday life; anger and worries are put into perspective in these moments. Apparently, not only endorphins but also spiritual energy is released here. When people pray with body and soul - be it through words, silence or dance - it appeals to them in a more holistic way than if faith were just a matter of the head. This is exactly what Msgr. Hernoga points out: Faith always involves senses and feelings; living faith even has a healing effect on people. Dance can be a form of therapy - both physically and emotionally - and genuine faith also has a healing and meaningful effect. *Faith is like dancing* therefore emphasizes that skills such as empathy, dialogue and self-acceptance require body, mind and soul to work together. Faith should be lived *"flexibly, courageously and with joy"* - this corresponds more to the lively dance step than the rigid genuflection.

Church in motion - dance as an expression of lived faith

If faith is like dancing, the question arises: *where does the church dance?* For far too long, there has been an unwritten rule of immobility in some parts of the church - pious bodies should be quiet, hands folded and faces serious. But this attitude is changing. Pope Francis, for example, tirelessly reminds us of the *joy of the Gospel* and that Christians should not be *"sourpusses"*. Although Francis did not literally speak of dancing, his vision of a church bubbling over with joy comes close. In fact, "today's Rome", i.e. the church leadership, would do well to promote dance more consciously as an expression of faith. Liturgy can be solemn and reverent - but reverence does not exclude joy. Think of King David: his ecstatic procession before the ark was just as much a worship service as the temple sacrifice cult, only more spontaneous. So why not make room for liturgical dance where it suits the culture? In many African and Oceanic communities, it is a matter of course to dance during the offertory or the Gloria. The Roman Church could learn from these "young churches" and also allow the joy of movement in European services without fear of losing control. Of course, tact is needed here - dancing in the chancel is not understood everywhere - but processions, rhythmic singing with body movement or meditative circle dances in prayer could be an enrichment instead of a threat.

An opening to the body would also be desirable in the training of pastors and theologians. Those who become priests or pastors learn a lot about dogmatics and liturgy, but little about bodily forms of prayer. A workshop on *"Prayer and Movement"* in the seminary for priests, a seminar on "Dance as Prayer" in theology studies - such impulses could help future clergy to overcome their fear of breaking new ground with their congregations. The French nun Sr. Geneviève Médevielle once said: "*When the spirit blows, the body must also be allowed to resonate.* This is where pneumatology (the doctrine of the Holy Spirit) and kinesiology combine to form a holistic spirituality. The church should understand that young people today are looking for other approaches - those who offer a Taizé dance or a hip-hop moves prayer evening as part of their youth work may reach hearts more directly than just by sitting and listening.

There are already encouraging new beginnings in church practice. Dance groups, meditative dance meetings (as reported by Krämer-Birsens) or even simple movement songs in family worship loosen up the atmosphere and make you feel that you can be *happy* here. The rigid seating arrangement of the church pews becomes a stage on which everyone is invited to get involved. Where believers *learn to dance,* literally and figuratively, the congregation comes alive. A sense of community is created - people move to the same beat, laugh and lose their fear of each other. Many a prejudice that faith is boring could be debunked if it became visible from the outside how lively it can be with Christians.

The theologian and dancer Hildegard Don Bosco once remarked with a wink that Jesus' first official act after the resurrection must have been a dance of joy - but none of the evangelists dared to write this down. Even if this remains in the realm of legend, the core is true: the *joy of resurrection* actually wants to be expressed in movement. So why shouldn't we celebrate Easter with liturgical dance instead of just singing "Christ is risen"? The church of the future can become bolder and dare to *take new (dance) steps.*

Dance your faith!

In the end, we are left with the invitation that the aforementioned training book and all the quoted voices have already extended: Come to the dance floor of faith! Anyone who engages with this comparison will discover that faith really is like dancing - an interplay of leading and following, of rhythm and improvisation, of seriousness and joy. The review of *"Faith is like dancing"* shows: The book combines inspiring theological insights with very practical assistance to get faith *moving.* It emphasizes that we can only live our faith authentically if we find ourselves in it - in harmony with the beat of our lives and yet open to the beat that God sets.

Faith wins when believers *dance* and learn to dance: symbolically, by letting their faith "swing" full of trust and joy, and also practically, by understanding their body as a gift from God. A dancing believer is the opposite of a dogged fanatic - then we radiate lightness, love and courage to face life. This is exactly the kind of witness the world needs. When God's melody resounds in our hearts, we must not be afraid to respond to it with our feet. The psalmists were already convinced that God dances with us: *"Praise him with tambourine and round dance!"* (Psalm 150:4). *"Because God dances, we dance too",* say many clergymen. Yes, the *"dancing God"* is at our side - now it is up to us to get involved in the heavenly music. With this in mind: *"Dance your life, dance your faith!"*. For he who believes may rejoice as one who dances before God and in the light of the Holy One (GN - W/D/M). Before the love of God that sustains us, let us have the courage to express this joy - in our congregations, our prayers, our whole life. Faith is like dancing: a risk, a gift and a heavenly joy. **Amen** - or should we say: *Àmen* (in 3/4 time).

List of illustrations

This volume is a *work of art by* artificial intelligence *algorithms*: the illustrations are generated entirely by AI: The image of the curator in the imprint was processed with AI filters and algorithms.

Supplementary online resources

- **ABC News** - abcnews.go.com - News portal of the US television channel ABC with current news and background reports.

- **Aleteia** - aleteia.org - International Catholic online portal covering news, spirituality, faith and life issues from a Catholic perspective.

- **ARD Tagesschau** - tagesschau.de - ARD's public news portal with news and background information on Germany and the world.

- **Berliner Morgenpost** - morgenpost.de - National daily newspaper with a focus on current news from Berlin, Germany and the world.

- **Bertelsmann Religion Monitor** - bertelsmann-stiftung.de - Regular study by the Bertelsmann Stiftung on religious attitudes, practices and social changes.

- **Catholic Answers** - catholic.com - Apologetic Catholic portal explaining and defending matters of faith and church doctrine.

- **Catholic News Agency (CNA)** - catholicnewsagency.com - English Catholic news agency specializing in reporting on the Vatican and the global Church.

- **CBS News** - cbsnews.com - US news site of the CBS television network with current news on international events.

- **CIDSE** - cidse.org - International alliance of Catholic development organizations committed to social justice, sustainability and poverty reduction.

- **CNA German** - de.catholicnewsagency.com - German language portal of CNA for Catholic news in German-speaking countries.

- **Crux** - cruxnow.com - Independent Catholic news portal from the USA with a focus on global church events and the Vatican.

- **German Bishops' Conference (DBK)** - dbk.de - Official website of the Catholic Bishops of Germany, with documents, statements and current news.

- **Die Presse** - diepresse.com - Austrian daily newspaper with detailed reports and commentaries on politics, society and the church.

- **Domradio** - domradio.de - Cologne Catholic online portal and radio station, offers comprehensive news and background information on the Catholic Church.

- **FAZ (Frankfurter Allgemeine Zeitung)** - faz.net - Leading German daily newspaper with extensive coverage of politics, business, society and religion.

- **Famvin** - famvin.org - International network of the Vincentian family, offers information on projects and news from the Vincentian community.

- **Frankfurter Rundschau** - fr.de - National German daily newspaper with socially critical articles and news on current topics.

- **Greenpeace** - greenpeace.de - International environmental organization committed to global climate protection, environmental protection and sustainability.

- **Heute** - heute.at - Austrian news portal with current reports on politics, society and the environment.

- **Kath-Kirche Kärnten** - kath-kirche-kaernten.at - Official Catholic information portal of the diocese of Gurk-Klagenfurt with regional and world church news.

- **Katholisch.de** - katholisch.de - Official news portal of the Catholic Church in Germany, offers news, background information and debates.

- **Kathpress (Katholische Presseagentur Österreich)** - kathpress.at - Austrian Catholic news agency with comprehensive reporting on church and religion.

- **Kirche+Leben** - kirche-und-leben.de - Catholic online portal of the weekly newspaper of the diocese of Münster with news, reports and commentaries on church and society.

- **Misereor** - misereor.de - Catholic relief organization for development cooperation, committed to fighting poverty and social injustice worldwide.

- **National Catholic Reporter** - ncronline.org - Critical and independent US Catholic news portal on church and social issues.

- **n-tv** - n-tv.de - German private news channel, reports on current national and international events.

- **ORF Religion** - religion.orf.at - Austrian news portal on religious topics, church news and interreligious dialogs.

- **PBS News** - pbs.org - US public news channel with background information and reports on international issues.

- **Sonntagsblatt** - sonntagsblatt.de - Protestant news portal, provides comprehensive information about church, religion and society.

- **Süddeutsche Zeitung (SZ)** - sueddeutsche.de - Leading German daily newspaper with comprehensive reporting on national and international topics, politics and society.

- **Vatican News** - vaticannews.va - Official news portal of the Vatican, reports on the Pope, the Vatican and global Catholic issues.

- **Watson** - watson.de - Online news portal with a young audience, reports on political and social issues in contemporary language.

- **Wikipedia** - wikipedia.org - Free online encyclopedia, offers comprehensive articles on almost all areas of knowledge, including religious and ecclesiastical topics.

- **Zeit Online** - zeit.de - Online portal of the German weekly newspaper DIE ZEIT, offers detailed articles and analyses on social, political and cultural topics.

Other more specific Catholic and ecclesiastical online portals:

- **Herder Korrespondenz** - herder.de/hk - A monthly Catholic magazine that critically examines ecclesiastical, political and cultural developments.

- **Katholische Nachrichten-Agentur (KNA)** - kna.de - German Catholic News Agency, provides up-to-date and independent reports on topics relating to the Church, religion and society.

- **The Tablet** - thetablet.co.uk - British Catholic weekly, offering in-depth reporting and analysis on the Church and international events.

- **Zenit** - zenit.org - International Catholic news agency focusing on events related to the Vatican and the global Church.

Work assignment in the annual internship with glossary

Work task in the annual internship:
Daily reflection on a glossary term

As part of an annual internship, you will receive a new **glossary term** every day, which you will deal with intensively. Your task is to carry out the following steps independently or in dialog with others:

1. **Understanding and contextualization**: Reflect on the content of the term, research additional information and sources if necessary, and clarify the central meaning of the term in the context of the Catholic Church.

2. **Personal reflection and evaluation**: Analyze what meaning, questions and impulses the term holds for you personally. Take a critical look at what thoughts and inner impulses the term triggers in you.

3. **Critical consideration in relation to the Catholic Church**: Evaluate how this term can be categorized with regard to current challenges, developments and necessary reforms within the Catholic Church. Identify clear reform approaches and possible needs for change.

4. **Local feasibility and development of measures**: Think specifically about which measures, actions or initiatives you can derive, discuss and practically implement locally (e.g. in a parish, in church groups or local networks) from dealing with this concept. Describe initial steps or suggestions for local implementation or thematization.

The daily processing should be documented in writing in order to obtain a comprehensive collection of your reflected findings, suggestions and reform impulses at the end of the annual internship.

(1) **#OutInChurch:** An initiative by queer (LGBTQIA+) employees of the Catholic Church who publicly acknowledged their identity and denounced discrimination in order to initiate necessary changes.

(2) **Abortion:** The termination of a pregnancy. Is fundamentally rejected by the Catholic Church.

(3)   **Abuse commissioner of the DBK**: A commissioner appointed by the German Conference of Bishops who deals with the topics of abuse and coming to terms with it.

(4)   **Abuse of power:** The misuse of a position of power or hierarchical superiority, which in the church context is identified as a key factor in enabling sexualized violence and its cover-up.

(5)   **Accountability:** The obligation of responsible parties to be held accountable for their actions (or inactions), especially in the context of abuse and cover-ups.

(6)   **Ad limina visit:** The mandatory visit of the bishops of a conference of bishops to the Pope in Rome, which normally takes place every five years.

(7)   **Adelphopoiesis (brotherly bond):** Rituals in the early Middle Ages for the liturgical blessing of same-sex, emotionally close relationships, known as "brother bonding".

(8)   **Alfred Delp SJ:** A German Jesuit and resistance fighter against the Nazi regime, whose quote "A Christian can never be a nationalist" is cited in the text as an expression of the incompatibility of radical nationalism and Christian faith.

(9)   **Amazon Synod**: A special gathering of bishops in the Vatican (2019) that addressed the challenges and pastoral needs of the Amazon region.

(10)   **Apostolic visitation:** An official examination of a diocese, religious community or other ecclesiastical institution on behalf of the Pope.

(11)   **Armaments policy:** Political measures and decisions relating to the manufacture, trade and use of weapons and military equipment.

(12)   **Artificial intelligence (AI):** Computer systems that can perform tasks that normally require human intelligence, such as learning, problem solving and decision making.

(13)   **Ascetic attitude / frugality:** A lifestyle that aims at voluntary renunciation, moderation and a reduction in consumption in favor of sharing and responsibility for creation.

(14)   **Assisted suicide:** Assisted suicide. Is fundamentally rejected by the Catholic Church.

(15)   **Association of German Dioceses (VDD):** A body that represents the common interests of the German dioceses and has its own budget.

(16)   **Authentic conversion and reform:** A profound and sincere change and renewal within the church, affecting both personal attitudes and structural aspects.

(17)   **Authentic development:** Development that is not only aimed at economic growth, but also takes into account the holistic well-being of people and the inclusion of all.

(18)   **Basic Regulations for Church Service:** The basic regulations governing the working conditions and loyalty obligations of employees of the Catholic Church.

(19)   **Basic rules of church service:** The basic set of rules that defines the conditions of employment and loyalty obligations for employees of the Catholic Church and has been reformed.

(20) **Bishops who are willing to shape things:** Clergy at episcopal level who are open to change and reform within the Catholic Church and would like to play an active role in this.

(21) **Blessing:** An ecclesiastical act in which God's blessing is invoked on people, things or situations; often refers to the blessing of couples.

(22) **Borg collective:** Fictional species from Star Trek, depicted as a cybernetic collective consciousness in which individuals lose their independence and are controlled by a central "hive mind". Used in the text as a metaphor for the desired adaptation of the seminar participants to a monolithic ideological structure.

(23) **Bundesarbeitsgemeinschaft Kirche und Rechtsextremismus (BAG K+R):** An ecumenical network that campaigns against right-wing populism, right-wing extremism and group-focused enmity and advises and supports church actors.

(24) **Call for disobedience:** A public statement by the Pastors' Initiative calling for civil disobedience against certain church rules.

(25) **Canon law:** The internal legal system of the Catholic Church, which regulates the structure, organization and rules for church offices, membership, etc.

(26) **Caritas:** An international association of Catholic aid organizations that is a major employer in many countries and is subject to church labor law.

(27) **Catechism of the Catholic Church:** The official summary of the teachings of the Catholic Church.

(28) **Cathedral chapter:** A body of priests that advises bishops and performs certain tasks within the diocese, often with its own finances.

(29) **Catholic Social Teaching:** The entirety of the Catholic Church's doctrinal documents on social, economic and political issues, beginning with Rerum Novarum (1891).

(30) **CEAMA (Conferencia Eclesial de la Amazonía):** An ecclesial conference for the Amazon region that brings together clergy and laity and is considered a model for synodal leadership.

(31) **Celibacy:** Voluntary celibacy for the sake of the kingdom of heaven, which is still obligatory for priests of the Latin rite in the Roman Catholic Church.

(32) **Central Committee of German Catholics (ZdK):** The official representation of the Catholic laity in Germany.

(33) **Centralism:** An organizational principle in which decisions and power are mainly concentrated in a central body or authority, in this context in Rome/Vatican.

(34) **Chance luck:** A meaning of the German word "Glück", which refers to random, unavailable events such as a win or the avoidance of danger.

(35) **Charisms:** Gifts and abilities given by the Holy Spirit to individual believers for service to the community.

(36) **Charity:** A central commandment in Christianity that calls for love and solidarity with all people, regardless of their origin or affiliation. It is mentioned as the opposite of hatred and exclusion.

(37) **Christian social ethics:** An area of theology that deals with the application of Christian values and principles to social, economic and political issues.

(38) **Christian Social Teaching**: The collection of principles and teachings of the Catholic Church on social, economic and political issues based on the Gospel and Church tradition.

(39) **Christian view of humanity:** The theological conviction that every human being is created in the image of God and therefore has inviolable dignity, regardless of origin, religion, sexual orientation, etc.

(40) **Church communion:** The full communion between churches based on agreement in matters of faith, sacraments and church structure.

(41) **Church of fear:** A church atmosphere characterized by mistrust, control and fear of deviation.

(42) **Church of the many:** A goal of synodal renewal in which priests, bishops and lay people work together at all levels.

(43) **Church of trust:** a church atmosphere characterized by appreciation, shared responsibility and the courage to explore new paths.

(44) **Church on the move:** The vision of a church that is more open to physical expressions of faith and allows dance as part of the liturgy and spirituality.

(45) **Church People's Movement "We are Church":** A Catholic reform movement that campaigns for more democracy and equal rights in the church.

(46) **Church structures:** The organizational hierarchy and the way in which decisions are made in the church.

(47) **Church Tax Council:** A body within a diocese that advises the bishop on financial matters and examines and approves the budget.

(48) **CIC (Code of Canon Law):** The collection of laws and norms governing the Catholic Church.

(49) **Clerical culture of silence:** The tendency within the church not to speak openly about difficult or unpleasant topics, especially sexuality and misconduct, but to make them taboo, repress them or cover them up.

(50) **Clericalism:** An attitude or structure that places the clergy above the laity and overemphasizes their role and authority.

(51) **Clerics:** Clergy of the church (e.g. priests, bishops).

(52) **Climate change:** The global, long-term change in the Earth's climate, in particular due to the increase in average temperature as a result of human activity.

(53) **Climate justice:** A concept that states that climate change has a disproportionate impact on poorer countries and populations, and calls for global action to address this injustice.

(54) **Climate protection concept:** A plan containing measures to reduce greenhouse gas emissions and adapt to the consequences of climate change.

(55) **Climate protection:** Measures to reduce greenhouse gas emissions and limit global warming, often seen as part of the responsibility for creation.

(56) **Clobber passages:** term used in queer theology for biblical passages that are often quoted in isolation and without historical context to condemn homosexuality.

(57) **Collective safe space:** A safe space created by the common attitude and actions of a group (e.g. a conference of bishops).

(58) **Collegiality:** The principle that bishops (or, in a broader sense, other groups in the church) bear responsibility and make decisions together as a college.

(59) **Coming out:** The process of recognizing one's own sexual orientation or gender identity and communicating it to others.

(60) **Commandment of respect for life ("Thou shalt not kill"):** A fundamental biblical commandment that emphasizes the sanctity of human life and serves as an ethical basis for the protection of human life in road traffic.

(61) **Common good balance sheet:** An instrument for measuring a company's contribution to the common good beyond purely financial indicators.

(62) **Common good:** The good of all members of a society, which is placed above individual interests. The church is committed to the common good.

(63) **Communio:** Community, a central concept in the understanding of the church as a community of believers.

(64) **Community-oriented sheep and watchdogs of the flock:** A metaphor for active, self-confident and cooperative lay people who are not passive "sheep", but who protect and shape the church community on their own responsibility and work together with the clergy.

(65) **Competence Center for Democracy and Human Dignity:** An institution set up by the Catholic Church to support the demand that right-wing extremists be kept away from lay positions in the church.

(66) **Compulsory celibacy:** The canonical obligation for priests of the Latin Church to live unmarried.

(67) **Comunidades Eclesiales de Base (base communities):** Small Christian communities, often rooted in Latin America, in which believers meet at eye level and shape the local church together.

(68) **Comunidades Eclesiales de Base (CEBs):** Base communities in Latin America, small communities of believers who gather for prayer, Bible study and social engagement.

(69) **Concept of ministry:** The theological understanding of church ministry (e.g. priests, pastors, bishops) and its legitimacy.

(70) **Conflict counseling and mediation:** Professional support to clarify and resolve conflicts between individuals or groups, especially between bishops or different camps within the church.

(71) **Conflict of loyalties circus:** A situation in which church actors are caught in constant conflict due to contradictory expectations (e.g. between Rome and the local church).

(72) **Congregation for the Doctrine of the Faith:** One of the oldest congregations of the Roman Curia, responsible for safeguarding and defending Catholic doctrine of faith and morals.

(73) **Co-responsibility (joint responsibility):** The theological principle that all the baptized are jointly responsible for the being and acting of the church.

(74) **Cover-up:** The deliberate concealment or disguise of cases of abuse by church officials in order to protect the institution or individuals instead of supporting the victims and clearing up the crimes.

(75) **Creative clergy**: A clergy member who is willing and able to actively develop the church and its community, characterized by openness, innovative spirit, participatory leadership and courage.

(76) **Credibility:** The capacity of the Church to be authentic and trustworthy in its teachings and practices, especially with regard to its consistency with the basic principles of the Gospel and social values.

(77) **Crisis of confidence:** A situation in which the trust of the faithful and the public in the institution of the church has been massively shaken as a result of the abuse scandal and the way it has been handled.

(78) **Critique of capitalism:** A critical examination of the basic principles and effects of capitalism, often from an ethical, social or ecological perspective.

(79) **Curia (Roman Curia):** The central administrative authority of the Holy See, which assists the head of the Church in governing the universal Church.

(80) **Dance of joy:** The idea that dance (and thus also lived faith) conveys joy and happiness and makes faith a holistic experience.

(81) **Dancing in the arms of God:** A metaphor by Madeleine Delbrêl that describes the relationship with God as an exhilarating dance full of devotion, in which one allows oneself to be led by God's rhythm.

(82) **Democratization (in the church):** Not the transfer of political democracy, but the expansion of genuine co-determination and participation in responsibility of all the baptized in the decision-making processes of the church.

(83) **De-pathologization:** The process by which certain behaviors, conditions or identities (such as sexual orientation) are no longer considered pathological or in need of treatment.

(84) **Diaconate:** The first level of ordained ministry in the Catholic Church. Deacons assist priests and bishops and may perform certain liturgical services.

(85) **Dicasteries:** The most important authorities or ministries of the Vatican that assist the Pope in the governance of the universal Church (e.g. Congregation for the Doctrine of the Faith, Dicastery for Bishops).

(86) **Digital native:** A person who has grown up in the digital era and has been familiar with technology and the Internet since childhood.

(87) **Diocesan council:** An advisory body at the level of a diocese, often with the participation of lay people.

(88) **Diocesan law:** ecclesiastical law provisions that apply to a specific diocese (diocese).

(89) **Diocese**: An administrative district of the Catholic Church under the leadership of bishops.

(90) **Diocese:** Another term for diocese.

(91) **Disciplinary regulations for clergy:** A provision in canon law that provides clear sanctions against male clergy for misconduct, particularly in relation to abuse or cover-up.

(92) **Disclosure of files:** The provision of church archives and documents relating to cases of abuse and the handling thereof for independent investigations and those affected.

(93) **Distanced baptized**: People who were baptized but later stayed away from the church, although they still formally belong to the church.

(94) **Diversity:** Described in the text as a richness within the church and society that brings in different perspectives on happiness.

(95) **Divestment**: The decision to withdraw investments or money from certain companies, sectors or funds, often for ethical or moral reasons (e.g. from companies that invest in fossil fuels).

(96) **Doctrinal preaching:** The official communication and interpretation of church doctrine.

(97) **Doctrinal reassessment:** The review and, if necessary, amendment of existing church teachings.

(98) **Dogmatic boundaries:** Beliefs and doctrinal provisions that are considered binding and can form the theological basis for demarcations between denominations.

(99) **Double standards:** The coexistence of public moral teaching (e.g. on sexuality) and secret, deviant behavior (e.g. secret relationships, affairs). Cited as a problem in the context of celibacy culture.

(100) **Duck and cover (in a church context):** Ironic metaphor for reflexive, passive or defensive behavior of clergy in the face of crisis or reform issues, an avoidance of conflict or uncomfortable discussion.

(101) **Dynamic vision of being a Christian:** An idea of being a Christian that goes beyond simply following rules and emphasizes an active engagement with oneself, others and the world with heart, hand and mind.

(102) **Ecclesia semper reformanda:** Latin expression that means "the church that is always being renewed", which emphasizes the need for continuous reform in the church.

(103) **Ecclesiastical labor law:** The specific labor law regulations and standards that apply to employees of the Catholic Church.

(104) **Ecclesiastical Magisterium:** The official teaching authority and doctrine of the Catholic Church, in particular by the Pope and the bishops.

(105) **Ecological conversion:** A change in mindset and actions that leads to a more responsible approach to the environment.

(106) **Economy for the common good:** An alternative economic model that is not based on profit maximization, but on values such as human dignity, solidarity, justice and sustainability.

(107) **Ecumenism:** The movement and striving for unity between different Christian denominations.

(108) **Emmaus disciples (Luke 24):** A biblical story of two disciples who wander away from Jerusalem disappointed, are accompanied by Jesus without being recognized and finally recognize him, which gives them new hope and joy. Serves as an image for the common search for happiness.

(109) **Encyclical Laudato si':** A papal circular issued by Pope Francis in 2015 that deals extensively with environmental and climate issues as well as social justice.

(110) **Episcopal chair:** special assets of bishops that are managed separately from the general diocesan finances.

(111) **Episcopate:** The office of bishops.

(112) **Equality and non-discrimination:** Principles that demand that all people are treated equally and are not disadvantaged, regardless of gender, sexual orientation or lifestyle.

(113) **Equality policy implementation:** The practical implementation of measures to ensure equal treatment and non-discrimination of a group.

(114) **Equitable participation:** The opportunity for all members of society to participate in economic, social and cultural life and to benefit from its fruits.

(115) **Error culture:** An attitude that allows people to make mistakes and learn from them without fear of excessive punishment.

(116) **Ethical consumption:** consumer decisions that take social, ecological and ethical factors into account, e.g. by buying fair trade products.

(117) **Ethics of responsibility:** An ethical approach that focuses on the individual's responsibility for the consequences of their actions and for the well-being of others, as opposed to rigid rules or commandments.

(118) **Ethnic nationalism:** A form of nationalism that is based on the idea of an ethnically or culturally homogeneous nation and often goes hand in hand with the devaluation or exclusion of other groups.

(119) **EU Supply Chain Act:** A law that obliges companies to identify, prevent and mitigate human rights and environmental risks in their global supply chains.

(120) **Eucharist / Lord's Supper:** The sacrament of the Lord's Supper in the Protestant Church and the Eucharist in the Catholic Church; joint participation in this sacrament as a sign of church communion.

(121) **Evangelii Gaudium:** A teaching letter from Pope Francis that begins with the "joy of the Gospel" and describes it as a source of joy for those who encounter Jesus.

(122) **Exploitation of raw materials:** The excessive or unfair use of natural resources, often with negative social and environmental consequences.

(123) **External expert opinion:** An investigation, e.g. into cases of abuse or the handling thereof, carried out by a non-ecclesiastical, independent body (e.g. a law firm) to enable a more objective assessment.

(124) **Faith is like dancing:** The central metaphor that describes faith as a dynamic, lively and active process, comparable to a dance that requires commitment, practice and dedication.

(125) **Feminist theology:** A theological approach that critically examines and reinterprets the Bible, tradition and church teaching from a feminist perspective in order to address inequalities and discrimination against women in the church.

(126) **Fig leaf:** Something that only serves as a cover or alibi, but has no real substance or effect.

(127) **Financial management:** The way in which financial resources are managed and used.

(128) **Focolare Movement:** An international movement in the Catholic Church that aims for communion and dialog between Christians of different denominations and people of different faiths.

(129) **Formation of conscience:** The process of developing and sharpening one's own moral judgment, often in comparison with teachings, traditions and personal experiences.

(130) **Fratelli tutti:** A social encyclical by Pope Francis from 2020 on fraternity and social friendship, which deals with globalization, populism and nationalism, among other things, and contrasts a "culture of encounter" with the "culture of walls".

(131) **Freedom of conscience:** The right and moral obligation of the individual to follow his or her own carefully formed conscience, even if this may contradict official teaching (based on the Second Vatican Council).

(132) **Full-time staff / volunteers:** People who work professionally (full-time) or voluntarily (honorary) in the church and are referred to as "ministering spirits" of the church.

(133) **Fundamental employee rights:** Fundamental rights of employees that are protected by state law (e.g. protection against discrimination, protection against dismissal).

(134) **Gaudium et Spes:** Document of the Second Vatican Council, which deals with the dignity of man and his role in the modern world and describes the conscience as the "hidden center of man".

(135) **Gen Z (Generation Z):** The age group roughly born between the mid-1990s and mid-2010s.

(136) **Gender equality:** The principle that men and women should be treated equally and have the same opportunities and rights.

(137) **Gender-sensitive:** Consideration of gender equality in church structures and practices.

(138) **General Assembly:** The highest authority of the Synodal Way, where decisions are made.

(139) **General Relator:** An important position at a synod, responsible for summarizing the discussions.

(140) **Generational conflict:** Tension and conflict between different age groups with different values, attitudes and expectations.

(141) **German Conference of Bishops (DBK):** The association of Catholic bishops in Germany.

(142) **Glücklichsein:** The deeper meaning of the German word "Glück", which describes a state of inner fulfillment, harmony and contentment.

(143) **Golden rule:** An ethical principle that exists in many religions and cultures ("Treat others as you would like to be treated") and is cited as a common denominator in interreligious dialog.

(144) **Good Friday and Easter:** Christian days of remembrance for the death of Jesus (Good Friday) and his resurrection (Easter), which symbolize the transformation from suffering to hope and new life.

(145) **Good news:** A term for the gospel that emphasizes that the central message of the Christian faith is a message of joy.

(146) **Grace theology:** From the perspective of the doctrine of God's grace.

(147) **Gray areas:** Areas within the church where certain practices or approaches are tolerated but not officially recognized.

(148) **Green electricity:** Electricity generated from renewable energy sources such as wind, sun or water.

(149) **Holistic well-being:** Development that encompasses not only economic growth, but also social, environmental and cultural aspects of human and community life.

(150) **Homines Probati:** Proven people, as a group of people in general, regardless of gender, who can work practically as priests.

(151) **Homosexual sensation:** A sexual orientation that is directed towards people of the same sex.

(152) **Homosexuality:** Sexual orientation in which a person is emotionally, romantically and/or sexually attracted to persons of the same sex.

(153) **HuK (ecumenical working group "Homosexuals and the Church"):** A working group that takes a critical look at the church's sexual morals and advocates the recognition of same-sex relationships.

(154) **Human dignity:** The idea, central to Catholic social teaching and ethics, of the intrinsic, inalienable worth of every human being.

(155) **Human sciences:** Disciplines that study human behavior and human societies (e.g. psychology, sociology).

(156) **Humanist and ecological conversion:** a demand to turn away from the "idolatry of money" and to focus on human life, dignity and the environment.

(157) **Idolatry (or idolatry):** The worship or deification of something other than God. In context, excessive nationalism is referred to as idolatry of one's own nation or people.

(158) **in persona Christi:** A theological term meaning that an ordained minister acts in the person of Christ when celebrating certain sacraments (especially the Eucharist).

(159) **Inclusive church:** A church that welcomes and includes all people, regardless of their characteristics or background.

(160) **Inclusive understanding of the church:** A vision of the church that sees diversity as enrichment and includes all baptized people regardless of their denominational affiliation or sexual orientation.

(161) **Inculturation:** The adaptation of church doctrine and practice to the culture of a particular place or group.

(162) **Independent Commissioner for Abuse of the Federal Government:** A government agency in Germany that advocates for the interests of those affected by abuse and critically accompanies the reappraisal process in various institutions.

(163) **Indoctrination:** The systematic inculcation of a one-sided world view or certain dogmas, often using manipulation and pressure techniques to suppress critical thinking.

(164) **Informal sector:** The part of the economy that is not regulated or taxed by the government and is often characterized by insecure working conditions.

(165) **Institutional homophobia:** Discrimination and prejudice against homosexual people that is anchored in the structures, rules and practices of an institution.

(166) **Institutional paralysis:** A state in which necessary reforms or changes within an institution (in this case the church) are blocked and do not make progress.

(167) **Institutional responsibility:** The responsibility of the church as an organization to acknowledge the systemic problems, to work through them, to make amends and to change structures in such a way that future abuse is prevented, over and above the individual guilt of individual perpetrators.

(168) **Integral ecology:** The concept that emphasizes the inseparable link between environmental problems and social problems and requires a holistic view of both.

(169) **Integrity of creation:** A theological term that describes the protection and care of the natural environment as a human duty towards God and the world.

(170) **Intercelebration:** The joint performance of a liturgical celebration (e.g. Eucharist or Holy Communion) by clergy of different denominations.

(171) **Interdiocesan peer networks:** Informal associations of bishops from different dioceses or countries who meet regularly to exchange ideas and support each other.

(172) **Interreligious dialog:** The exchange and encounter between people of different religions.

(173) **Isolation:** The feeling or state of being cut off from social or emotional ties. The text mentions isolation in connection with celibacy as a risk factor that can lead to loneliness and a problematic search for closeness.

(174) **John Jay Report:** Several studies conducted in the early 2000s in the USA for the US Conference of Catholic Bishops by the John Jay College of Criminal Justice investigating the sexual abuse of minors by Catholic clergy.

(175) **Joy instead of a religion of death:** a theological implication from Nietzsche's point of view that a faith without joy becomes implausible and can sink into nihilism.

(176) **Just peace:** A concept of Christian peace ethics that understands peace not only as the absence of war, but as a state of justice, reconciliation and the well-being of all.

(177) **Just war (Ius ad bellum/Ius in bello):** A traditional concept of Christian ethics that formulates conditions under which war can be morally permissible (Ius ad bellum) and establishes rules for behavior during war (Ius in bello).

(178) **Kingdom of God:** A central theme in the New Testament that describes the state of the world in which God's reign is realized and justice and peace prevail.

(179) **Laici Probati:** Proven lay people, lay persons (women and men) who are ordained on the basis of their experience and can be equated with clergy for their respective level of activity on site, also for the liturgical performance of sacraments.

(180) **Laity:** Baptized members of the church who are not clergy.

(181) **Laudato Si' (2015):** An encyclical by Pope Francis that deals with environmental and social issues and introduces the concept of integral ecology.

(182) **Leadership culture:** The way leadership and decision-making are practiced in the church, including the distribution of power and responsibility.

(183) **Learning organization:** An organization that continuously adapts, experiments and learns from its experiences.

(184) **Leavers:** people who have officially left church membership, often out of protest or disappointment.
(185) **Legal compliance:** Compliance with legal standards and procedures.
(186) **LGBTQIA+ inclusion:** The inclusion and acceptance of people who are lesbian, gay, bisexual, transgender, queer, intersex, asexual or have other sexual orientations and gender identities.
(187) **LGBTQIA+:** Abbreviation for lesbian, gay, bisexual, transgender, queer, intersex, asexual and other gender identities and sexual orientations.
(188) **Liberation theology**: A theological direction that reflects faith from the perspective of the poor and oppressed and emphasizes social justice.
(189) **Liturgical and meditative dance:** forms of dance that are consciously used in church services or as a prayer experience to combine faith and movement.
(190) **Liturgical organization:** The way in which services and rituals are conducted in the church.
(191) **Liturgy:** The entirety of the acts and forms of worship in the church.
(192) **Local churches:** The local or regional parts of the Catholic Church, typically dioceses.
(193) **Lone wolves**: Bishops who try to implement reforms or changes on their own, without broad support or networking within the college.
(194) **Lord of the Dance:** A hymn by Sydney Carter that sings of Jesus Christ as the dancing God who dances through life and death and invites the faithful into his dance.
(195) **Loss of credibility:** The loss of trust and reputation in the public eye, in this case in relation to the church, if it does not address obvious problems.
(196) **Lumen Gentium:** The dogmatic constitution on the Church of the Second Vatican Council, which, among other things, strengthened the concept of the "people of God".
(197) **Magisterium:** The authority of the Catholic Church to proclaim and interpret teachings.
(198) **Maria 2.0:** A Catholic reform movement that began in 2019 and is committed to full equality for women in the Church, including access to all ministries.
(199) **Marriage ceremony:** The sacramental marriage in the Catholic Church.
(200) **Marriage**: A lifelong and indissoluble union between a man and a woman, recognized by the Church as a sacrament (in the traditional teaching of the Catholic Church).
(201) **Meatless Friday:** A traditional Catholic practice of abstaining from meat on Fridays, often as penance or a reminder of Christ's suffering. Reinterpreted here as a possible contribution to climate protection.
(202) **Mentoring:** A process in which a more experienced person (mentor) advises and supports a less experienced person (mentee).
(203) **MHG study:** A 2018 scientific study on sexual abuse of minors by Catholic clergy. The text refers to its findings regarding perpetrator profiles and systemic factors.
(204) **Ministers:** Persons who hold an ecclesiastical office (e.g. bishops, pastors).
(205) **Minority stress:** Chronic stress caused by the stigmatization of and discrimination against members of minority groups.

(206) **Monocratic:** Administration or rule in which a single person has sole decision-making authority.

(207) **Moral theology:** An area of theology that deals with the morality of human behavior and develops criteria for morally good and bad behavior.

(208) **Narrow corridor:** A limited scope of action within which progressive forces within the church must operate.

(209) **Need for reform:** The need for fundamental changes in the structures, rules and culture of the church in response to the abuse scandal.

(210) **Need to shape:** The urgent need to actively change and develop the structures, practices or teachings of the church in order to remain relevant and vibrant.

(211) **Neoliberalism:** An economic system based on unbridled market thinking, profit maximization and minimal state interference.

(212) **Nietzsche and the dancing God:** reference to Friedrich Nietzsche's statement that we can only believe in a God who can dance, interpreted as a longing for a joyful and expressive God as opposed to a joyless religion.

(213) **Nuclear deterrence:** A security policy strategy in which a potential attacker is deterred from launching an attack because it fears a devastating nuclear counter-attack.

(214) **Open communion practice:** A practice that allows non-Catholics or remarried divorcees to receive the Eucharist under certain circumstances.

(215) **Open culture of debate:** A culture of discussion in which different positions can be discussed transparently, even if they are controversial.

(216) **Operational blindness:** The inability to recognize one's own mistakes, problems or outdated structures because one is too involved in the daily routine.

(217) **Opportunities for discrimination:** Practices in employment law that discriminate against or exclude certain groups of people (e.g. queer employees, remarried people) on the basis of their lifestyle.

(218) **Option for the poor:** A central principle of Christian social teaching, which states that Christians have a special obligation to care for the poor and vulnerable and to stand up for their rights.

(219) **Ordained ministries:** The offices in the church that are conferred by the sacraments of ordination (deacon, priest, bishop).

(220) **Ordinariates:** administrative units in the Catholic Church that are headed by an ordinarius (e.g. bishop).

(221) **Ordination of women:** The admission of women to church offices, in particular to the priesthood or episcopate.

(222) **Pacem in terris:** An encyclical by Pope John XXIII from 1963 on peace on earth, which is considered an important point of reference for the Catholic doctrine of peace.

(223) **Palaver:** Traditional forms of consultation in African cultures that are based on intensive dialog and consensus-building.

(224) **Paradigm shift:** A fundamental change in the way of thinking or in a system (here: Catholic sexual morality) that leads to a new perspective and different practices.

(225) **Paragraph 218:** The paragraph in the German Criminal Code that regulates abortion.

(226) **Parrhesía (boldness):** A term that stands for courageous and open speech that is allowed to express everything one feels.

(227) **Participation:** The active involvement of people in decision-making processes.

(228) **Participative leadership:** A management style in which employees or members are involved in decision-making processes.

(229) **Pastoral areas:** Larger pastoral care units that are created by merging smaller parish structures, often as part of structural reforms.

(230) **Pastoral care:** refers to the pastoral care and practical work of the church with the faithful.

(231) **Pastoral care:** The care and support of believers by clergy or other church employees in matters of faith and life.

(232) **Pastoral councils:** advisory bodies in parishes, deaneries or dioceses that deal with pastoral issues.

(233) **Pastoral dialog:** An approach to pastoral care that aims to remain in conversation with people, even if they hold political views that differ from church doctrine. The aim is often to encourage reflection and facilitate a possible return to the church line.

(234) **Pastoral realism:** The ability of church leaders to recognize and respond to the concrete needs and circumstances of the faithful and society.

(235) **Pastoral reality on the ground:** the concrete needs, challenges and realities of people's lives in the parishes and dioceses.

(236) **Pastoral solutions:** Practical pastoral responses to the needs of people who sometimes deviate from official rules.

(237) **Pastoral trials:** Temporally or locally limited experiments with new pastoral approaches that are monitored and evaluated.

(238) **Patriotism:** love of one's own country, which according to church teaching includes respect for other nations and cultures and is distinct from excessive nationalism.

(239) **Pax Christi Germany:** The German section of the international Catholic peace movement Pax Christi.

(240) **Peace ethics:** Theological and moral reflection on war and peace, violence and non-violence, based on Christian principles.

(241) **Peace to this house:** The title of the new basic peace ethics text of the German Conference of Bishops from 2024.

(242) **People of God:** The entirety of the faithful in the Catholic Church, as described by the Second Vatican Council as a pilgrim whole.

(243) **Permanent deacons:** A level of ordained ministry that is also open to married men. Also: the possible ordination of women as permanent deacons.

(244) **Permanent temporary solution:** A situation that exists but is not permanently secured or officially regulated.

(245) **Pfarrer:innen-Initiative:** An association of priests and believers in Austria that campaigns for reforms in the Catholic Church.

(246) **Physicality of faith:** The emphasis that Christian faith does not only take place in the head, but should permeate the whole person - heart, soul and body.

(247) **Pilot projects:** Experimental initiatives or reform trials carried cut on a limited scale to test their effectiveness.

(248) **Playful freedom:** The necessary quality of true faith that al.ows a certain lightness, creativity and courage of expression, similar to freedom in dance.

(249) **Pneumatology and kinesiology:** The combination of the doctrine of the Holy Spirit (pneumatology) with the doctrine of movement (kinesiology) to describe a holistic spirituality in which the body follows the movement of the spirit.

(250) **Practicing, letting go, daring:** steps of faith that are compared to learning to dance: Faith requires practicing (instruction, teaching), letting go (of fears, rigidity) and daring (courage to show and live faith).

(251) **Praedicate Evangelium:** Pope Francis' apostolic constitution on the reform of the Roman Curia, which enables greater participation of lay people, especially women, in leadership functions.

(252) **Pregnancy conflict counseling:** Statutory counseling in Germany for women who wish to terminate a pregnancy. Progressive voices are calling for this to be open-ended.

(253) **Prevention of sexualized violence:** Measures at various levels (primary, secondary, tertiary prevention) to prevent abuse, e.g. through training, rules of conduct, risk assessment and intervention.

(254) **Priestly ministry:** The second level of the ordained ministry, which authorizes the celebration of the Eucharist and the administration of other sacraments.

(255) **Primacy of conscience:** The theological doctrine that the conscience of the individual plays a paramount role in moral decision-making.

(256) **Primary prevention:** Measures aimed at preventing abuse in the first place, e.g. by creating safe environments, training staff and establishing a culture of mindfulness.

(257) **Primum non nocere:** Latin principle meaning "first do no harm", particularly relevant in a medical and ethical context.

(258) **Principles of commercial law:** Principles of accounting and financial reporting that are customary in the economy (e.g. according to HGB in Germany).

(259) **Priority option for the poor:** A central principle of Catholic social teaching, which states that the needs of the poor and marginalized should take priority in political and economic decisions.

(260) **Progressive theologians:** Theologians who are committed to the further development of Catholic doctrine and practice, often taking greater account of social changes and individual realities of life.

(261) **Prophetic:** In the context of the church, this refers to the task of denouncing injustice and proclaiming a vision for a fairer world.

(262) **Protection of life:** The fundamental principle in the Catholic Church that emphasizes the value and sanctity of human life from conception to natural death.

(263) **Psychosexual immaturity:** The lack of healthy, integrated and mature development in dealing with one's own sexuality, relationships and emotions. Cited as a risk factor associated with celibacy and abuse.

(264) **Public corporation:** A legal form that gives certain organizations special rights and obligations in the public sector, as is the case with the major churches in Germany.

(265) **Queer Catholics / LGBTIQIA+ Catholics:** People whose sexual orientation or gender identity is non-heterosexual or non-cisgender and who are part of the Catholic Church.

(266) **Queer Christology**: A theological approach that reinterprets Jesus Christ from the perspective of LGBTQIA+ people - understood as queer or homosexual, among other things - and critically questions what significance such an image of Jesus can have for the faith and spiritual identity of queer people.

(267) **Queer community:** A comprehensive term for people who are not heterosexual and/or cisgender (LGBTQIA+).

(268) **Queer employees:** Church employees who identify as lesbian, gay, bisexual, transgender, intersex or queer.

(269) **Queer theology**: A theological approach that reinterprets and questions the Bible and theological traditions from the perspective of LGBTQIA+ people.

(270) **Queer:** A collective term for people whose sexual orientation, gender identity or gender expression deviates from social norms; in a broader sense also for LGBTQIA+.

(271) **Queer-sensitive pastoral care:** Pastoral care and attitudes in the church that recognize, value and include the needs, identities and experiences of queer people.

(272) **Reappraisal:** The process of comprehensively investigating, documenting and understanding past cases of sexual abuse in the Catholic Church and their background, including institutional failures, in order to draw lessons for the present and future.

(273) **Reconciled diversity:** An ecumenical concept that sees the unity of Christians not in uniformity, but in the recognition and appreciation of different traditions.

(274) **Reform backlog:** A situation in which necessary structural or substantive changes are not implemented, leading to stagnation or decline.

(275) **Reform efforts:** Efforts within an institution to make changes to existing rules, doctrines or practices.

(276) **Reform of Catholic sexual morality:** The process and efforts to renew the traditional teaching and practice of the Catholic Church with regard to sexuality, partnership and family and to adapt it to current knowledge and the reality of people's lives.

(277) **Regens:** The leadership of a seminary.

(278) **Relationship competence:** The ability to enter into and shape healthy, sustainable and reflective interpersonal relationships. Considered essential for effective pastoral care, especially in relationship issues.

(279) **Religious competencies:** Abilities and dispositions in people that make faith possible and can be encouraged and trained, similar to practicing steps when dancing.

(280) **Remarried divorcees:** Catholics who have remarried civilly after a divorce.

(281) **Representatives of victims:** Organizations and groups of people who have experienced sexualized violence in the Catholic Church and who campaign for the rights, support and appropriate processing of the cases. They often demand a central role in dealing with these cases.

(282) **Repression:** Suppression or punishment of people or initiatives that deviate from the official line.

(283) **Rerum Novarum (1891):** The first major encyclical of Catholic social teaching to address the conditions of the working class.

(284) **Resilience:** The psychological resistance or ability to survive difficult life situations and setbacks without lasting impairment.

(285) **Resonance:** The ability to make a connection and be understood; in the context of the text, the ability to connect with the world in which young people live.

(286) **Responsibility for creation:** the theological duty or mission of man to protect and preserve the world created by God.

(287) **Retreats with collegial exchange:** Planned time-outs or retreats that offer targeted space for open dialog, spiritual reflection and mutual strengthening.

(288) **Right-wing populism:** A political stance or strategy that is often characterized by an emphasis on "ordinary people" as opposed to "elites", nationalism, criticism of immigration and often anti-democratic tendencies.

(289) **Risk aversion:** An attitude that aims to avoid possible negative consequences at all costs, even if this blocks necessary changes or innovations.

(290) **Roman Catholic World Church:** The entirety of the Catholic Church worldwide, with Rome as the central seat of leadership.

(291) **Roman norms:** Rules, instructions and doctrinal statements issued by the Vatican or the head of the Church.

(292) **Rome/Vatican:** Refers to the Holy See and the central administration of the Catholic Church, often synonymous with the position of Pope.

(293) **Rule of law:** The application of principles such as transparency, consultation, clear rules and independent control also within church procedures and decisions.

(294) **Sacrament of marriage:** The sacrament of marriage, which is understood as a sacred bond between a man and a woman.

(295) **Sacrament:** Holy signs and acts in the Christian church through which grace is imparted according to the teachings of the church (e.g. baptism, marriage, Eucharist).

(296) **Sacramental marriage:** The marriage between a man and a woman recognized by the Catholic Church and confirmed by a sacrament.

(297) **Sacraments:** Sacred acts in the church that are considered a sign of God's grace (e.g. baptism, Eucharist, marriage).

(298) **Safe spaces for innovation:** Protected contexts (places, projects, initiatives) in which new pastoral approaches, liturgical forms or participation models can be tried out without immediate fear of sanctions.

(299) **Same-sex partnership/marriage:** A relationship based on love, fidelity and responsibility between two people of the same sex that is recognized by the state or the church (in some contexts).

(300) **Second Vatican Council (Vatican II):** An important council of the Catholic Church (1962-1965) that led to significant reforms and a reorientation of the Church.

(301) **Secondary prevention:** Measures aimed at identifying borderline behavior at an early stage and intervening to prevent it from escalating.

(302) **Self-defense:** The right of an individual or state to defend itself by appropriate means against an unlawful attack.

(303) **Self-determination (sexual):** The right and ability of individuals to make free and responsible decisions about their sexuality.

(304) **Seminarian:** A person in training to become a priest in a seminary.

(305) **Separation of powers (in the ecclesial context):** The principle of introducing control mechanisms and shared responsibilities within church structures (checks and balances) to limit the concentration of power in individuals and ensure accountability.

(306) **Sermon on the Mount:** A central discourse of Jesus in the New Testament that contains ethical teachings, including the commandments on non-violence and love of enemies.

(307) **Sexual ethics:** The Church's teaching on human sexuality and sexual relationships.

(308) **Sexual morality:** the Church's teaching on sexuality and sexual relationships.

(309) **Sexualized violence:** Acts of abuse of a sexual nature committed within the Catholic Church by clergy or other church employees, often by taking advantage of positions of power.

(310) **Shalom:** A Hebrew word that means more than just peace, but also includes wholeness, well-being and inner peace.

(311) **Shame and guilt culture:** A culture in which natural human feelings, needs or experiences (such as desire, longing, sexuality) are regarded as suspicious, sinful or shameful, which can lead to repression and a lack of integration.

(312) **Sin:** In Christian theology, an action or attitude that is considered a separation from God or a violation of God's commandments.

(313) **Social framework conditions:** Social and economic factors that influence the living situation of families and pregnant women and are considered by progressive voices to be relevant for the protection of life.

(314) **Social market economy:** An economic model that combines a market economy with a strong social security system and state regulation.

(315) **Social responsibility:** The obligation of companies and politicians to assume responsibility for the well-being of society and the environment beyond the mere generation of profit.

(316) **Speed limit 130:** A maximum speed limit of 130 kilometers per hour on freeways.

(317) **Spiritual depth:** An anchoring in faith and spirituality that serves as a source of strength and inspiration for shaping church life.

(318) **Spiritual director:** A person who accompanies seminarians or believers on their spiritual journey, often through conversations about questions of faith, inner conflicts and conscience.

(319) **State truth commission:** An independent commission set up by the state to carry out comprehensive investigations into cases of abuse in institutions (here: the church) in order to bring the truth to light and make recommendations for the future.

(320) **Structural exclusion:** Systemic barriers and discriminatory practices within an institution that disadvantage certain groups.

(321) **Structural violence:** Violence that does not originate directly from individuals, but is anchored in the structures of society, the economy or politics and causes injustice, suffering or disadvantage (e.g. through unfair trading conditions, arms exports to conflict areas).

(322) **Subsidiarity:** A principle of social doctrine which states that tasks and decisions should be taken at the lowest, smallest or most local level that is capable of doing so.

(323) **Sustainability:** A principle in which resources are used in such a way that they serve the needs of the present without compromising the opportunities of future generations. In the Catholic Church, often in the sense of preserving creation.

(324) **Synodal Council:** A planned joint advisory and governing body of bishops and laity at national level, the establishment of which was stopped by the Vatican.

(325) **Synodal path:** A discussion and reform process of the Catholic Church in Germany over several years, in which bishops and lay people are involved.

(326) **Systemic causes:** Problems that are not limited to individual persons, but are rooted in the structures, rules, cultures and power relations of an institution (here: the church) and promote misconduct.

(327) **Tertiary prevention:** Measures taken after an offense becomes known that aim to deal with cases professionally, prevent further offenses by the offender and support the victims.

(328) **The image of God:** The Christian doctrine that human beings are created in the image of God, which forms the basis for the inviolable dignity of every human being.

(329) **Theologians:** Scientists and scholars of theology (the doctrine of God and religion) who are mentioned in the text as important voices for reform and a critical examination of the systemic problems of the church.

(330) **Theological impoverishment:** The state in which theological discourse and the development of doctrines within the church stagnate or wither, often through the avoidance of controversial topics.

(331) **Thomas Aquinas:** An important Doctor of the Church who recognized the natural human pursuit of happiness.

(332) **Those who are distant:** People who have little or no contact with the church or who belong to other religions/worldviews.

(333) **Togetherness instead of loneliness:** A topic of overcoming isolation through community and mutual support among bishops.

(334) **Torn loyalties:** The inner conflict that progressive church leaders experience when they have to mediate between official norms and the pastoral reality on the ground.

(335) **Training book for religious skills:** A workbook that guides you to practice and develop faith through reflection questions and learning areas (such as dialog, empathy, self-acceptance).

(336) **Transhumanism:** A movement that aims to improve and transcend human existence through the use of technology.

(337) **Transparency:** The openness and accessibility of information about cases of abuse, processes for dealing with abuse and institutional decisions for those affected, the public and external auditors.

(338) **Treaty on the Prohibition of Nuclear Weapons (TPNW):** A treaty under international law that prohibits the possession, development, production, deployment, transfer and use of nuclear weapons.

(339) **Tuning work:** The process of finding one's own faith in harmony with the rhythm of one's own life and at the same time in harmony with God's great melody.

(340) **Turnaround in gender equality policy:** A fundamental shift in policy and practice towards equal treatment of all people regardless of their sexual orientation.

(341) **Ultima Ratio:** The last resort; a means that is only used when all other options have been exhausted.

(342) **Unavailability of life:** The theological view that human life is a gift from God and is not subject to the free will or control of the individual.

(343) **Understanding marriage:** The theological and legal definition of marriage by the Church.

(344) **Unity in reconciled diversity (communion):** An ideal of the church in which unity is not enforced by uniformity, but by enduring and integrating differences in an atmosphere of reconciliation and communion.

(345) **Universal basic salary (basic income):** A regular, unconditional income paid to every citizen or resident of a country.

(346) **Vatican Council II:** A major council of the Catholic Church (1962-1965), whose documents (such as Gaudium et Spes) are often quoted, e.g. in relation to the Church as a "sign and instrument" of joy and hope.

(347) **Vicar General:** main representative of bishops in the administration of the diocese.

(348) **Victims of abuse:** Persons who have experienced sexualized violence and abuse in the church by church officials.

(349) **Viri Probati:** Proven men, usually married men, who can be appointed as priests (older paradigm).

(350) **With burning concern:** An encyclical by Pope Pius XI from 1937, written in German and critical of National Socialism and its racial ideology.

(351) **Women's self-determination**: The right of women to make independent decisions about their bodies and their lives, a point that prog‐essive voices bring to the debate on abortion.

(352) **World Church:** The Catholic Church as a global community.

(353) **World Economic Forum Davos**: An annual meeting of leaders from business, politics, science and other fields to discuss global problems.